Fears, Doubts and Joys of Not Belonging

Editors
Benjamin Hart Fishkin
Adaku T. Ankumah
Bill F. Ndi

Langaa Research & Publishing CIG
Mankon, Bamenda

Publisher:
Langaa RPCIG
Langaa Research & Publishing Common Initiative Group
P.O. Box 902 Mankon
Bamenda
North West Region
Cameroon
Langaagrp@gmail.com
www.langaa-rpcig.net

Distributed in and outside N. America by African Books Collective
orders@africanbookscollective.com
www.africanbookcollective.com

ISBN: 9956-791-53-9

© Authors 2014

DISCLAIMER
All views expressed in this publication are those of the author and do not necessarily reflect the views of Langaa RPCIG.

The Editors

Benjamin Hart Fishkin in his research has emphasized Nineteenth Century British Literature through each phase of his education. Prior to earning his Doctorate from the University of Alabama in May of 2009, he obtained a BA in English and Film from the University of Michigan, Ann Arbor, and an MA from Miami University, Oxford, Ohio where he examined the interest of Charles Dickens in the theatre and how the stage influenced his novel writing. He has published *The Undependable Bonds of Blood: The Unanticipated Problems of Parenthood in the Novels of Henry James*. He recently co-edited, with Adaku T. Ankumah, Bill F. Ndi and Festus Fru Ndeh, *Outward Evil Inward Battle: Human Memory in Literature*. His recent research interest now include amongst other things the problems of marriage and the American family, and the relationship between the Blues and the single-parent home in the works of William Faulkner, August Wilson, and F. Scott Fitzgerald. Professor Fishkin joined Tuskegee University in the fall of 2009. Before taking up this position at Tuskegee University, Professor Fishkin was a Junior Fellow in The Blount Undergraduate Initiative at the University of Alabama. He has won several distinguished awards, including the Buford Boone Memorial Fellowship, the Oregon Shakespeare Festival Scholarship Award and the George Mills Harper Graduate Student Travel Award.

Adaku T. Ankumah received her PhD in Comparative Literature from the University of Wisconsin-Madison. With a minor in drama, her dissertation and initial research interests focused on revolutionary playwrights from the African Diaspora, such as Kenyan Ngugi wa Thiong'o, Martiniquais writer Aimé Césaire, and African American Amiri Baraka, who use their creative efforts to work for the destruction of what they consider to be the colonial/capitalist foundation of post-colonial Africa. Ngugi's play *The Trial of Dedan Kimathi*, a play that examines the arrest and trial of one of the famous leaders of the Mau Mau revolt against the British in Kenya in the 1950's, has been the subject of her published research. She has also done research on the role of women in revolutionary theatre, voicelessness of African women, and gender and politics in the works of African women authors like Mariama Bâ, Ama Ata Aidoo and Tsitsi Dangarembga.

Dr. Ankumah's recent research interest includes the writings of women in the African diaspora. This includes research on memory in literature and its role in helping those dealing with painful, fragmented pasts forge a wholesome future in Edwidge Danticat's *The Dew Breaker*. She has also examined memory and resistance in the poetry of South African performer and writer Gcina Mhlophe. She recently co-edited, with Bill F. Ndi, Benjamin Hart Fishkin and Festus Fru Ndeh, *Outward Evil Inward Battle: Human Memory in Literature*.

Bill F. Ndi earned his Doctorate from the University of Cergy-Pontoise in 2001. He joined Tuskegee University in the fall of 2011. His areas of teaching and research comprise among others English Languages and literatures, French, Professional, Technical and Creative Writing, World Literatures, Applied/Historical Linguistics, Literary History, Media and Communication Studies, Peace/Quaker Studies and Conflict Resolution, History of Internationalism, History of Ideas and Mentalities, Translation & Translatology, 17th Century and Contemporary Cultural Studies. He has published numerous articles and book chapters in these areas. Professor Bill Ndi has also published 10 volumes of poetry in English, 3 in French, a play and 3 works in translation. Amongst Professor Ndi's peer reviewed publications are the following: Edward Coxere's *Adventures by Sea*, (2012), *Letters of Elizabeth Hooton, The First Woman Preacher,* (2011), Thomas Lurting's *The Fighting Sailor Turn'd Peaceable Christian,* (2009) (Annotated French Translations); "Names, an Envelope of Destiny in the Grassfields of Cameron" and "Extending educational boundaries" in Kumar, Pattanayak, Johnson – **Framing My Name,** (2010); Venuti, L. (ed.), *The Translation Studies Reader* in *Australian Review of Applied Linguistics* (2008), [Vol. 31, No. 1: Pages 11.1-11.4,] « Discours de la vengeance dans les journaux confessionnels Quakers » in Marillaud, P & Gauthier R. **La Vengeance et ses discours,** «La première contestation de l'esclavage», *(A Translation)* Paris, Présence

Africaine, « Quakerisme Originel et Milieu Maritime », in Augeron & Tranchant *La Violence et la Mer dans l'Espace Atlantique (XIIe-XIXe)*, « Littérature des Quakers et Clinique de l'Âme » in *Arts Littéraires, Arts Cliniques* (*Literary Arts, Clinical Arts*), « Traduire le discours Quaker », in *Traduire 2*, «Globalization and Global Ethics: A Quaker Concern» in *Questioning Cosmopolitanism*. Finally, he recently co-edited, with Adaku T. Ankumah, Benjamin Hart Fishkin and Festus Fru Ndeh, *Outward Evil Inward Battle: Human Memory in Literature*.

Authors

Antonio J. Jimenez-Munoz is lecturer at the University of Oviedo, Spain. His research takes on the influence of Romantic literature and culture upon the present. His main line of research deals with the influence of Romantic legacies in modern poetry and art and particularly the material continuity of Romantic modes of expression in contemporary art-forms. His fields of interest are Literary Criticism, Theory, and World Poetry. Before his current position, he was a Teaching Fellow at the universities of Kent at Canterbury-UK (2001-2004) and Hull-UK (2004-2006), after graduating in English Studies at the University of Cordoba (Spain) in 2001.

Blossom N. Fondo is Senior Lecturer in Postcolonial Theory and Commonwealth Literature at the Higher Teacher's Training College of the University of Maroua, Cameroon. Her publications have appeared in the *IUP Journal of Commonwealth Literature*, *Labyrinth: A Journal of Postmodern Studies* and *Kaliao; The Multidisciplinary Journal of the Higher Teachers' Training College Maroua*, and *Reflections on World Literature* edited by Nilanshu Agrawal. Her main areas of interest are postcolonial feminist theory, Anglophone Caribbean, African and African-American Literatures. She is currently working on a monograph on the representations of history in the postcolonial novel with a focus on the novels of Michelle Cliff.

Emmanuel Fru Doh holds a Ph.D. from the University of Ibadan and has taught in colleges and universities in Cameroon and the United States since 1990. Poet, novelist, social and literary critic, his research interests, with a remarkable interdisciplinary approach, include Africa's literatures, cultures, and politics; the African diaspora; and colonial and postcolonial literatures. Doh has published numerous substantial scholarly works, including *Africa's political Wasteland: The Bastardization of Cameroon*, and *Stereotyping Africa: Surprising Answers to Surprising Questions*. He is currently teaching in the Department of English at Century College in Minnesota.

Gloria Nne Onyeoziri is a professor of French at the University of British Columbia. She published *La Parole poétique d'Aimé Césaire* (L'Harmattan, 1992) and *Shaken Wisdom: Irony and Meaning in Postcolonial African Fiction* (University of Virginia Press, 2011). Other recent publications include "In the Face of the Daughter: Feminist Perspectives on Métissage as a Gendered Concept in the Works of Maryse Condé" (in *Emerging Perspectives on Maryse Condé*, African World Press, 2006) and "Gisèle Pineau et l'oralité mondialisée" (*Nouvelles études francophones*, 2012).

Robert Alvin Miller teaches French and African Studies at the University of British Columbia. He has published studies on J.M.G. Le Clézio and other francophone authors including Simone and André Schwarz-Bart, D. T. Niane and Aminata Sow Fall. Recent studies include "Interface and Erasure in Le Clézio's 'Mondo' and Gatlif's *Mondo*" (*International Journal of Francophone Studies*) and "Communes hippies et autres communautés improvisées chez Maryse Condé et J.M.G. Le Clézio" (in *Diasporiques*, F. Paré & T. Collington, eds., Ottawa: Éditions David, 2013).

Adaku T. Ankumah is an Associate Professor of English at Tuskegee University. She holds a Ph.D. from the University of Wisconsin-Madison. Her areas of interest include women's literature (with a focus on African and Diaspora women) and the short story genre.

Bill F. Ndi, poet, playwright, storyteller, literary critic, translator, historian of ideas and mentalities as well as an academic has held teaching positions in several universities in Australia, France and elsewhere. He now teaches in the Department of English and Foreign Languages at Tuskegee University, Tuskegee, Alabama, USA. He has published numerous scholarly works on Early Quakerism and translation of Early Quaker writings. He has also published poetry and plays extensively in both the French and the English languages.

Benjamin Hart Fishkin is an Assistant Professor of English at Tuskegee University, where he specializes in teaching Nineteenth Century British Literature. He holds a Ph.D. from the University of Alabama where he served as a Junior Fellow in The Blount Undergraduate Initiative.

Table of Contents

Preface..ix
Introduction..xi

Section I: Prose and Verse on the Verge......................1

Chapter 1
Bill F. Ndi's Social Angst and Humanist Vision: Politics, Alienation and the Quest for Freedom in *K'cracy, Trees in the Storm and Other Poems*. **Emmanuel Fru Doh**...................................3

Chapter 2
In Moments Like These: Emmanuel Fru Doh and the Mirrors of Romanticism. **Antonio Jimenez-Munoz**............................31

Chapter 3
Warring Estrangement in Edward Coxere's Adventures *by Sea*. **Bill F. Ndi**..55

Section II: Outside Looking in....................................81

Chapter 4
The Oppressed Out of the Circle: United Marginals in Francis B. Nyamnjoh's *The Travail of Dieudonné*. **Adaku T. Ankumah**.........83

Chapter 5
F. Scott Fitzgerald and the Pain of Exclusion. **Benjamin Hart Fishkin**..107

Chapter 6
Minority Identity and the Question of Social Failure in John N. Nkengasong's *Across the Mongolo*. **Blossom Ngum Fondo**.........125

Chapter 7
Changing the Status Quo from the Margins" in Bill F. Ndi's *Gods in the Ivory Towers* **Adaku T. Ankumah**............................. 153

Section III: Strangers at Home and Abroad...................... 173

Chapter 8
A Costly Gift to the Receiver: Francis B. Nyamnjoh and the Alienation of the African. **Benjamin Hart Fishkin**............... 175

Chapter 9
Willful and/or Imposed Alienation in Recent African Emigration Narratives: Fatou Diome's *Ventre de l'Atlantique*, Henri Lopes's *Une enfant de Poto-Poto* and Chimamanda Adichie's *The Thing Around Your Neck* **Robert Alvin Miller and Gloria Nne Onyeoziri**............197

Chapter 10
Blighting Companionship: Emmanuel Fru Doh's *The Fire Within*, A Tale of Passion and Alienation. **Bill F. Ndi**...................... 215

Preface by Dr. Kenneth Wilburn, Department of History, East Carolina University

The authors of this provocative book explore distinctions of individual and group belonging, as well as manifestations of not belonging. Written for advanced undergraduates, graduate students, faculty, and those seeking knowledge about the complexity of identity, *Fears, Doubts and Joys of not Belonging* examines variations of imposed and self-imposed alienation. Ndi, Ankumah, and Fishkin explore the rich historiography of estrangement in fiction and non-fiction to demonstrate the universality, timelessness, and varieties of alienation. For example, Muslim leaders like Nana Asma'u of the Sokoto Caliphate disseminated educational poems of inclusiveness to the Africans of Gobir alienated by conquest. In contrast, Europeans who organized the Atlantic slave trade sought power and material wealth through mechanisms of intimidation and force that resulted in widespread hopelessness and exclusion. Both groups were victims of alienation, but those of the caliphate were invited in language they understood to participate inside the new society; those who survived the Middle Passage were addressed in languages they did not understand, transformed into chattel, and kept outside settler societies.

Thus, whether inclusive or exclusive in nature, alienation can be imposed, as heretics have often been painfully reminded by the orthodox. Yet alienation can also be willful, as Christian and Sufi ascetics have frequently demonstrated. In this book's ten chapters, the authors seek balance in our understanding of estrangement by asserting that joy can also come out of willful alienation. From that half-filled glass of life's serendipity one can often drink just as deeply of joy as one can of despair. This is what Steve Biko meant when he wrote about Black Consciousness, about discovering joy in one's identity. Alienation can be transformed from a lock into a key to open the collective Global African in us all. *Fears, Doubts and Joys of not Belonging* moves forward that recent scientific discovery.

Introduction

Fears, Doubts and Joys of not Belonging comes at an appropriate moment. In the wake of the Trayvon Martin shooting and the subsequent "not guilty" verdict pronounced to his murderer, a large number of Americans as well as people from around the world (familiar with this case) find themselves in the grip of fears, doubts and joys of not belonging/belonging. Inasmuch as the present book does not focus on this specific tragedy, it gives the reader in general and the American reader in particular an array of scenarios and reflections on the orchestrated/calculated estranging process and consequences that have driven the world to this point. Bringing together scholars of different literary confessions and professions, this book explicates the concept of alienation as engendered by fears, doubts or joys of either belonging or not belonging. The texts explored by the various scholars span from 17th Century Quaker autobiography through canonic writers of the 20th Century (F. Scott Fitzgerald) to contemporary literary texts produced from around the world. The chapters of the present work explore the shrill thrill and terror of this type of indelible, lasting hurt. Just like the alienation experienced by a person who is banished from his or her home country—who is forced to survive without the compassion he or she needs the most—estrangement changes the way people think. It shapes or distorts the ways characters develop and more often than not creates antiheroes who are hostile to the system that has spurned them.

As in real life, various writers, even before Max and Engels, have addressed this topic of alienation. In most of these works, alienation is generally conceived as a negative sometimes associated with psychosis and other forms of mental health issues. In some recent literature, however, especially from Africa and some of the relatively unknown works coming from Anglophone Cameroon, alienation takes on a new dimension as those who are alienated devise means of coping with their estrangement, whether it is religious, political, social or linguistic. The various chapters in this volume, to a greater extent, shed light on this topic.

Thus, the primary objective of this book is to consider the various approaches to the fears, doubts and joys of not belonging and/or belonging by writers and the unforeseen effects on literature, literary theory, social relationship, etc., among other matters. This book is a collection of essays and not a monograph *stricto-sensus*. However, the book focuses on a number of areas in which alienation and estrangement have been directly influential in matters of creativity and poetization.

Melvin Seeman, the noted sociologist and professor at UCLA, classifies alienation and its attendant problems as a "pervasive theme" in sociology and in contemporary society. He then quotes Erich Kahler who goes further in his own observation that "the history of man could very well be written as a history of the alienation of man" (qtd. in Seeman 783). This statement very well characterizes human existence, with alienation intensifying in the twentieth century, especially after World War II. In contemporary society, alienation becomes an even more pressing issue with globalization and the movement of peoples from their natural environments to unfamiliar locations just to be gainfully employed. Even technology, regardless of its many positive usages, has contributed to our estrangement from each other. Thus, in many contemporary families, communication via cell phone and mobile devices such as email, Skype, Twitter, is more common than connecting face-to-face with each other. In his award-winning essay "Old MacDonald had a Farmer's Market," Bill McKibben notes, "Even the people who share our houses are becoming strangers not just due to our lack of meaningful relationships but also architecturally as we wall ourselves away in 'internet alcoves,' locked-door 'away rooms,' and his-and-her offices on opposite ends of the house" (153). This last scenario underscores the pervasive nature of alienation and the need to address this topic, which is not a recent topic, but has been tentacling out to different areas and different groups of people.

Fears, Doubts and Joys of Not Belonging is about setting, environment and surroundings that do not afford room for us all. Some of these exclusions are determined by geography, but more often than not these challenges are symptomatic of a pervasive psychosis and conformism that has no limits (Breitinger 562). When a person is an outsider, there is a romance associated with that. However, this is usually the appraisal of a very young audience, and it is usually temporary. It is not easy to be unacquainted or unconnected. Similar to the experience lived by a child who is forcefully snatched from the hands of a loving parent, severing one's ties with his or her roots is always traumatic. The famous author Ken Kesey describes an asylum patient who as he was being born looked out of his mother and "…somehow realized what he was being born into, and had grabbed on to everything handy in there to try to stave off being born" (15). This is what *Fears, Doubts and Joys of Not Belonging* is about. That feeling of panic, what may well be a universal panic, is what the authors isolate and tease out in their individual attempts to tap into an emotional pain that is more severe than any blood-inducing wound to produce this collective work.

While all the respective authors to the individual chapters tackle works of different authors from different clime, it is worth noting that these scholars all seem to come to the consensus that the driving force of literary venture as well as societal endeavor is marked by the fears, doubts and joys of not belonging which are animizing. They are the engine of literary aesthetics and even human behavior. Human action, be it in the real or the fictive world, is egged on by these qualities. In fiction, plot as well as character development becomes stunted if these aspects of human interaction are taken away. Besides, only the author sticks his or her neck out fearlessly without doubt, joyfully or sadly, to belong or not to belong. Like a warrior prepared for an ordeal and on the lookout, the author remains the only one to give a detailed account of every grip of the fears, doubts and joys of not belonging. And this explains why Delmore Schwartz considers that "in the unpredictable and fearful future that awaits civilization, the poet must be prepared to be alienated and indestructible" (qtd. in Gibbons 91).

It is in line with the above-mentioned fact of an unpredictable and fearful future that awaits civilization that *Fears, Doubts and Joys of Not Belonging* dwells on cultural, political, racial and economic outsiders in a globalizing world. The book chapters examine how things got that way and why things *stay* that way. Furthermore, while acknowledging there is nothing wrong with acquiring wealth, the scholars explore why people want to be part of the wealthy elite or class when it comes at the expense of others' sufferings—and suffering to a degree that outstrips any degree of enjoyment to be procured. Again, dissecting the resistance of the wealthy to accept any who happens to originate from the lower stratum, the book brings to life most of the elements associated with alienation.

Alienation, according to Raymond Williams is "one of the most difficult words in the language" (qtd. in Monroe 5). The challenge of arriving at an all-encompassing definition, though, does not prevent critics from attempting to shed light on this term. For some, alienation implies a separation or estrangement from the self or from the natural world around. Alienation, William Monroe notes, suggests "dissatisfaction, discontent, boredom" (Prologue 5). The alienated feel estranged from themselves or their surroundings, leaving them with the feeling of no longer belonging. The issue of alienation has to do with endurance, stamina and tenacity. How much anxiety and depression can people struggle and battle against without this lack of fulfillment changing them? If through tremendous heat and pressure a rock changes in a process measurable to a geologist, it is the goal of the creators of this book to ascertain meticulously the extent of the equivalent metamorphosis in people. The physical scientist who documents the extent and quantity of lifeless minerals is replaced by or transformed into a social scientist who has his or her instruments on the vital signs of living, breathing literary characters.

A query like this is compulsory because so many are unwelcoming, be it through language, laws or finance, without being aware that their behavior is injurious or defamatory. It is true that some are cognizant but simply do not wish to be bothered; however, we think that these are in the minority. Many, like Jesus in the Gospel of Luke indicates, "do not know what they are doing." More to the point, there is no empathy. There are no open relationships that are filled with genuine concern as opposed to lip service. *Fears, Doubts and Joys of not Belonging* excavates and exposes the horrifying callousness of those who are comfortable and materialistic, as well as the bitter, severe and justifiable complaints of the poor who have no recourse. There is a universality of theme at work here that links all of these stories together, regardless of age or era. The setting may change, but the exertion of force does not. The technology may change, but the construct does not. The person who is not protected, who is not on the right side of the moat, is the one who is not like the others and is not considered likely to win or succeed.

When a person is purposely subjugated, there is almost always a transfer of economic influence. People want to belong. If they are unable to integrate with their surroundings successfully, money, or the lack thereof, becomes a source of distance between the player and the company that is staging the production. A person without means needs savings because without it the individual is a spectator. He or she can see other people enjoying themselves or read of other's privileges, but he or she is cut off from the layers or levels that will grant the same advantages. What is crucial to this collection is that those without the means are also cut off from their own lives. Their own thoughts must become secrets, and their own words must become part of a memorized script.

The very fact that Karl Marx lived much of his adult life in London says something about his affinity for the disenfranchised who want society to be reformed and reconstructed. Most people, according to Marx, have no power. Scholars and specialists like Marx talk about how people cede because the world is out of balance. There is no creativity in their work, and they have no niche or foothold within it that they can cling on to and take pride in. Just as the author was a nineteenth century intellectual who was separated from Germany, the worker is separated from a career of his or her choosing. A person is reduced to an object, an article of trade that cannot feel, cannot think and cannot decide. He or she "sinks to the level of a commodity and becomes indeed the most wretched of commodities" (qtd. in Scott Appelrouth and Laura D. Edles 47). People are so spun around that they do not know if they are coming or going. The biggest price that is given up, a psychological one, is that the person becomes estranged from his or her own personality—there is a split or separation between two things which naturally belong together.

Marx is certainly clever—regardless of one's political preferences. His emphasis is on politics and economics. His poignant phrasings, such as when he states that "[l]andlords, like all other men, love to reap where they never sowed" (qtd. in Marchionatti 8), are a glaring example. This belies the fact that language was not his emphasis. In other words, there were methods of creating division within a culture that he did not think about. And above all, he did not decide on avoiding to write about them. So, scholars like Mikhail Bakhtin took linguistics and rhetorical criticism and became detectives who invigilated and studied the nuances of the written word. Bakhtin's critical theories and areas of expression differed thus from those of Marx. Whereas Marx felt people were left out because of how they worked and how that work defined them, Bakhtin argued that a word, what he termed a spoken "utterance," did the very same thing. One does not need money or position; one only needs the air in his or her lungs to speak and a disciplined mind. An ill-intentioned word aimed at the "other" could alienate with an immediacy of which Max never dreamed. If a culture is embedded with expressions, those expressions have power that a skilled orator can use to control the response of the recipient. In *Speech Genres and Other Late Essays*, the author states:

> From the very beginning, the speaker expects a response from them [the others], an active responsive understanding. The entire utterance is constructed, as it were, in anticipation of encountering this response. (94)

In other words, everything that is spoken is reliant upon what has been said before. If a speaker is aware of this and is informed about the power of language, these words cease to be mere elements of contextual conversation and become weapons.

If the theory of alienation is rooted in biblical tradition and has been talked and written about before the twentieth century, in the twenty-first century it is assuredly a creative concept that has changed with modern experience and experiment. In the middle of the twentieth century there was an increase in the study of alienation that leaned upon the building blocks put into place by Karl Marx and Mikhail Bakhtin. More modern thinkers, like social scientist Melvin Seeman, state that alienation is burdened with an antiquated meaning that is no longer well-suited to the modern fields of sociology, psychiatry and psychology (Heinz 213). The rules, systems and pedagogies have changed; therefore, the means of inquiry have to change with them. Seeman attempts to quantify alienation, just as would an accountant, a financial analyst, or an actuary who needs raw numbers to get his or her job done properly. A person's status, class and gender now matter, whereas earlier, according to Marx, people were considered to be interchangeable (Seeman, qtd. in Shafritz Jr. 104). The issue of human disconnectedness is no longer enough; what *kind* of human beings are we talking about? Alienation needs a new definition and that definition has to fit in the world of modern social science. Seeman singlehandedly creates five components to describe this term: powerlessness, meaninglessness, normlessness, social isolation, and self-estrangement (783). In doing so, isolation and detachment become terms that apply to more than just people. They apply to the literary critic, the literary theorist, readers and the characters they are reading about. Not only could people reluctantly confront the culture around them, but they could, by choice, withdraw from it and insulate themselves from actual hostility by reading about it.

When it comes to the task of ordering the various sections and chapters of *Fears, Doubts and Joys of Not Belonging*, the idea was to create a volume that adhered to an actual philosophy. This book is organized in three sections. The ten chapters echo a need for some sort of change—a need to eliminate alienation, marginalization and conflict in formerly colonized societies especially. As scholars of literature (and increasingly social science), we have decided that a burden that lies so heavy on the psyche requires, first and foremost, poetry to commence our study. It is our conviction that poetry is one of the sharpest tools of protest and discontent. Just as the continent of Africa cannot always fight back with physical ammunition, weapons or hard currency, it has become clear over the decades since the alleged independences that those commodities are not needed. They are temporal. Clever verse is timeless. It is amongst the best art form to battle inequity. It has a structure that cannot be taken away, dismantled or forgotten. The first section of *Fears, Doubts and Joys of Not Belonging* is called "Verse on the Verge." The question that immediately comes to mind is on the "verge" of what? This is intentional. There are so many socio-political ills in society that even the most optimistic African would have to say that equity is as elusive as ever. The individual is on the verge of creating a "clean and well-lighted place" à la Hemingway to rest, reflect and formulate a resistance for a diaspora that is not of his or her own making.

While this book is not a religious text, it does, indeed, follow a spiritual process. When people find themselves on the brink of the destabilizing of their own consciousness, they struggle against the power structures that have placed them within the walls of such a spiritual, metaphorical or literal prison. The use of the number *three*, like the trinity, invokes the notion of a journey or odyssey. The speaker is a pilgrim, like Chaucer or Dante, but a pilgrim in the very land which has birthed him or her. The search is for a home or sanctuary for an individual and a population that have for centuries been looking in through a glass at others enjoying the benefits of their birth. This thread that connects this book is a story like the one of Joseph in the Old Testament, where he is sold into slavery and cut off from the hearth that once nurtured him. Thus Section 2 of this book suggests that the African, regardless of geography, is on the "outside looking in" in bewilderment, just as Joseph looks back with a sense of frustration from an Egypt that is not his home to an Israel that he does not recognize.

Though the concept of feeling like a stranger and questioning where one belongs evokes memories of Ellis Island and the plight of the immigrant, it is, indeed, universal and timeless. Many of the Bushfallers (Nyamnjoh 2011) from sub-Saharan Africa wind up in America and Western Europe only to realize that relocation has cost them a terrible price. The third section of *Fears, Doubts and Joys of Not Belonging* involves all the optimism of the American Dream without the saccharine Hollywood ending that is never part of the actual story. A "Stranger at Home and Abroad" speaks to immigration, but also to a subset of this category that is uniquely African. The chaos of colonization is daunting for even the most persistent traveler who does not even know what or who constitutes authority. People are pushed to the fringes and the perimeters of society. The job of the editors here is to cull a sampling of chapters that examine why people are marginalized and why other people are so eager to erect barriers rather than tear them down. This topic deals with not being welcomed and examines issues involving religion, money, class, birth, and race. If in 2013 we do not yet live in a post-racial and religious tolerant era, it is worth reminding ourselves that these are not the only problems we have yet to transcend.

As warranted by the spiritual process mentioned above, i.e. to open this book with possibly the sharpest tool and weapon of protest and discontent that there is, this first chapter of the book and of Section One takes the reader through a close reading of Bill F. Ndi's *K'cracy, Trees in the Storm and other Poems*. The analysis reveals a restless and somewhat tormented spirit. One might ask: "tormented by what?" The socio-political ills that have left him on the verge and with one desire: find a place to rest, to reflect and to formulate a resistance, an awakening. It is through the resilient and powerful medium of poetry that Ndi's anguish, engendered by misguided priorities and the seeming lack of patriotism on the part of the leaders of his native Cameroon, primarily, comes to light. However,

Ndi chooses self-exile only to find out that self-exile comes with its own woes that are no less momentous. Through the analysis of representative poems from *K'cracy, Trees in the Storm and other Poems,* Chapter One takes a brief look at Ndi's life so far. It unveils Ndi's experiences of unsympathetic treatment and estrangement in the hands of fellow human beings either at home or abroad. These experiences have cast Ndi into the mold of a socially engaged poet and a literary warrior poetically indulged in guerrilla warfare. He is out to appeal to the consciences of his people. Also, he aims at chastising and redirecting the alliance of thieves and worst citizens who have hijacked power and imposed one of the worst autocracies on his people. This maddening deadlock has led his country of birth to self-destruction. Finally, Ndi has made his life a mission of righting the wrongs in a nation in shambles before his own eyes as a result of the lack of purposeful and competent leadership. His attack on societal ills is universal, though with a critical focus on Cameroon. His hope to start with a solution to Cameroon's problems will nonetheless serve as a first step to eventually improve upon the human lot as a whole.

In Chapter Two, "In moments like these: Emmanuel Fru Doh and the mirrors of Romanticism" reconfirms Emmanuel Fru Doh (EFD) as a major voice in Cameroonian poetry. Here, Dr. Jimenez explores a number of poetry collections by EFD: *Wading the Tide* (1995), *Not Yet Damascus* (2007), *Oriki'badan* (2009) and *Shadows* (2011). He taps from them the tensions between a pulsating voice in contemporary Anglophone Cameroon poetry and the legacies of the forms, rhetoric and versification that British Romanticism imposed for lyrical expression in English. This imposition thus renders writing poetry, for those whose colonial legacy amongst others include the English language, a struggle between received poetic means and the need for a poetic expression which is current. These poets like EFD have the need to belong to both a tradition but also the present. This binary of belonging and not belonging warrants EFD's poetry to be viewed in terms of its influences as well as in terms of the poet's vocalization of the inner depth of his belonging to the bulk, stripped and left on the margin of his society. It also unveils EFD's commitment to writing through his quest for a poetic voice. Through study, EFD's poetry turns out to be politically-charged with potent images that reveal his caustic reproof of human abuse and corruption. He thus celebrates hope and enthusiastically pursues freedom from the constraints of fears and doubts.

This first section concludes with Chapter Three, "Warring Estrangement in Edward Coxere's *Adventures by Sea.*" It takes the reader into the exclusive seventeenth century Quaker experience of the pain of exclusion and Quaker endeavors to overcome it. This activism is in line with claims by the distinguished historian of Quakerism Jacques Tual about Quaker contribution and input to modern society:

> Some concepts in this century stem directly from Early Quakerism. To this effect, mention must be made of the active contribution by Quakers in the evolution of dress code, language, education, trade and industry, humanitarian attitude in the treatment of the alienated and slaves in the 17th and 18th centuries… and international peace in the 19th and 20th century. (447)

Thus, this chapter explores and elucidates Coxere's war on the orchestrated process of pushing others onto the fringes and margins of society as he clenches onto his religious conviction. He is enjoined by his faith to break or tear down the walls and barriers that fears and doubts erect to bar free thinking and peace loving beings from bathing in inclusiveness. Also, the chapter exhibits the inward and outward scars left by willful and imposed marginalization. Inasmuch as Edward Coxere's *Adventures by Sea* comes across as a spiritual autobiography, the narrative is not devoid of the central doctrinal fights early Quakers put to warrant a level playing field for all human beings on earth and at all times, a place where "fearing" and "doubting," and above all "not belonging" will forever be banished. As a consequence, this gives grounds to joys of belonging. Coxere's is, therefore, a series of journeys by sea that plunges the reader into a rather eye-opening journey in the process of estrangements and marginalization as the relevant focal and central point rather than otherwise.

The chapter "The Oppressed out of the Circle. . ." examines the lives of people in post-colonial societies who find themselves marginalized after independence and in their environments have become "outsiders looking in" as their leaders exploit them. Their exclusionary status, invariable stemming from their class, pedigree, and linguistic orientation, renders them voiceless and powerless in a society that has no regard for the downtrodden. In older research on alienation, much attention is given to the negative psychological effects of such powerless, meaningless, isolationist existence which leads to identity crisis, depression, alcoholism and other mental illnesses as attempts to deal with these challenges. Writers like Frantz Fanon, the philosopher, activist, and psychiatrist born in Martinique, have dealt with the psychological impact of internalizing negativity from the oppressor. These fears and doubts about their existence are present in the chapter, as the protagonist of Francis Nyamnjoh's novel *The Travail of Dieudonné* experiences abandonment, dismissal, and rejection. The author notes that far from feeling estranged due to their circumstances, the alienated turn their fears into the joys of not belonging as they gather together to hear the protagonist's narrative. In Nyamnjoh's novel, the solidarity of the oppressed is vital in overcoming the challenges of their situation. In this new group forged out of the commonality of their experiences at various places near the margin, members support each other as they cope with life.

The final and only North American based chapter in this collection shows us that in the Africa of the present we are meeting a series of old "friends" that have brand new names. F. Scott Fitzgerald knew, almost ninety years ago, that literature and language, all too often, are about the psychological challenges of living and accepting what one cannot rise above. "An Attempt At Redemption: F. Scott Fitzgerald and the Pain of Exclusion" portrays how the ancient blow of rejection really has no balm. Not being welcomed by high-class families haunted him just like a film on a continuous "loop" and it is this persistent irritant—this very canker sore planted firmly between his cheek and gum—that urged him on and compelled him to place his indelible suffering before the public.

Like a father punishing a child and saying between each whack or wallop, "This is going to hurt me more than it hurts you!" Fitzgerald put an end to the genteel romance. The individual did not have control of his/her destiny. There were limits, and society was going to enforce them, often gleefully. The nineteenth century was over. The girl, not the boy, had the power. The individual did not deliver. Real life was not a Horatio Alger, Jr. story. Fitzgerald's literature is so psychologically revealing and so memorable because he could not solve what was troubling him.

The unanswerable question is: would it have been better had Fitzgerald been a less talented writer? Or would it have been better had he been happier and more content in his personal life? In essence, is alienation and exclusion the bit of sand that acts as an irritant resulting in the smooth pearl that is his literature of the nineteen twenties? If this is, indeed, the problem, why didn't his success at twenty-four years of age solve the problem and enable him to move on with a brand new view of the world? These are questions not only about wealth and power, but also about borders and boundaries that are translucent.

While colonialism continues to spark discussions in history, cultural studies, politics, globalization, gender, health and environmental concerns, its impact on the lives of nations and peoples around the world remain topical. With more than fifty years since most African countries attained independence, one would expect the trend obsolete. However, one of the least explored areas of colonialism has been the impact on "inter/intra" human relationships. It created a dichotomy amongst the colonized and colonizers in the first instance and amongst the colonized, the end of colonialism notwithstanding. This situation, Chapter Six contends, seems to have been aggravated by the formal end of colonialism. The hierarchization that characterizes post-colonial societies, making one group to dominate another, is based on aspects of identity such as ethnicity, language, religion amongst others. The subjugated group, as a result of the fears, doubts, and joys of not belonging, ends up on the fringes of society. Exploring the various traumas and conflicts resulting from this, the present chapter, informed by John Nkemngong Nkengasong's novel *Across the Mongolo,* shows how through his narrative, this Anglophone Cameroonian author captures the estranging tensions within post-colonial Kamangola. The author's struggle with these issues of identity as well as with those of social failure is the focus of this chapter. Framed within the theoretical construct of *subalternity* as viewed by Gramsci and Gayatri Spivak, this chapter establishes the relationship between social identity and failure and whether such a relationship should serve as a basis for defining identity. Over and above, the chapter underlines social failure as experienced by minority groups in terms of identity and the groups "not belonging."

"Changing the Status Quo from the Margins. . . " confronts the alienation that exists in so many post-independent African nations from corruption at the highest levels of administration, as outlined in the one-act play *Gods in the Ivory Towers* by Bill F. Ndi. The new shibboleth for advancing in this corrupt society which resembles the playwright's country of birth, Cameroon, is French; thus the Anglophone citizens find themselves at the margins of society, unable to progress. Their exclusion from belonging leaves the majority of society paralyzed by fear and adopting defeatist attitudes about their future. The author examines how one father proposes to challenge the status quo in the naming of his son and the son's determination to live up to his name and identity, to survive and overcome the limitations of his culture. In his attempt to achieve what the rest of the citizens consider laughable, the protagonist is rejected both by the oppressed and the oppressor. In fact, his alienation from both groups becomes his catalyst for change. Ndi uses the protagonist's tenacity and strength of will to challenge the complacency of his countrymen, asserting that each one of them holds within himself or herself the power to bring about change.

When the marginalized reject the status quo like the protagonist does, then they will move from the margins to the center.

From the moment that the congregation gathers in church, in the opening chapters of Francis B. Nyamnjoh's *Mind Searching,* and looks up (literally) at the heavens because the building does not have a roof to cover the congregants with anything other than sawdust, it is clear that the identity of the African is fading away. The chapter, "A Gift That Costs the Receiver: Francis B. Nyamnjoh and the Alienation of the African," takes the reader on an unwelcome tour of what has become a sticky cauldron of censorship, mistrust, confusion, colonialism, ceremony and crocodile tears. Cameroon is a nation that is more than half a century into its independence from the French and the British and nearly a century into its independence from the Germans. Yet, here, the reader is an unwelcomed guest in this toxic bitches' brew that keeps Cameroonians disoriented, excluded, and incapacitated in the very nation that has nurtured them.

Was there not value in Africa before Europeans used religion to help colonize it, and now that we are beyond this stage, does any of it remain? Nyamnjoh's tracing of Judacious Fanda Yanda is like a medieval morality play with Yanda showing us the ills that are all around him. In a spiritual sense, people are not living right. They have lost sight of what is important and from the west have learned only how to consume and display worldly riches. Colonialism and the strings attached to it force people into positions where they are disoriented, depreciated and devalued. The frustration embedded within Nyamnjoh's text indicates that not only does nothing remain of any value, but no one seems to miss it or remember when it got away. In a Cameroon replete with French currency and German coupes, the citizens find themselves increasingly as spectators in their land where someone else decides what is justice and what is sedition.

Chapter Nine tackles the everyday experience of Africans in a world where emigration to destinations in Europe and North America is a common part of life. It explores narratives focusing on the life and witness of Africans living in foreign cultural contexts. This analysis unveils a shift from those of alienation and return, à la

Cheikh Hamidou Kane's the *Ambiguous Adventure* of the early post-colonial period, to that of entrenchment. This new generation of African writers have been compelled to reconceptualise the experiences of fears, doubts, and joys of African men and women leaving their countries of birth. Alienation from their communities of origin becomes more of a negotiation, a game of frustration, deception and misunderstanding than an absolute existential rupture. This present rift is marked by a complex and multi-faceted alienation from and within the new community, involving rejection by that new community as well as betrayal by the very people supposed to be the closest representatives of one's origins. This new trend is revealed in critiquing Fatou Diome's *Ventre de l'Atlantique*, Henri Lopes's *Une enfant de Poto-Poto* and Chimamanda Ngozi Adichie's collection of short stories *The Thing Around Your Neck*. None of these authors suggests that this moral-cultural confusion takes place in a world of reciprocal global acceptance; rather, they portray old forms of prejudice and systemic exclusion persistent in their finding a place in the magma of changing experience. This leaves the writers with the contention that old languages compete in new contexts with futures and destinies in a maze of conflicting and contradictory claims to cultural identity and moral value. In the world of fiction, the history of African communities, as a consequence, takes a new form in the newly imagined spaces of alienation and conflicted memory.

This final chapter of both the last section and the book portrays how Emmanuel Fru Doh (EFD), by confronting new trends and traditional values in *The Fire Within*, does not only revert to the primal affirmation of the unrest and possibly tragedy engendered by such an endeavor but goes a step further to explicate the process of estranging people in a nation where two inherited colonial cultures (one from the French and the other from the English) stand at variance, leaving a cross section of the population plagued with woes brought about by alienation. This chapter addresses some of the following critical questions: how does one accommodate a child who is not his or her biological child? This question is replete with political undertone, given that the minority English/British

Cameroons appended to *"La République du Cameroun"* faces the same if not worse challenges and harassment than those suffered by EFD's protagonist who is a motherless child shortly after birth. It is this same circumstance that led British Southern Cameroons to be appended to *La République du Cameroun,* former French East Cameroons. Also pried into in this chapter is the question of why it is impossible for any to make plans and follow them through to realization in contemporary Africa. Are the forces out there too powerful to be averted? Are they man-made, natural or supernatural? In exploring these questions in the light of *The Fire Within,* the author has translated EFD's art and craft as one beginning with a flight aimed at conquering and conscientizing as a result of the tremendous burden of alienation weighing down the author's homeland fictionalized as Caramenju.

Fears, Doubts and Joys of Not Belonging will certainly fulfill the needs of those who have an interest in the historical, social, and political plight of not just the fictive and imaginary characters but that of people in general. It will also provide grounds for empathizing with fellow human beings irrespective of their race, profession, gender, age, sexual orientation, creed, class, etc. It would also be of significance to anyone interested in literary theory, for the different chapters are approached from various theoretical perspectives: Marxist, ethnic, historical, biographical, socio-critic, psycho-critic, feminist, New Historicist, as well as the New Reader Response criticism, etc. All in all, the use of literary evidence by the respective authors to inform scholarship on opinions and beliefs relating to alienation has been critically assessed as anchored in the eponymous *Fears, Doubts, and Joys of not Belonging* or of belonging.

Works Cited

Gibbons, Richard. *Poets at Work: 29 Poets on the Origins and Practice of Their Art.* Chicago: U of Chicago P, 1989. Print.

Griffith, Kelley. *Writing Essays about Literature.* Fort Worth: Brace Harcourt College, 1998. Print.

Heinz, W.R., "Changes in the Methodology of Alienation Research." *International Journal of Sociology and Social Policy* 11. 6/8 (1991): 213-221. Print.

Ken Kesey, *One Flew Over the Cuckoo's Nest.* New York: Penguin, 2002. Print.

Marchionatti, Roberto, ed. *Karl Marx: Critical Responses.* New York: Routledge, 1998. Print.

McKibben, Bill. "Old MacDonald Had a Farmer's Market." *Patterns of Exposition.* Ed. Robert A. Schwegler. 20th ed. Boston: Pearson, 2012.152-156. Print.

Bakhtin, M. M. *Speech Genres and Other Late Essays.* Trans. Vern W. McCree. Ed. Caryl Emerson and Michael Holquist. Austin: U. of Texas P, 1986. Print.

Monroe, William. *Power to Hurt: The Virtues of Alienation.* Urbana: U of Illinois P, 1998. Print.

Nyamnjoh, Francis B. "Cameroonian Bushfalling: Negotiation of Identity and Belonging in Fiction and Ethnography" *American Ethnologist,* 38.4 (2011): 701-713. Print.

Scott Appelrouth and Laura D. Edles, *Classical and Contemporary Sociological Theory: Text and Readings.* Los Angeles: Sage, 2007. Print.

Seeman, Melvin. "On the Meaning of Alienation." *American Sociological Review* 24.6 (1959): 783-791. *JSTOR.* Web. 5 Apr. 2013..

Shafritz, J.M. Jr., *International Encyclopedia of Public Policy and Administration,* Boulder: Westview, 1968. Print.

Tual, Jacques. *Quakers in England, 1649-1700: Illuminism and Revolution* Diss. Paris 3 Sorbonne-Nouvelle, 1986. Print.

The Editors

Bill F. Ndi
Adaku T. Ankumah
Benjamin Hart Fishkin

Section I:
Prose and Verse on the Verge

Chapter 1

Bill F. Ndi's Social Angst and Humanist Vision: Politics, Alienation and the Quest for Freedom in *K'cracy, Trees in the Storm and Other Poems.*

By
Emmanuel Fru Doh

After reading *K'cracy, Trees in the Storm and other Poems*, it is obvious that the poet Bill F. Ndi would have been banished from Plato's republic with all speed. Because there are hardly any songs in the volume praising the gods, Plato would have seen Ndi as a true poet focusing on people's emotions and thereby a perverter of morality and a deformer of minds besides all else. This is definitely a simplistic representation of Plato's position towards poets; notwithstanding, it is because of Plato's knot with poets that I prefer Victor Hugo's idea of the poet:

> C'est surtout à réparer le mal fait par les sophistes que doit s'attacher aujourd'hui le poète. Il doit marcher devant les peuples comme une lumière, et leur montrer le chemin. Il doit les ramener à tous les grands principes d'ordres, de morale et d'honneur; et pour que sa puissance leur soit douce, il faut que toutes les fibres du cœur humain vibrent sous ses doigts comme les cordes d'une lyre. (xviii)

The poet today has to preoccupy himself with the goal of setting right the wrongs of the sophists. Accordingly, he has to go ahead of society like a guiding light. He has to reconnect the members of society with the great rules of order, morality, and honor; therefore, for his authority to be appealing to society, he must be in total control of the sensibilities of the human heart. (My translation)

This definition is quite a breakaway from the classics in a manner reminiscent of Arthur Miller and his definition of what a modern tragic hero should be in spite of Aristotle's.[1]

Bill F. Ndi is from the politically sensitive and turbulent North West part of Cameroon. A multi-linguist, Ndi grew up schooling and earning certificates with the hope of ultimately serving his beloved country. In the process, he earned his Ordinary level Certificate in Bamenda,[2] then went on to Government Bilingual Grammar School in Yaoundé, the nation's capital, for his Advanced Level Certificate. With this move, Ndi had left behind his familiar English-speaking territory and ventured into a somewhat unfamiliar part of his country where French was and remains the main language spoken. It is not surprising then that Ndi decided to pursue a double Honors BA in English-French (Bilingual Degree) in the University of Yaoundé. He was later to pursue graduate studies in French, an experience which degenerated into a nightmare after he had virtually completed the program. Ndi was about to defend his dissertation, "La Quête des indépendances dans le roman africain: L'exemple de *l'Harmattan* de Sembène Ousmane et de *Le cercle des tropiques* d'Alioum Fantouré," when some narrow-minded examiners refused to partake in the exercise. Ndi's crime, according to one of them, was that Ndi had written his dissertation in French because he wanted to take the place of Francophones. Yet Cameroon is a bilingual country, at least administratively, that has imposed the study of French on English-speaking Cameroonians.[3] Unable to find any recourse, Ndi gave up.

After a brief stint teaching in Sacred Heart College, Mankon, Ndi left for Nigeria for his graduate studies. His departure, again true to Cameroon, was turbulent. First of all, acquiring a Cameroonian passport was and remains a herculean task, with corrupt officials who would not approve that a passport booklet be issued, let alone append their signatures to such booklets without the price being right. The result was clashes between Ndi and some police officers—a certain four-star "Commissaire Mbida"[4] comes to mind here. He must be retired now, the days these miscreants fail to see coming in all their corrupt and vain ways. Mbida had Ndi locked up and was about to frame this young citizen against the president of the country such that Ndi would have evaporated somewhere along the chain of command responsible for so-called "National Security."[5] Ndi managed somehow to get a passport and found his way to Nigeria where he studied Translation and Conference Interpreting at Imo State University.[6] From Nigeria, Ndi won a French Government scholarship and left for France to study at the Institut Supérieur d'Interprétation et de Traduction (ISIT), Paris. He was later to earn his doctorate in France, carrying out his studies in French without the French feeling threatened he was trying to take the place of French people as was the case in the Francophone-dominated land of his birth. Ndi later left France for Canada, came back to France, then off to England, Australia, back to France again and then the United States where he is currently resident.

I have traced Ndi's life this far, albeit without the juicy details, which are beyond the scope of this work, to throw some light on the mind that has yielded forth the sometimes disturbing poems one encounters in *K'cracy, Tree in the Storm and Other Poems (K'cracy)*. It is obvious that it did not take a day, nor was it some solitary, yet damaging, experience that fired Ndi. His problems started from his native Cameroon, the main playground, climaxed in the diaspora where his angst soared greatly before engendering the philosophy of his humanist vision.

One thing then is obvious at this point—Ndi has always belonged to an oppressed minority in his life's journey. In Yaoundé, in his own native Cameroon, Ndi was an Anglophone oppressed by an overwhelming Francophone majority; in Nigeria, he was a Cameroonian, a foreigner; in France and the rest of the West, he was a foreigner but above all black in societies extremely color sensitive with regards to human hue. The outcome is that in life, Ndi has always been running away from or running towards something. His otherwise vivacious mind was forced by an unfeeling and impersonal world to become lonely and solitary, hence the characteristic existential angst usually endued by such characters. Ndi, at one time, had to learn to fight back or, at the very least, speak up for himself when he felt oppressed or discriminated against as an individual or a member of any group.

Ndi fought back in many ways, but above all by writing poems, like Walt Whitman who exposed his frustrations, his anger sometimes, at the socio-political state of his world in his poems. Ndi became a true poet in our modern sense of the word for as Diana Greene points out, "The authentic poet must be one who works against all forms of injustice and destruction…"; she was later to add that the role of the poet is to awaken and engage the reader (15). This is Ndi's purpose in *K'cracy* as this study, using poems from this volume, will illustrate. Ndi had become too nauseated by repulsive ontological feelings generated by fragmented societies to remain without throwing up. After all, justice, fairness, and freedom as fundamental essentials of an authentic human world have had their advocates throughout history in the likes of poets and other committed members of society such as Wole Soyinka of Nigeria, Voltaire in France, Vladimir Mayakovsky of Russia, Gabriel José García Márquez of Colombia, and Pablo Neruda of Chile, to mention a few. In the same vein, Jimmy Reid, the Scottish trade union leader, journalist, broadcaster, and rector was to declare in his Glasgow University rectorial address about alienation as a result of what he saw as humanity suffering at the hands of humanity:

> It is the cry of men who feel themselves the victims of blind economic forces beyond their control. It's the frustration of ordinary people excluded from the process of decision-making.

The feeling of despair and hopelessness that pervades people who feel with justification that they have no real say in shaping or determining their own destinies. ("Alienation - or 'The Rat Race' Speech.")

This definition of alienation is a crown of jewels that could fit Ndi perfectly given his experience of life.

To begin with, a look at the title of Ndi's volume itself gives off the poet's frustration at the state of things around him. It is interesting that the first word of the volume's title is a richly loaded pun, the expression "k'racy," which brings to mind several interpretations in view of the words it echoes: "kakistocracy," "kleptocracy," "khaki," and "crazy." Ndi is fed up with this kakistocracy he is exposing, which is fomented by the kleptocrats in power. These power-drunk kleptocrats protect themselves with layers of khaki-dressed officers turned idiotic by corrupt leaders who usually pay them money they do not deserve; what layered meaning in just a word. One is also forced to think of "crazy" followed by the image of trees in a storm as concretizing a world with its people and their activities which, according to Ndi, has gone crazy dancing to dastardly unpredictable rhythms reminiscent of trees in a storm. For this reason, the very first poem of the volume "Happy Birthday," is a bitter irony marked by Ndi's disdain: yes, this birthday would have been worth celebrating, but the Cameroon nation has nothing remarkable to celebrate at all, having mainly distinguished itself as a "Champion of corruption." Besides, the persona asserts his belonging to the deprived masses kept away from uphill by the unpatriotic brooms of the witches in government: "But one, like all, kept away from uphill / By their broom and briar downhill" (1). Ndi makes no secret of his wish to have these witches masquerading as leaders while perpetrating corruption, hunted down and made to pay for their misdeeds.

The next poem, "Letter to Our Deaf Father of the Nation: Mr. Dict…" (2), is a direct chastisement of Paul Biya, Cameroon's despotic leader, and possibly any other dictator, who seems not to hear the desperate cries of the suffering masses, or else he just does not care and so ignores them. It is no wonder the poet qualifies him as "Master of mischief and ingratitude! (2). To the poet, if this birthday must be celebrated, then that which renders the nation physically and spiritually untidy must be swept away. This will make space for a spiritually healthy environment to emerge in which citizens can find love and better living conditions for themselves. Until such a time, the people will remain disappointed about Mr. Dict…'s manner of governing and will continue "nudging [him] to the head" (3), which head they now know to be "empty" (3). The emptiness referred to here also alludes to and emphasizes the pangs of hunger the people feel, as well as their angst and the poet's:

> We now know your head as empty
> As the bellies of our fellow human beings
> 'Littering' your streets
> & wanting in food and water;
> We know it emptier
> Than the calabash of that
> Desert Wanderer whose thirst
> Harried him to you
> And you ushered him
> To the garrotte chamber!
> Breaching the Contract! (3)

In "Platitudesmaybe," the persona wonders about the plight of the ordinary members of society. Mindful of the ways of the corrupt politicians who do not seem to listen to anyone before doing whatever they set their minds to, the persona is wondering if these members of society are nothing. Not even the voices of writers who complain about what is going on seem to matter to them. Hence the persona wonders why they are the citizens they are if their plight means nothing. This poem, therefore, is a call to those in power to begin understanding what being in power means: serving the citizens instead of lording it over them with events taking place above them like clouds in the air: "All nothing see / And like clouds'/ Story told… / They passed / No doubt/ Above us" (28).

In "Fools Themselves" (38), we encounter a frustrated persona who, just like in the previous poem, damns these pilfering unpatriotic leaders as "fools themselves." Ndi's persona points out that even though these corrupt leaders are doing all the terrible things against the poor citizens and seem to be doing well with all that they need at their disposal, the latter would know how to survive better difficult times than these irresponsible barons in office: "With ease, in storm espouse New Vanes" (38). The calligraphic nature of the poem, with words scattered in an ostensibly chaotic manner on the page, is in itself a replication of the angst engaged by Ndi's humanist vision.

In "Hurdles" (40), Ndi sees his vision for society always being thwarted by impediments. It is his hope that everyone would be able to rise to the moon and be, if not like the moon, then like a shooting star beside the moon:

> The skies, rising from the ground.
> Yet beneath sinks all the ground.
> From the earth's four walls,
> Proceeds the journey; the coming earth,
> But Arêtes and Pyramidal Peaks
> The calories sap, and the quarries,
> To the mire them down,
> Up to the large moon, look we
> Yet, identify we but a star. (40)

Ndi is obviously aware of the potentials for a good life that his people have. Regrettably, it is not going to be easy for them, given the status quo, to acquire such a life. Yet, they must keep trying; even if in the end they cannot identify with the moon, they should be able to identify with the stars.

In "Rain Dance" (41), Ndi's anger at leaders, Africans typically, whom he sees as tyrants without a vision, boils over. Hence, these selfish leaders set aside by their "swine Greed" (41), surround themselves with tight security: "These tyrants / steel hemmed / Daunt skunks...! (41). It is obvious Ndi has no respect for these leaders as he insults them, a practice almost totally alien to Africans who show a lot of respect for age, let alone their leaders. That he compares them to filthy swine is indicative of Ndi's frustration, disgust, and burning rage at these traitors.

To Ndi, this clinging onto power and its fringe benefits amounts to vanity as revealed in "Vain Glory" (51), yet he is unable to understand why such a simple fact is beyond the comprehension of these moral dwarfs passing for political leaders especially in Africa and his native Cameroon in particular. The poet laments the discrepancy in society, that rejection experienced by a child growing up with great expectations, hoping that she is striving toward equality in society only to realize things have never been as they seem; her world is tortured by vanity as some look down on others, "And with the greenest eyes drinking / Others..." for the simple reason that "[...] they eject dejectedly / Thoughts of supremacy ..." (51).

In "K'cracy," the title poem, Ndi makes a comparison of Cameroon's former president, Ahmadou Ahidjo, and the incumbent, Paul Biya. To the poet, the former looked evil but the latter is, indeed, evil even though he wants to paint his predecessor as bad. Hence Ndi describes Biya's succession to Ahidjo's throne in "The Shoots" (62), which is an imagery of those in power recklessly abandoning themselves to a vegetative state by doing nothing to address the plight of the people they are supposed to be governing:

> The change that ever place took
> Never was anymore than night followed by
> An eclipse profounder than night.
> And replaced Mask
> Though nightly painted is cleaner
> For the darker genotype is the cleaner phenotype. (62)

In "We see, Only Mourn. *Cities' Debacle*" (71), there is another comparison made of Ahidjo and Paul Biya while playing with their skin color — Ahidjo being darker than Biya. We are made to understand that the whites exploited the blacks just as Biya, the light-skinned leader, has been exploiting our nation. It is not surprising then that all the displeasure culminates in "Dragon-like Friday (April Sixth)" when an attempted coup against the Biya regime was staged in Cameroon but failed.

Meanwhile, in "The Versatiles" (63), Ndi goes on to damn the former speaker of Cameroon's House of Assembly, Solomon Tandeng Muna and his House of Assembly for refusing to give in to the idea of democracy when it was first voiced: "On our knees forced we him and his House hear say "No!" (63). To Ndi, this was a leader who was most unwilling to give anyone a chance who was not his own true blood: "Never is he not unwilling to let any, / No matter whom but his embryo him replace" (63). It is not surprising then that in "Our House" (76), Ndi, like other Cameroonian poets, such as Christmas Ebini Atem in "Applause Applause" (31 – 32), and Emmanuel Fru Doh in "Njangi House" (5 – 6), reminds these members of the House about their role as members of the House instead of them spending time nodding and approving whatever comes their way:

> Beguiled we stand agape
> Sinking in swamps' forest.

> Our fertile village land
> Needs a hitch and courage
> And there we'll bask ourselves
> Like playing eagles at dawn
> 'planing across the sky in the morning sun
> With backs on walls, we must
> To the last wan, wailing, fight. (76)

Appropriately then, in "Assassinating Democracy (Insurgence)" (79), Ndi celebrates advocates of democracy who were slaughtered by Cameroon's security forces, which to him are "forces of regression" (79), on the occasion of the launching of democracy in Cameroon in the guise of the Social Democratic Front (SDF) political party. Ndi considers the six who were murdered on this occasion national martyrs and is waiting for the day they will be formally recognized:

> Martyrs are these six
> In this nation where no dead is a hero
> For what we live for is the here and now
> A less conducive one for a penman!
> Yet, I long for that day this Mayday
> Shall itself fit into our official commemorations!
> Our Martyr's Mayday
> Victory over dictacracy! (79)

Within the national problem, Ndi isolates and personalizes his dissatisfaction as an Anglophone-Cameroonian in "Caught" (82). He does this by presenting the Anglophone as trapped in his predicament within the Cameroon nation, a predicament the late firebrand scholar and critic Bate Besong described as being beasts without a nation in his play *Beasts of No Nation*. According to Ndi, as Anglophones try to reason together, the president of the nation appoints an Anglophone to a high office and the rest from this ethnic group stop seeing the need for change in the country. Thus, the Anglophone effort to improve upon their lot in their fatherland remains thwarted.

The seriousness of the Anglophone problem is again touched upon in "IUD" (90), which stands here for an intrauterine device. In this poem Ndi explores a one-time attempt by those in power to control the Anglophone population from exploding. This is a poem certainly influenced by attempts several decades ago, to sterilize girls in Bamenda while masking the dastardly act as a vaccine program. Its discovery led to the death of a Roman Catholic priest in Kumbo, Cameroon.

Ndi returns in "The Real Guano" (94) to confirm that in the struggle for citizens' national rights and specifically those of Anglophones as a people, the real drive has always come from the Grassfields. There was Gorji at first (Gorji Dinka, I dare suggest) and then came Fru Ndi who brought about neo-colonial democracy in Cameroon when he and a crowd in Bamenda stood their ground against soldiers trying to stop them from launching the SDF party. Interestingly, the one who was trying to block such a process by unleashing his dogs of war on Fru Ndi and members of the public, Paul Biya, is today claiming to be the one who promoted democracy in Cameroon. Yet, it was his ministers cum intellectuals who went about embarrassing themselves by chanting hymns against multi-party politics. Hence the poet calls out for all to join hands with Fru Ndi whose name is spelt by the initials of "**F**or **R**esourceful **U**nison / **N**ot **D**iscouraging **I**ntellectualism" (emphasis mine, 94). The same feeling of the Grassfields as a place advocating our freedom is encountered in "Grassfield" (103) where the people are ready to pay the price for "liberty" (103). A look at the allusions to places, people, the weather, and historical events hints at the fact that to Bill F. Ndi, this part of the country shall be responsible for bringing down the oppression he decries. Extending this allusive field, Ndi makes mention of General Winter, the harsh 1812 winter, which was responsible for bringing the tyrant Napoleon to his knees when he attempted to overrun Moscow in his 1812 campaign. This specific case in Ndi's work is not just one of allusive embellishment but of corroborating allusiveness: Ndi is possibly suggesting that nature too will bring down this dictator.

Ndi's social angst in a world made uncomfortable by political minions and questionable academics soars as he continues to wonder about the socio-political situation in Cameroon where the citizens have been transformed into prisoners in their own country by a leadership that would not conduct dialogue with them and is always overseas, completely oblivious to what is happening at home:

> We as prisoners
> Seeking escape sneaked out
> As he took to his chambers;
> came to the parlour while we're out,
>
> he hate [sic] this fresh air
> and loves French air
> enjoyable only abroad
> not this waste intoxicated one aboard
>
> our one real father
> has children at heart
> depriving them of fresh air
> his prerogatives found abroad. (64)

It is no wonder then Biya is called "Pope of Camsima" in the poem with the same title. Convinced that "Cam" stands for Cameroon and "sima" for Silicate and Magnesia, i.e. the earth's crust, and also remembering that Pope John Paul II was the travelling Pope who covered virtually all of the earth, the analogy between the Pope and Biya becomes obvious. The Pope, however, did travel for good reasons: to unite his followers and show his love for them and the rest of the world, thereby assuming the responsibility of his office as Pope. This is not the case with Biya, who travels abroad to avoid dealing with important socio-political issues at home, thus destroying all the good work his predecessor had begun: "Intelligently thou fly over the world. / Bat! Bittering the sugared pills" (73) Ahidjo had put in place. Indeed, the past glories of the Sahel, a symbol of Ahidjo's birth place, which means the good work done by Ahidjo and the glories of his reign have all been wasted by Biya: "Past glories of the Sahel all gone" (73). This same fear of leaders Ndi wants to see unseated is once more echoed in "The Plebs: Their Chair" (70). The trouble, though, is doubt about their reactions to such efforts on the part of the oppressed. However, the persona is convinced that such leaders, though tyrants, cannot afford to wipe everybody and rule in a vacuum: "With their armed arms / Can they rid us / And in vacuum reign?" (70).

In "In Our Manger: Are We Strangers?" (74) Ndi continues lamenting the fact that as a whole, Cameroon treats her citizens, even before the Anglophone problem, as if they are strangers, or as if their country belongs to someone else. Simply for taking to the streets to protest against the status quo, citizens end up with "hounds" (74)—the police—chasing, brutalizing, and putting them behind bars, thereby intensifying the feeling of alienation and estrangement even when the poet is still at home. This poem also comes across as an opportunity for Ndi to educe one of the darkest moments of Africa's history, the apartheid system which was practiced in South Africa until the early 90s. To this effect, Ndi extends his angst and humanist vision to the plight of the iconic Nelson Mandela encrypted in this poem as "**M**anly **A**frican **N**ationalist **D**enied **E**very **L**egal **A**menities" ([sic], emphasis mine 74). This encryption is a symbolic representation of the one who has beaten all the odds to survive any obstacle alienation might have erected in his path. When it is realized that Ndi wrote this poem five years *before* the fall of apartheid, his humanist and equally prophetic vision becomes remarkable. In spite of all the horrors brought the way of this "Manly African…" by the evil forces of apartheid, Ndi declares with so much conviction his becoming the liberating force: "Yet, his goblin would and our ship will respire" (74) Yes, that part of our continent, comparatively speaking, is respiring today thanks to the "Manly African…" [7].

Ndi's frustration with his country peaks when in "Dredging Mokolo Market" (78), he points out the madness that governance amounts to through the abusive use of the nation's resources and facilities against the citizens. At a very basic level here, Ndi laments the fact that "Extinguishers never their job did" (78). He uses a fire incident in Yaounde when Stamatiades, a well-equipped drug store, got burnt down without the fire brigade showing up to help put out the flames only for this same brigade to show up with water cannons on another day to brutalize and hose market women from their spots where they displayed their wares because the council was about to develop the market. What mismanagement of resources, amounting to an embarrassing display of the absence of dialogue and democracy in society as Cameroonians are abused by their own government instead of being educated and convinced why certain decisions are being taken, such as the need for the market to be developed or redesigned in a particular manner. As a result, Ndi trashes the general, Gaston, in charge of this operation by qualifying him as a Lilliputian. By this allusion to Jonathan Swift's *Gulliver's Travels*, Ndi stands on the shoulder of his angst to decry the meanness, pettiness, and brainlessness of those oppressing his people. An allusion like this which echoes the infirm cast at the head of his country does not merely amplify Ndi's angst, that feeling of alienation and not belonging but also his humanist vision.

Ndi's angst, along with his frustration and anger, was triggered by his native Cameroon, hence the need for him to look elsewhere so as to remain calm and sane like a soldier retreating from one battle to better plan on how to engage another. Upon leaving Cameroon, the budding scholar hoped to encounter greener pastures; alas, in Nigeria, he was classified a foreigner. The poet's angst also intensified and was to be most traumatizing in the West. In France, Ndi was no longer only a foreigner, he was now both a foreigner and "le petit nègre," deepening more his anxiety about human existence. Ndi's angst about the human predicament, even beyond Africa, causes him in "Thirst: Would Our Heads Understand" to warn before observing:

> Stage the biggest war
> Create the supreme fight
> To show your might
> And in the name of fame
> . . . .
>
> Greatness does not come by war
> Greatness never passes through a door
> He dwells inside
> And shows the light. (11)

Even then, the ingredients that spiced further his state of anxiety and worry keep popping up every now and then. Accordingly, Ndi's poems present scenes in which people live on the edge of an isolated, insecure, and equally fragmented existence through exploring the gloomy, lethargic, and seemingly hopeless struggle for survival in a miserably harsh world poisoned by humankind's inability to be decent and fair. In this light, Ndi's writing amounts to a social act, thereby confirming him a genuine example of Jean-Paul Sartre's "new" writer to whom he accorded a three-pronged task here effectively executed by Ndi:

> ...to discern behind the surface chaos of the times the interdependent processes that pattern human lives and orient humanity toward its future forms of collective existence; through

conscious practice in his personal and political life and relentless self-criticism, to participate effectively in the shaping of that future; and through his writing, to communicate to as broad a public as he could reach the nature of the patterns in the making, the issues they involved. (qtd. in Brée 26)

In "The Racist Black" (12), a discomfiting experience is presented as big black men are used as cultural heralds to deliver scathing messages to other black men whom the hypocritical white population cannot face. The "gorilla-like" black culture envoy is a bouncer keeping out other black men from nightclubs where white men do not want them. While telling black men "To night, the pub is all women" (12), white men are being let in. Racism is the new flavor to spice up the angst sauce already nauseating the poet.

In "Presence" (13), unable to take lightly the alienation caused by such isolation, the persona escapes into love for some comfort which is only ephemeral as indicated by the ever present Joycean idea of flight concretized in the bird image—the swallow—"And me in the bird fly," (13). Isolation, alienation, and angst, are all feelings drowning the persona. This is certainly a mirroring of the poet's own state.

In "Sweet Exile" (15), Ndi's persona relapses into a state of anguish again parallel to the poet's. He laments the fact that he is away from home albeit with plans to return, "And in hope to go home" (15), but before that day, like our ancestors, Africans in the West remain laborers. In this capacity, they are drained of their energy and even their earnings such that they return home worse than half the people they were when they left, for they return "maimed" (15). According to Ndi, African immigrants in the diaspora are a new breed of slaves who work and leave everything behind only to return home empty-handed and maimed.

The poet's social angst is again heightened as revealed by the persona's encounter in "Glen" when an Irishman, a scallywag by the name of Glen, thinks the persona cannot understand his problem simply because the persona is African: "You can't understand / Being African the problem is Irish" (16). The persona, like the poet, is thereby reminded of his alien status in a most condescending manner, his knowledge of the pain of alienation notwithstanding. The persona, however, parries Glen's ignorant remark by recalling his interest in, and his awareness of the universality of the plight of the alienated worldwide from as far back as during his days as a schoolboy:

> I laughed
> At the remembrance
> Of those days as a schoolboy
> When scanning
> 'An Irishman Foresees his death'
> 'The Bloody Sunday'
> And playing Singe's 'Show-boy...'
> And a host of others
> Were all with my world one! (16)

It is with a certain aloofness that the politics of his inherited nation is dealt with while in exile; his plate is already too full with the problems of his native soil. And so in "Another Messiah is Born" (19), a poem which echoes views about Jacques Chirac's 1995 victory on "Seventh May," the presentation of the victory scene is lackluster: Chirac's arrival is presented as the same old song—just another election brouhaha void of any significant promise. Chirac's victory is similar to what takes place in the other major Western capitals: Washington, Kremlin, and Westminster, of course. These leaders always come to power in style, yet upon their departure nothing much would have changed with regards to the plight of the downtrodden, the neo-colonized, and the alienated.

Exile and the feeling of alienation are again strongly experienced in "The Seine By Night" (27) in which a regular visitor to the river spends time thinking about liberty of which exiles are in some way deprived, since they cannot really be where they would love to be—their native shores. His disillusionment is compounded by the fact that even while in exile in France, the country of "liberty" turns out to be the grave in which she is buried as liberty becomes an elusive creature magicking away like "Faustus' Queen in raid" (27). Comparing her parade to that of the French military only gives meaning to the illusion liberty has become. This idea echoes the image of the French military parading to kill thoughts of liberty in French dominions like Cameroon. Along with the feeling of alienation, such a soul relapses into doing battle with himself as revealed in "The Inner Being" (30) in which the inner and true self begins to wonder about and question what is becoming of human beings as everyone seems to be aping the West with its moral conflicts and vainness.

Solitude, alienation, and the feeling of frustration are again experienced in "Pari(s) Ah" (42). This poem, with an evocative title, cages "Paris" and "Pariah." In it, should the parenthetical "s" be dropped, the reader would undoubtedly be left with "Pariah." This highlights the revelation that the beauty, along with all the lights, is experienced only from afar as the reality of Paris is morbid: the neglected poor one encounters, the disparity between the rich and the poor:

> Bleak city heart so bright
> Outward villas at night
> . . . .
> We started shouldering
> Trash
> We're
> T'mark twilights' dawn west .... (42)

The same spirit of disillusionment with Paris continues in "Paris: Is It?" (44), as the persona considers things in the city as artificial, fake, and unreal. A smile, for example, is not genuine, emphasizing thus the solitary lifestyle which then intensifies the outsider's feelings of loss and alienation. Hence in a subtle metaphor the poet writes comparing Paris to a desert, "...so deserted / That not even a date was in sight" (44). Ndi's persona is puzzled then by an atmosphere of gloominess, isolation, discord, and disillusionment where his hope for a better life is crushed as his existence is now cheated of its humanity by sordid forces like racism, ostracism, and loneliness. As a result, the persona wonders about the meaninglessness of French colonialists indoctrinating those they "civilized" with the notion of France being home, their real motherland, when there seems to be nothing there for these exiles, aliens who have paid over and over for being colonized by the French: "For the chattel, he thrice paid / ... / Hands looking only west" (45).

Ndi left home bitter about the political backwater it is, hoping to find relief, peace, and calm in the West, yearning to be free of angst triggered by his native soil, only to be slapped in the face with racism, discrimination, and a disturbingly solitary lifestyle. It is no wonder Ndi's personae, like he himself, had to deal with frustration, disillusionment, and melancholia which, after all, culminated in a humanist vision for himself in particular, Cameroon, and the entire human situation. Ndi's anxiety, therefore, heightens with his determination to make the world a better place. As a result, in "Hearing the Voiceless" (7), it is Ndi's wish that that which is overwhelmingly important should prevail:

> The connection
> Of the inner voice
> And the voiceless, their voice
> Within telling their travail,

> Hopes and aspirations shall prevail. (7)

The poet urges further that poverty, not materialism, only strengthens and grants resolve to the oppressed to survive but with the barest to survive on.

Exile, then, were one to pit Ndi's personae as his alter egos, has not been wonderful. Being away from Africa in exile in the West, the poet has come to realize that the West has its own problems, a realization that continues to torment his views on human existence. To make things worse, Africa's profitless exploitation by Western governments becomes more evident. As the poem "In my herd" (23) reveals of the "herd" of nations owned by Western powers, African nations are "The one cattle standing / As the greatest menace" (23), which is milked over and over, depleting natural resources while presenting the nations as deserts with nothing to offer.

In "Transparency" (24), another poem generated by Ndi's troubled psyche as a result of the ontological bareness of his world, the persona calls out for writing that communicates so the audience could use the words from these writers like weapons to bring down the oppressors. This is Ndi's humanist vision for the world beginning to take shape in his writing. He has identified himself as an oppressed citizen of the universe—at home and abroad—so what next? Ndi's vision intensifies in "May Be in a Dream" (26), in which he compares St Lucian poet and playwright Derek Walcott and "hit-la" (Hitler). Ndi is later to confirm this interpretation when he writes:

> He and him are down in History
> And we have at least a story;
> The one in the military
> The other in the literary
> And I bow to the literate,
> His militancy not the military illiterate
> Against literacy. (26)

To Ndi, writers can be better mentors of society than soldiers of the likes of Hitler backed by nothing else but military mettle.

Ndi is, therefore, calling upon the oppressed in "Beyond Sentient Patience" (10) to do something in order to improve upon their lot instead of sitting back complaining and doing nothing. He confirms in "Come's the Time" (34) that it is time for action so as to bring about change, even as a few corrupt and corrupted citizens are still clinging to the dishonest ways of the incumbent dictator:

> But, come is the time
> Lulling its forward march?
> No way? To let it, we must slump then
> Put on our last putrid rags. (34)

Ndi's commitment brings to mind Jay Parini's expectation of poets:

> It is important for poets to read the world around them and to respond to that world in their own fashion: not in slogans that can be printed on posters or slapped on to bumpers but in urgent, astute ways that reflect injustice and immorality everywhere in evidence, even sad abundance. (116)

Through the reverse juxtaposition which opens the poem with "Sunset" and closes it with "Sunrise," Ndi assures the oppressed in "Sunset / Sunrise" (49) that they have, indeed, been crushed until they are living in darkness, but they shall arise. Besides, the configuration of these words on the page is also revealing of Ndi's angst and vision. "Sunset" appears on the top (i.e. Priority) left of the poem (geographically, West) and "Sunrise" occupies bottom right (geographically East), an indication of Ndi's last hope for an unfailingly bright future for humanity. Everything else happens in-between, replicating the internal torment, dark thoughts and angst in the persona's psyche. It is a flashback on the persona's "boyhood" which is "gone" and in its place the imposition of alienation by extraneous forces.

In "Stale-Word (Hope)" (66), the persona takes one last sweep at his life from childhood to maturity, acknowledging the difficulties and challenges in his way growing up. As an adult, he becomes completely disappointed with the tide of events in life such that he wishes for his blissful ignorant childhood days when he was unaware of the ills he became conscious of as an adult. Regrettably, he has been unable to do much to improve upon the situation because of the corrupt and hostile forces in the path of change:

> In those long gone days
> Adulthood I thought nice;
> Now for my childhood I long
> For it is better stay in dark;
> We in ignorance
> See everything bliss,
> Than live in light that is bleak
> Unable to effect change
> 'Cause of the thousand bayonets
> screening the pavements
> those leading to the doors of change. (66)

In his vision of an ideal society, Ndi wants to eliminate oppression, poverty, and bad governance so as to emerge with a world that is peaceful, calm, provided for, and free. For this reason, he is not afraid to call for an uprising if that is what would bring about positive change in society. Robert Bly has posited that the true political poem does not order us to take any specific acts, but like the personal poem, it moves us to deepen awareness (134). To Ndi this is only part of the effort as he goes beyond deepening our awareness into urging his readers into action. In Lenore Kandel's opinion, "Poetry is never a compromise. It is the manifestation/translation of a vision, an illumination, an experience. If you compromise your vision you become a blind poet" (450). Accordingly, Ndi will not compromise his syncretic vision; instead, his poetry inspires political and social awareness among readers, opening their hearts and minds to possibilities never quite imaginable without it (Parini 24). No, Ndi's poems are not idle or written simply to enjoy the sound of words, not with all that is going on around him. In Ndi's predicament, there is no point in poetry which exists mainly as an exercise in dexterity, for "…craft is valuable in so far as it serves as a brilliant midwife for clarity, beauty, visions; less it degenerates into producing word masturbation only" (Kandel 450).

Indeed, Ndi's craft serves a purpose: it is an eye opener, a desperate cry for mankind to revisit his environment and rethink his deeds by reorienting his worldview so that humankind can face humankind without guilt or animosity because of the deeds of the one to the other. The poet's hope that all will be fine in the end is so strong, yet at times he doubts this vision which seems to stall when urgently needed such that he names hope "Mr. Dixeption" (67). Even with this sporadically shaken hope, Ndi has no other way out than to urge the oppressed to be "[h]opelessly hopefully optimistic" (68). Ndi succeeds in communicating his message which is sometimes difficult to arrive at because of a style that can be disturbingly peculiar such that it leaves one wondering, since it is no accident, given the way this quality recurs. Ndi's words have a way of springing out meaning and possible interpretations at one. His words are often like compressed verbal springs in a box with a latch which, when released, toss out meanings at an involved reader. The difficulty is in releasing the latch, which happens when the first correct idea intended by a word is arrived at; virtually all else falls in place then with a kind of domino effect. It must be a similar technique that led Owen Barfield to write in *Poetic Diction*: "The full meanings of words are flashing, iridescent shapes like flames—ever-flickering vestiges of the slowly evolving consciousness beneath them" (qtd. in Bradbury 14). Only a common background could help decipher some of Ndi's lexemic puzzles, else the reader is lost. Because this happens often, Ndi comes across as a difficult poet in spite of his mostly simple diction. Ndi's layering and texturing of both word and meaning prick the mind to search beneath and beyond the surface as he renders his apparently simplistic words unrecognizable to reflect the imperceptibility of a visionary made possible by the ills he challenges. This smack of the magical in Ndi's poetry is tantamount to a replication of his own life in particular as well as that of the bulk of the alienated underdogs of this world in general.

Writing about Ndi has been a challenging yet interesting task as his travels, triggered by haunting socio-political encounters, has led to angst and his quest for a way out—physical, mental, and emotional freedom. The overall effect is a culmination into a rich and equally culturally diverse depth of experiences, albeit often depressing, that fascinate and as well enthrall the mind. It is in this light that Ndi's poems in *K'cracy* amount to ideological avenues that portray, highlight, and inspire an ever-refreshing connection with the poet's experiences and his vision for society. With his humanist vision so clear and poised, Ndi cries out to God for help in "My Prayer" (48). He could care less about theories on religion as the opiate of society; if all else has failed or is taking too long and leaving the oppressed in doubt and misery, then he is not afraid to turn to a force his life has assured him will not fail. In this light, I see Ndi, the poet, as a visionary; however, beyond William Blake's submission (Galvin 16). Ndi's inspiration does not only arise from within but also from without as he struggles to reconcile himself with the unnecessary conflicts and evil around him. The result is a committed poet who, after confronting his angst initiated by his experiences in life, is aflame with the desire to communicate his humanist vision—the possibility of a congruous and peaceful co-existence—to an embattled humanity. In times like these, by communicating his humanist vision, Ndi hopes he is contributing to the gradual, yet invaluable, remaking of a world currently disfigured by greed, myopia, parochialism, and moral recklessness so that human beings can, in the end, thrive in solace, understanding, and true freedom moderated by the fear of God:

> God
> Let all your own light
> See and not for a fragment shine bright
> Amen. (48)

Notes

1. In his essay "Tragedy and the Common Man," Arthur Miller presents his ideas on what a tragedy and a tragic hero are today. In a nutshell, tragedy, to Miller, is not supposed to be pessimistic, but rather an optimistic display of human qualities. He argues that the tragic hero does not necessarily have to be a king or of a noble background; thus even the common man can be considered a tragic hero. He points out that if tragedy were to only apply to kings, then it would be impossible for everyone else to cherish and comprehend it. Miller makes the point that the tragic flaw is the idea that the tragic hero is unable to accept anything that may affect his status or self-image. Accordingly, the only quality needed for a character to be a tragic hero, according to Miller, is the readiness to lay down his life, if need be, to secure his sense of personal dignity.

2. Ndi prepared for his Ordinary Level certificate at Government Bilingual Secondary School Bamenda, but had to write the exam as an external candidate at another center, Bambili. He was sent away from his school at the behest of his teacher who felt insulted when Ndi questioned his methodology vis à vis that of another teacher, when it came to teaching Shakespeare.

3. French is one of three subjects a student in the English-speaking part of Cameroon must have a pass grade in so as to move to the next class. This is the case all through secondary school; Math and English are the other two.

4. This is all the name one ever got of this rapscallion of a superintendent (*Commissaire*) of police.

5. There is the need to point out that national security in dictatorships like Cameroon has nothing to do with the welfare of the citizens; instead, it has everything to do with ensuring the safety and maintenance of power by the incumbent dictator. So ordinary citizens could be hurt or even killed to ensure this and it will all be

categorized as efforts at maintaining law and order—national security.

6. When Ndi started school in Nigeria, his university was known at the time as Imo State University; it was renamed Abia University by the time he was graduating.

7. During an interview with Ndi, the awkwardness of this poem as a post-apartheid venture, a feeling I had when reading the volume, came up. The poet pointed out that this poem, like a number of others in the volume, was written in 1985, hence his conviction and humanist vision about the future of apartheid South Africa.

Works Cited

Atem, Christmas Ebini. *Partners in Prison: Selected Poems*. Douala : Lycee Bilingue de Bonaberi, 1991. Print.
Besong, Bate. *Beasts of No Nation*. Limbe: Nooremac, 1990. Print.
Bly, Robert. "Leaping up into Political Poetry." *Poetry and Politics: An Anthology of Essays*. Ed. Richard Jones. New York: William Morrow, 1985. 129-37. Print.
Bradbury, J. G. "Poetic Vision: Owen Barfield and Charles Williams." *Renascence* 63.1 (2010): 13-22. Print.
Brée, Germaine. *Camus and Sartre: Crisis and Commitment*. New York: A Delta Book, 1972. Print.
Doh, Emmanuel Fru. *Wading the Tide*. Langaa: Mankon-Bamenda, 2009.
Galvin, Rachel. "William Blake: Visions and Verses." *Humanities* May/June (2004): 16-20. Print.
Greene, Diana. "Denis Levertov: A Poet's Pilgrimage." *National Catholic Reporter* 27 (2007): 14-15. Print.
Hugo, Victor. *Odes Et Ballades*. Paris : Novelle ed. Librairie de L. Hachette, 1862. Print.

Kandel, Lenore. "Poetry is Never Compromise." *Poetics of the New American Poetry*. Ed. Donald Allen and Warren Tallman. New York: Grove, 1973. 450-52. Print.

Ndi, Bill F. *K'cracy, Trees in the Storm and Other Poems*. Mankon Bamenda: Langaa, 2008. Print.

Parini, Jay. *Why Poetry Matters*. New Haven: Yale UP, 2008. Print.

Plato. *Republic*. Trans. Robin Waterfield. Oxford: Oxford UP, 2008. Print.

Reid, Jimmy. "Alienation - or 'The Rat Race' Speech." On the Occasion of His Inauguration as Rector of Glasgow University. Glasgow. 1972. Speech.

Chapter 2

In Moments like These: Emmanuel Fru Doh and the Mirrors of Romanticism

By
Antonio Jimenez Munoz

Despite both the French and English languages being official in the country, the Anglophones who form the minority in Cameroon have long denounced marginalization by the Francophone majority. They have claimed that their language, disfavored against French as the language of the administration, limits their participation in the decision-making of the country and also in the provinces where they live, which they believe are deliberately backward in socio-economic development compared to the rest of the country.[1] They see their position close to subjugation, since many feel that "nation-building has been driven by the firm determination of the Francophone political elite to dominate the Anglophone minority in the post-colonial state and to erase the cultural and institutional foundations of Anglophone identity" (Eyoh 249). Contrasted with Francophone output, English-writing poets are themselves in an uneven situation. Their writings are often equated to oppression. Despite recent efforts, the status of Anglophone poetry within Cameroonian culture can still be considered marginal at best. While there is intrinsic value in poetry being written by Anglophone Cameroonian poets, its dissemination to their primary readership is relatively small. Abroad,

---

[1] As Juliana Nfah-Abbenyi notes, to be "Anglophone or Francophone in this postcolony is to be much more than a speaker of English or French"; and these labels are "codes fraught with meanings that can simultaneously conjure cultural, political, linguistic complexities/tensions complicated by concepts of nation and/or ethnicity" (24).

within an already decentered position for African literature, their poetry seems to be even more painfully disregarded. Though English poetry commands a bigger readership and market globally, or precisely because it is the case, their poetry is nevertheless a contribution to the larger body of global poetry.

As a consequence, Cameroonian poets writing in English see their work doubly marginalized: politically from within and economically from without. As Oscar C. Labang complains in the introduction to a recent anthology of Cameroonian Anglophone poetry, these poets are the "margin in a marginal society," often "regarded as a pariah" and also "the subject of derision and misgiving" (xi). Their poems act accordingly to this derision; these are often irate speech acts against the political frivolity, economic ineptitude and downright abuse of power which has characterized the governance of the country. This is deeply distinct from the themes and function of poetry in most parts of the Western world. While these Cameroonian poets mostly have a strong trend of an eminently social poetry, in most of Europe and America this function has long been considered a mid-twentieth century phenomenon, restricted to those countries where dictatorships were in power. As Western countries transitioned towards democracy, the need for socially-geared poems seemed to be no longer justified. In contrast, contemporary Cameroon Anglophone poetry often results in harsh contestations to the perceived oppression, marginalization and discrimination which deliberately put these poets and their poems, despite their cultural triumphs and wealth of expression, in the difficult place of a minority struggling not to be silenced.

Despite their causes being different, when compared to the sorry state of poetry in the Western world, with falling sales and lack of media attention,[2] the status of Cameroon poetry in English is remarkably similar to that of poetry elsewhere. While poets struggle to make some impact, their voices are part of a system which favors their silence. Whether politically or economically determined, poets write in an environment which is unfavorable. Poetry is either innocuous to question power and status quo and thus inherently irrelevant to the community they serve, or else it would struggle not to be silenced. The end result is remarkably similar: poetry which is socially relevant by design, as well as one which is eminently personal or experiential, seems to end up not reaching its target audiences. As disseminating, editing and publishing poetry become scantier and the readership narrower and narrower, the blame can be easily put on poetry itself. It is no longer relevant for moments like these.[3] Times for poetry are hard, but, as I aim to show here, the ways in which different poets and poems face that challenge can differ wildly while illuminating upon each other.

While Western poets have turned inwards towards self-expression and have largely relinquished the social roles of poetry, Anglophone poets in Cameroon, such as the late Bate Besong, John Ngong Kum Ngong, Vakunta Peter, Ba'Bila Mutia, Bill F. Ndi,

---

[2] According to governmental reports, between three to four per cent of UK book sales were poetry, and these were already "highly concentrated" at the turn of the century, as one author – Seamus Heaney – concentrated "sixty seven per cent of sales of contemporary volumes" (Bridgwood 1). The American Poetry Foundation sales lists for the last three years show that only Mary Oliver and Derek Walcott have managed to sell over a hundred thousand copies of their poetry collections, but only as an aggregate of their latest five books (Poetry Foundation 20); which gives an indication of a tendency that, at least in Western societies, reveals the reading of modern poetry as a dwindling activity.

[3] Particularly in Western societies, many have actually called for the cultural decline of poetry. Dana Gioia, poet and former chairman of the American National Endowment for the Arts, complains that poets "are almost invisible" to Western societies (94) – a sentiment which has been radicalised by others into the death of poetry (Wexler) – while influential critics such as Joseph Hillis Miller acknowledge that "if Shakespeare were alive today" he would not be writing poetry at all, as he would have done "if he had lived in the Romantic period" (111).

Kangsen Feka Wakai, Gahlia Gwangwa'a, Alembong Nol, Sammy Oke Akombi, Mathew Takwi, Giftus Nkam, Oscar C. Labang, Emmanuel Fru Doh, etc., have consistently denounced in their poems the various abuses of power, the monetary exploitation of the vast natural and human resources of their country, and the tendency of governments to cause social disunion. Whether in the diaspora or at the home front, these poets have sustained a social role which goes beyond aspects of self-expression and into matters of social as well as personal identity.[4] Poetry can thus serve as a weapon; it can be thrown at leaders, officials and people in an attempt to change their attitudes, to raise awareness, to denounce injustice, without renouncing other forms of poetic expression.[5] Taking Doh's poems, I want to show here that verse can also serve as a mirror; it can reflect not only other poetry produced in other parts of the world, but also the poetic tradition of those poems written in the same language.

Much of Cameroonian and African poetry explores how gender, ethnicity, class or culture interact with state power and traditional forms and institutions as these continue to shape postcolonial conditions in a global society. Few of these institutions are more entrenched in the language of poetry than the legacy of Romanticism. There is a general consensus between poetry scholars worldwide that the influences of British Romanticism upon the poetry produced in English have been largely unacknowledged throughout the

---

[4] When contrasted to European poetry, the weight of the social in African culture has been often noted in seminal studies to be a quintessential, distinctive feature, as "this insistence on the social role of the African artist and the denial of the European preoccupation with individual experience has been one of the most distinctive features in the assertion of a unique African aesthetic" (Ashcroft, Griffiths and Tiffin 125).

[5] Bate Besong, perhaps Anglophone Cameroon's most charismatic playwright and poet, has always maintained that the Anglophone creative writer "must arouse his Anglophone constituency from the apathy and despair into which it has 'sunk' and transform his writing into 'hand grenades' to be used against Francophone oppressors" (qtd. in Ngwane 35).

theorizations of the twentieth century. Prominent theorists such as Isaiah Berlin, Alan Badiou, Philippe Lacoue-Labarthe, Jean-Luc Nancy or Jerome McGann have raised questions which call for the persistence of Romanticism. Berlin views Romanticism as the

> [G]reatest single shift in the consciousness of the West that has occurred, and all the other shifts which have occurred in the course of the nineteenth and twentieth centuries appear to me in comparison less important, and at any rate deeply influenced by it. (1)

To Badiou, we do not know whether we will "be delivered, finally delivered, from our subjection to Romanticism" (23). Romantic poetry has been associated in both Germany and the UK to a literary absolute (Nancy and Lacoue-Labarthe), while other critics such as McGann have denounced how poetic criticism has been "dominated by a Romantic ideology, by an uncritical absorption in Romanticism's own self-representations" (1).

Whether by sales and critical success, theorizations or sheer aesthetic achievement, the result is one of domination: in the English language, Romantic poetry replaces poetry as a whole, and even if formal changes occur later, its aesthetic tenets still largely fuel the production and appreciation of poetry at present. More recently, some scholars have called the attention to this dominance of Romanticism in contemporary poetry: "[J]ust as it has often been claimed that Modernism is essentially a remoulding of Romanticism, [...] Postmodernism is also yet another mutation of the original stock" (Larrissy 1), so that Romanticism is "not only [...] the root of our modem times, but also as its trunk, branches and leaves" (Moscovici 3). Scholars have begun to trace these romantic modes of expression in both American and European poets writing in English.⁶ That influence, to my knowledge, has rarely been acknowledged outside these two continents, and particularly, it has never been applied in African poetry. Taking the case of a prominent Cameroonian poet, I hope to show here, however, that Anglophone Cameroonian poetry can mirror the ways in which literature itself travels across lands and time, that poets manage implicit heritage and tradition, and that poetic legacies shape the form of poetry at present, even in cases such as Doh's in which tradition is not so apparent.

In recent years, Doh has become a major voice in Cameroonian poetry because of his harsh denunciations of the terrible damage caused to his country by successive regimes. He is consistent and his literary merits are beyond reproach. Before moving to the USA at the turn of the century, he had already gained a literary reputation at home throughout the nineties while teaching at the University of Yaounde. Acclaimed as a scholar and a critic, he is progressively acquiring relevance abroad, to which this chapter humbly aims to add. Collections such as *Wading the Tide* (1995), *Not Yet Damascus* (2007), *Oriki'badan* (2009) and *Shadows* (2011) have created a noticeable body of work which deserves more attention[7] and can

---

[6] O'Neill has identified Romantic traits in a number of poets such as Wilfred Owen, Robert Frost, Denise Levertov, Robert Lowell, and other many British, American and Irish poets (O'Neill, The All-sustaining Air: Romantic Legacies and Renewals in British, American, and Irish Poetry Since 1900), backed up by other studies of the modalities of that romantic influence upon Victorian (Martens) and twentieth-century poetry (Davies and Turley) which aim to show pervasive aesthetic legacies in these last two centuries (Casaliggi and March-Russell).

[7] Doh has written consistently in the last two decades. Apart from the poetry volumes referred to here, he is the author of two perceptive, devastating critiques of kleptocracy (*Africa's Political Wastelands: The Bastardization of Cameroon*) and of African clichés on foreign eyes (*Stereotyping Africa: Surprising Answers to Surprising Questions*). He has also penned fiction (*The Fire Within*) as well as his recent memoir (*Nomads: the Memoir of a Southern Cameroonian*) in which he gives a bleak account of the destruction of Cameroon as a nation on the grounds of linguistic disaggregation.

serve as an example of a kind of eminently social poetry which has been lost in most of the Western world. This social perspective of poetry makes it relevant in this new century. It is also one which is not at odds with other expressive modes. Doh's poems offer a wide thematic palette which, beyond their social emphases, can also be linked to lyrical, 'identitarian' and self-expressive modes used by other contemporary poets as well as those of the past.

An ever-present constant in his work, the aforementioned oppression towards the Cameroonian Anglophone culture is patent in Doh's frequently iterated maledictions, particularly in his most political poems in his first two collections. His first volume is notably dedicated to "the oppressed minority of this once beautiful country, that as we struggle for freedom and our integrity, our sacrifice and the blood of all those who have died in the struggle may not go in vain" (*Wading the Tide* v). In the same vein, other volumes have been offered to "all those who have died, sacrificed a limb, or simply been genuine part" of the attempts to get African leaders to think "about the welfare of their citizens instead of betraying each other for worthless positions governments distinguished by corruption, pilfering, and illegal piling of public funds in private accounts overseas" (*Not Yet Damascus* iii). Considering these offerings only, Doh's work would put him clearly as one of the "radical poets" (Ambanasom, *The Cameroonian Novel* 202); it is the case, however, that social criticism can hardly amount to radicalism. It has been noted as a common trait of African poets to engage with their times and contemporaries in an attempt to stir up change. Ashuntantang points out that it is often claimed that "the hallmark of African literature lies in the social role of the African writer" (88). However, while Chidi Amuta holds this to be true in the case of Soyinka, Achebe and other household names who "use their talents to challenge the ruling class and thus champion the cause of those who bear the burden of oppression" (177), it is hardly the case that their poetry can be reduced to that mere function. To reduce Doh, in the same fashion, to a purely militant position would be a disservice to the perception of the subtleties of his poetry, to his place within tradition and to the deeper resonances which his poetry could represent in a wider context.

It is a common misconception on the part of literary historians and critics such as Janowitz who claim that to "ameliorate this constitutional doubleness by narrating it as a life history" would avoid figuring "the poet as both an isolated consciousness and as a socially orientated poetic radical" (11). Romanticism imparts that a poet can be both. Wordsworth[8] notices how "I communed with all that I saw as something not apart from, but inherent in, my own immaterial nature" (468). The radical solitude of poem-writing is not at odds with those democratic, social and communal aspects of the poetic self: Shelley can be the radical solipsist of *Epipsychidion* as well as the communitarian of "The Mask of Anarchy" who braves the lower classes of impoverished England to "rise like lions after slumber" (216) in acts of rebellion. In contrast, to consider Doh against the mirror of Romanticism would show, however, how such double social and personal poetics can effectively be sustained in times like these, while also unearthing how aesthetics and tactics for such difficult balance are effectively in a constant dialogue with those of poets who were in a similar position in the past.

This legacy of Romanticism can be considered Eurocentric and even linked to cultural subjectivity. As it has been noted elsewhere, educational models in African universities caused the relegation of African languages to liminal positions while at the same time spreading English and French cultural and value systems. Similarly, the production of a poetry which could be considered *europhonism*, a set of cultural products "whose initial aspirations were triggered by

---

[8] Wordsworth's *Lyrical Ballads* can be considered an attempt "to speak out of and into a community forged through sympathetic links across the borders of status and wealth, and drawing on the counter-hegemonic metres of oral tradition" (Janowitz 12).

the admiration or disagreement with the models they read" in English and French (wa Thiong'o 5). We can wonder whether this presence of Romanticism in contemporary poetry should be constrained to those Western societies in which these texts were first disseminated. The case that British Romantic poetry reached English-speaking colonies is well documented, especially in Anglophone countries. The aim, to Oakley, is "to inculcate love for the English countryside through Romantic poetry" (192). In early anthologies of post-colonial poetry, it is often recognized how contributors share a British heritage. They are in Harold Head's views "schooled in Shakespeare, Wordsworth, Blake, Byron, Shelley, Keats, and Browning," and are from "all former British colonies," while their compositions "return, in spirit, to origins, to Africa where the work of the artist is even today at one with his community" (7-8).

Themes could be local, but poetry would be global; as in the rest of the world, Romantic poetry was disseminated through education as the highest form of the lyric, thus equated to poetry as a whole. Particularly in Africa, where the weight of literary models for those pursuing education beyond primary school was heavier, it is not surprising that Romantic poetry was the model for many African poets, regardless of the language they wrote in.[9] More recently, Ehling thinks it is difficult to argue against "the validity of detecting an autobiographical element in Romantic poetry" in modern poets like Soyinka (363) even if that is not the only influence on their

---

[9] Such is the case of B. W. Vilakazi, who "wrote Zulu poetry in the 1930s strongly reminiscent of nineteenth-century Romantic poetry" (Westley 2).

poems.[10] This poetry, in principle, can be observed as foreign, as Doh's "Of Changing Tides" attests:

> What strange rhythms are those
> Bare of the voluptuous cadences
> Of the tam-tam, the kora, the xylophones
> On banana or plantain tree-trunks? (*Shadows* 7)

However, the persuasive forms of Romantic poetry in English cannot be neglected as influences to the way poetry is written when using the language: it slowly replaces traditional forms and approaches to poetry through education and reading, as Doh's *Oriki'badan* chronicles.[11] The basic terms of the relationship between poet and reader are altered. The poem becomes a "transparent lyric" in which by "replacing the lyric speaker with the reader as the center of dramatic attention, the poem itself becomes a transparent medium through which the reader is led to see the world in a particular way" (Walker xii). It is impossible to read a single Doh poem, precisely as these are closer to the lyric, and not be convinced by its message. He targets his reader precisely through this trope. Doh may criticize the

---

[10] Ehling makes an argument against considering Soyinka as a mere romanticist "when [influence is] applied to the modernism of Soyinka, whose practice is obviously more in line with that of T.S. Eliot" (364). Similarly, the classical topoi and rhetoric in Doh is a noticeable trend, perhaps a direct result of his education (*Oriki'badan* 28), but one which is restricted to certain recurring images – the Odyssey and the gorgon, notably – and themes, such as a Villonian nostalgia in "Of Changing Tides": "Where are the tam-tams? / I hear them no more, / No more in the morning rising" (*Shadows* 7).

[11] This entails changes in the form of the poems; after Romantic lyric there is a paradigmatic shift which entails a move from the "hegemony of the external" towards "interiorization" from "description" to "interpretation" from "seeing" to "perception" from "transparency" to "mediation" "denotation" to "connotation" "personification" and "allegory" to "symbol" "metonymy" to "metaphor" "message" to "meaning" "rhetoric" to "literariness" from talking to an "audience" to talking to a "scene" (Furst 12-18).

government or popular cainism – positions which the reader might not share—in poems such as "The persecution" or "The Thing about Progress" (19-20) in *Shadows* but it is hard, however, for the reader to make an abstraction as he/she is hearing the lyric voice. The poem becomes all that there is and cannot be relinquished as Coleridge would have it; "willing suspension of disbelief" (174) is a prerequisite for the appreciation of modern literature.

In Africa and elsewhere, modern poetry in English has been shaped by the unprecedented success of Romanticism in a period of mass readership, which has lodged the very conception of the poets' role in society, the functions of their work and the shape and aesthetics of their poems for centuries. Poetry since Romanticism has had what Clifford Siskin calls a "lyric turn"—a change from the dominance of form to the rule of subjectivity into an aesthetics of spontaneity in which meter and versification which are "trivialized as the poet's expressiveness naturally transcends inherited form" (27). For the first time in the history of poetry, form becomes secondary to voice and thus gradually becomes less and less important when poets write. There is a quintessential lack of form, noticeable in later romantics such as Shelley or Byron whose poetic form, O'Neill contends, "strays beyond aesthetic space even while occupying it, and exists as a device through which sentiment is expressed" (49). The fact that Doh, like most contemporary poets, very rarely uses rhyme rather than syntax[12] to bring rhythm to his poems, uses blank verse or no recognizable stanzaic structure, writes generally short poems and aims at reproducing natural speech takes his diction closer to Romanticism than Postmodernism. After Romanticism, modern poetry follows sprung rhythm and the vernacular. Poetry's implicit readership is the lay people. Wordsworth states that it addresses them in their own "language of men" (853). Doh would mix English,

---

[12] With the notable exception of "Mea Culpa" (*Not Yet Damascus* 25-26), Doh's poems never rhyme fully; incidentally, as in some lines of *Oriki'badan*, the rhyme is caused by lexical repetition but not sought to be sustained.

French and other minority languages in his poems, which greatly resemble spoken language with his use of exclamations, punctuations, as well as the use of well-known cultural and religious icons he shares with his readers.

Regardless of the different intentions, his poetry takes the form of a monologue. According to Duff, Romanticism entails a displacement of earlier modes of poetic expression as "the sonnet, the local poem, and the ode" and evolves "into one comprehensive category" (207). Except the more narrative impulses of *Oriki'daban*, Doh's poetry moves within the lyrical forms, where there is a self-communicating to others. Analyzing *Shadows* would illuminate on the use of the lyric on the part of the poet; Doh's lyric is often meditative, as in "Cheap Talk" or "Disillusioned," where the poetic voice includes itself as the focus of the poem:

> After this Odyssey
> On me imposed by man
> Through which I plodded,
> My life became a lonely bloody cell
> With metaphysical bars restraining:
> Victim of charity,
> Victim of humility. (*Shadows* 25)

The effect of such inclusion is theatricality of some sort; if the poet does not depart from the truth, there is an implicit staging of his emotions. This is a Romantic institution, as the "continued reliance on dramatic or performative modes of address over the past two centuries will be traced in exemplary Romantic lyrics and odes [...] to the present day, and in the 'performance' of the self in contemporary poetry" (Brewster 72). The interesting aspect in Doh is that he manages to operate that performative power into a communication with his implicit audience. Whether by addressing the reader directly or deferred through the target of an addressee in poems such as "The

African Dinosaur" (former heads of state), "Bobolo Oath" (foreign companies), Doh effectively manages to give his poetry a sense of pertinence and urgency which is highly welcomed as part of the creation of his lyrical discourse. By implicitly talking to oppressed Cameroonians and Africans, as well as addressing their oppressors, Doh makes poetry relevant regardless of form. He is in line with postromantic poetry which, according to Duff, helps "sustain a heightened lyricism" and "confer[s] aesthetic unity on a seemingly disparate poetic structure" (209). The lyric after the alterations of Romanticism becomes, then, the vocative form of the poem into modernity – a model which, as the reader will observe in Doh's intense, pertinent and socially geared poems, is flexible enough to incorporate all other poetic forms and is devoid of formal allegiances.

While other authors such as Ambanasom in *Homage and Courtship: Romantic Stirrings of a Young Man* would offer, on face value, a much clearer case of conventional Romantic aesthetics, Doh may ultimately serve as a perfect example of an all-inclusive Romantic. He combines a socio-political emphasis with the lyrical and self-expressive in a way which is remarkably similar, both conceptually and aesthetically, to that of the major figures within the Romantic period. A word of caution must be noted here. Influence does not make poets less original or less worthy of attention; on the contrary, it brings attention to the rich tradition in which their poems are inserted. As Linus T. Asong remarks in the introduction to Doh's first collection of poems, there is always the danger "to compartmentalize the new poet in a manner that deprives him of his individuality, his uniqueness" as "it is an assertion of the poet's singular identity" (*Wading the Tide* xi). I am also deeply aware that, in the light of postcolonial theorizations, there is the risk that linking an African poet to Romanticism can be observed as a cultural, Western imposition. Contrary to that, it is my view that prejudice would come from treating African poetry differently. Doh himself, in "Telling

Africa," criticizes how Africans are often singled out as different, even in the most good-hearted intentions. This amounts to bias:

> When they talk of Africa,
> You think of a termite hole,
> Of my people as some strange species.
> Our ways in alien colours they paint, castigating,
> Then their ignorant laugh and celebrate our misery
> Conjured by vain pens and minds
> (*Shadows* 3)

My aim here is, precisely, not to consider Doh differently from other poets writing in English. It is rather an attempt to insert his poems within a modern poetic tradition whose denial is wishful thinking rather than acknowledgement of an unavoidable reality which stems from the complexities of the value systems of cultural dissemination. The study of Romantic legacies is not reductive. Contemporary poetry can illuminate our understanding of the past, just as Doh can prove to be a valuable example to modern Western poets as he belongs to a tradition, but also reacts to the present. The aim is not only to perceive Doh's poetry in terms of influence, but also to disclose a bravado engagement with his times as part of the search for an individual poetic voice, one which can be meaningful to others – and one which is sorely needed elsewhere.

One of the key features of the Romantic poets is that, despite how much their image has been distorted, simplified and reduced by subsequent criticism, their poems cannot be simmered down to a single line of thought. Blake cannot be considered just a visionary poet, just as Shelley cannot be considered a mere social radical; Keats cannot just be reduced to a contemplative aestheticist, nor Wordsworth simply to a nature poet. A defining feature in the versification of these poets as highlighted by Helfer is that they use various "self-conscious reference[s] to and exploration of various modes of artistic representation within the literary text meant to highlight the fragmentary and referential nature of art" (369). Romantic poets, interestingly, alternate the social with the personal or expressive, and combine the tensions between these two modes as the poem reveals itself as a medium for both self-expression, but also social communication.[13] Doh's poetry seems to follow this to the dot. In poems such as those in the "Uprising" section of *Wading the Tide* (3-19), "Guardians of the Peace," "Fear-Fear King," "Like serpents" (*Not Yet Damascus* 5-10), or in "Lamentation," the harsh first half of his latest collection (*Shadows* 3-46), Doh denounces injustice and oppression in both Cameroon and Africa.[14] But his poetry does not only confront the powers that be; its social strand also criticizes the unethical attitudes and implicit acceptance of that oppression on the part of Africans. In *Wading the Tide,* poems such as "The Seasons,""Kwashiorkor Graveyard," "Land of Prawns,""Shame Africa" (4-5,7,14), "Their Turn to Party," "That Learned Professor," "The Conspirators" in *Not Yet Damascus* (11-13,21-22), "Consultation" and "Losing Track" in *Shadows* (33-35) have a clear social emphasis which aims at stirring up awareness that change must be driven from within. Social unrest would be, in his formulation, always preferable to subjection:

---

[13] Even obscured by previous purely aesthetic theorisations, the social undertones of Romantic poems such as "Tintern Abbey" have propelled the need to re-read Romantic poetry "against its historical background" which they represent (Butler 9).

[14] Whether from within – "The Bloody Caps" (*Wading the Tide* 8), "Guardians of the Peace" or "The Persecution" (*Shadows* 19) criticize the alienation of brute police taskforces, while "Lament of the Town-Crier" (*Wading the Tide* 10), "Fear-Fear King," "Like Serpents" or "The African Dinosaur" (*Shadows* 11-12) severely question rulers as a solution to African problems – or from abroad, in poems such as "The Black Queen," "Who Do They Think They Are Fooling" (*Wading the Tide* 16-18), "Africa" (*Not Yet Damascus* 16) or "Gang-raped" (*Shadows* 5) denouncing foreign exploitation, Doh uses poetry to attack those institutions preventing Africa to thrive and prosper.

> Hear the echoes of laughter from 'Mvomeka'a,
> Witness the sullenness of a betrayed proletariat
> The lion and tiger in a dance?
> What is this lethargy? (*Not Yet Damascus* 12)

And, even for this social emphasis, Doh's use of irony helps put the poem's message into question: the tolerance on the part of the oppressed may have a part in their subjugation. In poems such as "The Seasons," the people with "Faces radiant with smiles / at the arrival of a 'messiah' / the start of a new season" are up for "disillusionment, / the trademark of the contents of the heart"; in "Kwashiorkor Graveyard," the country's scarcity is blamed on "the tapper who [...] drinks the oil / and says the kernels were barren"; in "Land or Prawns," people are caged, packed just like prawns in a confined space, but "Calm / the water appears, but the bubbles will rise." Consistently, he presents situations which are superficially something, but may enclose an altogether different reality. There is a methodical use of irony in presenting one stable, albeit miserable, situation which is destabilized by another factor, an intimation which puts the rest of the poem's meaning into question. From questioning the meaning, knowledge arises. As in Blake, Wordsworth or Coleridge, irony in Doh has an explorative, heuristic function by presenting both conflicting ideas to be negotiated and reconciled by the reader. Thus, the message in Doh's poems can often be read, prima facie, as contradictory. Many of his poems end with an implicit menace, which can be read as a call for an impending revolt against oppression: the bubbles rising in "Land of Prawns"; the threat that "When the tide shall turn, / many shall go overboard" in "Lament of the Town-Crier," echoed in the final line in "The Black Queen"; the hope that "it may take forever, but virtue/ in the end will win" in "Africa's Journey"; the assurance that exploitative "persecution" of natural resources by "legalized pilferers [...] will end, yes it will." The means for this deliverance are in a predicament: sometimes Doh envisages violence as a natural, potential reaction, so that "it were better like the bee / To sting and be killed" rather than "thy sting / In shame and servitude adorn" (*Not Yet Damascus* 19); he, however, quite clearly warns against the dangers of violence as a response to subjugation. Like Shelley's *Alastor*, *The Revolt of Islam* and *The Triumph of Life* (Frosch), many of Doh's poems can be seen as studies of the potential and horrors of violence as a means to social revolution. Doh, like Shelley before him, explores the potentials of violence, but advocates for passive civil disobedience and self-affirmation.[15] Several poems reinstate the idea that, despite Africa being "ridiculed and slighted," violence cannot be matched with violence. Revenge will not bring ultimate freedom:

> From of old, errors must be acknowledge
> And a price paid that the forces
> Violated may be placated,
> Only then do we begin to heal.
> Such vainness only incenses. (Doh, *Shadows* 6)

Thus, Doh compels his implicit readers to be "like the grass that / Will not tell of the dung's stench / So as to freely feed thereof"; with unblemished vision and an envisaged program for his country and continent, Doh warns against the dangers of using violence as it would naturally entail a counter-reaction:

---

[15] It has been noted that the political project of Shelley, Leigh Hunt and other members of the Cockney School was to "consistently [stand] out against violence, both that of governments and that of their opponents" as they "sought to change society by creating a better community for themselves" (Cox 60). The impact of the French Revolution and its horrific aftermath for popular classes on the Romantics can be paralleled to Doh's anxieties towards his own country and his fellow people.

> Do not bite and not expect a scream,
> Do not stab and not expect blood,
> Plant and there shall be growth
> Nurture and there will be a harvest.
> Bless and in return be blessed,
> Curse and in return be thyself damned.
> If we be not this wise
> But go on stabbing our backs
> With suicidal strokes
> Then doomed we are as a people. (*Not Yet Damascus* 22)

Doh is being true to African traditional values, seeking reconciliation rather than revenge. As he writes, "Western style jurisprudence that instead of promoting justice tends to create injustice, enmity, and animosity, unlike the traditional African system which emphasized reconciliation and the reinstatement of the guilty individual to his society" (*Africa's Political Wastelands* 175). It is only then that his seemingly threatening endings illuminate optimistic vantages of a poet who sees beyond actuality, beyond the reality of the present into a hopefully better future. As the end of "Anti-Clockwise" attests, when time figuratively reverses – and African countries can freely decide on their future – then "This hour of darkness" will be gone since, as the poet notes, "in the East I see the glimmer, / It will be dawn eventually" (*Not Yet Damascus* 7). Despite the bleakness of the present, there is a future, and it will be a better one. Returning to Shelley with whom he shares many images of winds and gales as transformative, his optimistic use of the Promethean myth to foretell a new and better world is paralleled by Doh in the second part of *Shadows*, called "Celebration." After devastating poems such as "Losing Track" or "The News of Death," (34,42) Doh is far from a defeatist in the second half of his latest collection. He rises as a voice to claim hope in a better future as built from the present. The commendation in "The Lighthouse" becomes less a desire than a prediction:

> May you thrive,
> Your children and your children's children.
> May people wake up to you, husband and wife
> Who have the tears from so many
> Cheeks in silence dried. It must not a whole nation
> Be, but to the very least of my brothers and
> The Master's reward awaits you. (*Shadows* 62)

Doh, like many of the Romantics, can be seen as a visionary who combines sensibility with individual perception of common welfare. This is often linked to their role as outsiders and often seen as over-imposing righteousness;[16] despite addressing a given community, they are somehow partly alien to it. From his position as an expatriate, Doh is, indeed, an impassionate patriot poet who aims at leading his people, considered as outsiders within their own country. In that sense, should his voice be heard, he would become – in a twist to the famous Shelleyan quote – an acknowledged legislator of the world (57), a voice that would make a difference to the lives of many of his fellow Cameroonians. As the other chapters in the present volume attest, the ambivalence of both belonging and not belonging and the mixed feeling towards it, capture in Doh the essence of a self which becomes an "existential paradox / just being me" (*Not Yet Damascus* 31) and yet is a member of a community. In poems such as "Claustrophobia," the fragmentariness of that identity is exposed:

> At one place I am Anglo-minority

---

[16] Friedrich Schlegel notes how the "first commandment" of Romantic poetry is "that the will of the poet can tolerate no law above itself" (31), but that seemingly totalitarianism stems more from the monologic aspects of writing than actual socio-politic stances.

> And so I do not belong,
> And could very well go elsewhere,
> My responsibility it is to survive
> Amidst the chosen ones
> Of the malnourished Francophonie assembly. (*Not Yet Damascus* 23)

Revelation, we learn with the Romantics and Doh, is both personal and communal. This is in line with Michael O'Neill's reflection on the poetry of the period when he writes: "the desire to escape mere self-expression cannot stifle the sense of the poem as a place where modes of self-revelation occur" (*The All-sustaining Air* 1). Just as Shelley or Byron did centuries before in the turbulent times which engulfed them, Doh's poetic voice reveals a particularly pungent denunciation against human abuse and corruption which is fully compatible, as the second part of *Shadows* attests, with the celebration of hope and the enthusiastic pursuit of the light of freedom. His power resides in that engagement with his times as well as his confidence in the future. Western poets should follow suit, and those of the Romantics, if they want to take poetry out of the self-centered, disengaged hole it has written itself into. Rather than aiming at revealing a heritage or indebtedness which makes a dent on the prestige of Doh's poetry, his poetry in the mirror of Romanticism serves as a reminder of what has been lost in Western poetry – of what is paramount to recover. Put against Romantic poetry, the central role of the poet is that of a self-proclaimed, yet essential leader and warrior against estrangement, who is most incisive when placed against the liminal position in which poetry and poets serve in contemporary First-World societies.

Works Cited

Ambanasom, Shadrach A. *Homage and Courtship: Romantic Stirrings of a Young Man*. Bamenda: Langaa RPCIG, 2010. Print.

———. *The Cameroonian Novel of English Expression: An Introduction*. Bamenda: Langaa RPCIG, 2009. Print.

Amuta, Chidi. *The Theory of African Literature: Implications for Practical Criticism*. London: Zed, 1989. Print.

Ashcroft, Bill, Gareth Griffiths and Helen Tiffin. *The Empire Writes Back: Theory and Practice in Post-Colonial Literature*. London: Routledge, 1989. Print.

Ashuntantang, Joyce. *Landscaping Postcoloniality: The Dissemination of Cameroon Anglophone Literature*. Bamenda: Langaa RPCIG, 2009. Print.

Badiou, Alan. *Theoretical Writings*. London: Continuum, 2004. Print.

Berlin, Isaiah. *The Roots of Romanticism*. Princeton: Princeton UP, 1999. Print.

Brewster, Scott. *Lyric*. London: Routledge, 2009. Print.

Bridgwood, A. *Rhyme and Reason: Developing Contemporary Poetry*. 1 Jan. 2000. Web. 25 June 2013.

Butler, Marilyn. *Romantics, Rebels, and Reactionaries: English Literature and its Background, 1760-1830*. Oxford: Oxford UP, 1982. Print.

Casaliggi, Carmen and Paul March-Russell. *Legacies of Romanticism: Literature, Culture, Aesthetics*. London: Routledge, 2012. Print.

Coleridge, S. T. *Biographia Literaria; or Biographical Sketches of my Literary Life and Opinions*. New York: W. Gowans, 1834. Print.

Cox, Jeffrey N. *Poetry and Politics in the Cockney School: Keats, Shelley, Hunt and Their Circle*. Cambridge: Cambridge UP, 2004. Print.

Davies, D.W. and R.M. Turley. *The Monstrous Debt: Modalities of Romantic Influence in Twentieth-Century Literature*. Detroit: Wayne State UP, 2006. Print.

Doh, Emmanuel Fru. *Africa's Political Wastelands: The Bastardization of Cameroon*. Bamenda: Langaa RPCIG, 2008. Print.

——————————. *Nomads: the Memoir of a Southern Cameroonian*. Bamenda: Langaa RPCIG, 2013. Print.

——————————. *Not Yet Damascus*. Bamenda: Laanga RPCIG, 2007. Print.

——————————. *Oriki'badan*. Bamenda: Laanga RPCIG, 2009. Print.

——————————. *Shadows*. Bamenda: Langaa RPCIG, 2011. Print.

——————————. *Wading the Tide*. Patron: Mankon-Bamenda, 1995.

——————————. *Stereotyping Africa: Surprising Answers to Surprising Questions*. Bamenda: Langaa RPCIG, 2009. Print.

——————————. *The Fire Within*. Bamenda: Langaa RPCIG, 2008. Print.

Duff, David. *Romanticism and the Uses of Genre*. Oxford: Oxford UP, 2009. Print.

Ehling, Holger G. *No Condition is Permanent: Nigerian Writing and the Struggle for Democracy*. Amsterdam: Rodopi, 2001. Print.

Eyoh, Dickson "Conflicting Narratives of Anglophone Protest and the Politics of Identity in Cameroon." *Journal of Contemporary African Studies* 16.2 (1998): 249-276. Print.

Frosch, Thomas R. *Shelley and the Romantic Imagination: A Psychological Study*. Newark: U of Delaware P, 2007. Print.

Furst, Lilian R. "Autumn in the Romantic Lyric: An Exemplary Case of Paradigm Shift." *Romantic Poetry*. Ed. Angela Esterhammer.Vol.7. Amsterdam: John Benjamins, 2002. Print.

Gioia, Dana. "Can poetry matter?" *Atlantic Monthly* . May1991 : 94-106. Print.

Head, Harold. *Canada in Us Now: the First Anthology of Black Poetry and Prose in Canada*. Toronto: NC Press, 1976. Print.

Helfer, Martha B. *Rereading Romanticism*. Amsterdam: Rodopi, 2000.

Hillis Miller, Joseph. "The Future of Literary Theory." Østreng, W. *Consilience. Interdisciplinary Communications 2005/2006*. Oslo: Centre for Advanced Study, 2007. 111-114. Print.

Janowitz, Anne. *Lyric and Labour in the Romantic Tradition*. Cambridge: Cambridge UP, 1998. Print.

Labang, Oscar C. *Songs for Tomorrow: Cameroon Poetry in English*. Yaounde: Miraclaire, 2010. Print.

Larrissy, Edward. *Romanticism and Postmodernism*. Cambridge: Cambridge UP, 1999. Print.

Martens, Bruno. *Browning, Victorian Poetics and the Romantic Legacy: Challenging the Personal Voice*. Aldershot: Ashgate, 2011. Print.

McGann, Jerome J. *The Romantic Ideology: a Critical Investigation*. Chicago: U of Chicago P, 1983. Print.

Moscovici, Claudia. *Romanticism and Postromanticism*. Lanham, MD: Lexington Books, 2007. Print.

Nancy, Jean Luc and Philippe Lacoue-Labarthe. *L'Absolu Littéraire: Théorie de la Littérature du Romantisme Allemand*. Paris: Le Seuil, 1978. Print.

Nfah-Abbenyi, Juliana. "Anglophone Cameroon Poetry." *Free Verse* 22 (2012): 24-26. Print.

Ngwane, George. *Bate Besong, or the Symbol of Anglophone Hope*. Limbe: Noomerac Press, 1993. Print.

Oakley, Seanna Sumalee. *The Creole Ghost: Language, Geography and Community in Recent Jamaican Poetry*. Madison: U of Wisconsin P, 2002. Print.

O'Neill, Michael. "Inextinguishable Energy: Byron and Poetic Form." Ed. Cochran, Peter. *Byron's Poetry*. Cambridge: Cambridge Scholars, 2012. 49-58. Print.

_____. *The All-sustaining Air: Romantic Legacies and Renewals in British, American, and Irish Poetry Since 1900*. Oxford: Oxford U P, 2007. Print.

Poetry Foundation. "Best-selling Books - Contemporary." *Poetry Magazine* (2011-13): 20. Print.

Schlegel, Friedrich. *Athenaeum Fragments*. 1798. Minneapolis: U of Minneapolis P, 1991. Print.

Shelley, Percy Bysshe. *The Complete Poetical Works*. London: Edward Moxon, 1840. Print.

Siskin, Clifford. *The Historicity of Romantic Discourse*. Oxford: Oxford U P, 1988. Print.

wa Thiong'o, Ngugi. "Europhonism, Universities, and the Magic Fountain: The Future of African Literature and Scholarship." *Research in African Literatures* 31.1 (2000): 1-11. Print.

Walker, David. *The Transparent Lyric: Reading and Meaning in the Poetry of Stevens and Williams*. Princeton: Princeton U P, 1984. Print.

Westley, David. "Choice of Language and African Literature: A Bibliographic Essay." *Research in African Literatures* 23.1 (1992): 159-171. Print.

Wexler, Bruce. "Poetry is Dead. Does Anybody Really Care?» *Newsweek* 5 May 2003: 3.Print.

Wordsworth, William. *The Complete Poetical Works of William Wordsworth*. Basingstoke: Macmillan, 1893. Print.

Chapter 3

Warring Estrangement in E. Coxere's *Adventures by Sea*

By
Bill F. Ndi

Edward Coxere in his *Adventures by Sea* indulges in a war against what would indubitably be styled endemic and systemic forms of oppressions and exclusion. To explore and comprehend this autobiography today, a quick glance must be cast at the early Quaker movement of the mid-1600s. This movement was founded upon the idea of challenging the status quo. It aimed at infusing new ideas into the stale and sterile debate that marked the world thus far. This left England at the time with chiliastic upheavals that, in the view of the historian Christopher Hill, are summed up in the title of his 1991 opus magna *The World Turned Up-side-down*. The logical consequence of "the world turned up-side-down" would follow that of a world turned inside-out. That is to say a multitude would be left on the fringes of the society. Coxere's writing indulges in the exploration of this phenomenon as a representational act of the struggle for a free and equal society engendered by fears, doubts and joys of not belonging and/or of belonging. This probe is all in keeping with Quaker founding father George Fox's vision as expressed in his *Journal* that it is needful to have a sense of all conditions to be able to address them. In this vision he "saw the infinite love of God..." (21).

Quakers in their endeavor and strife for an egalitarian society vehemently fought against any tendency that left other human beings on the margins and made of them some strange beings. The art of warring estrangement is among the glories of Early Quaker endeavors: creativity, peace mongering, creedlessness, global egalitarianism and the desire to globalize the world. Early Quakers strove at defying the hegemonic views of Christianity as presented by the Established Church as indispensable. They were goaded by the urge to reconstitute the tenets of primitive Christianity. At the same time, they obstinately refused to set themselves apart. Seventeenth Century Quakers fought to right the wrongs of the oppressive forces that characterized England and the world. They understood what Harold Loukes underscores in *Quaker Contribution* as "the basic facts of human existence: 'I' and 'others' and so reaching out towards the misty frontiers with [...] commitment to the teaching" (118). Quakers did all they could to take the fight for equality everywhere they set foot. It is in this light that Christopher Hill underlines "...the attempts of various groups of the common people to impose their own solution to the problems of their time, in opposition to the wishes of their betters who had called them into political action" (13). In this vein, Edward Coxere as a Quaker clenches unto his religious convictions and wages a war against the orchestrated process of pushing others onto the fringes and margins of society with baseless claims of gender, age, race, creed, class, sexuality, profession, etc. Quakers believe all of these to be attributions influencing men to distance others and/or themselves through the acculturative process of alienation. He is enjoined by his newfound religion to help tear down the walls and barriers that fears and doubts erect to bar free thinking and peace-loving human beings from joyfully bathing in inclusiveness and in a single human community devoid of all the aforementioned assumptions of estranging social values. Quakerism thus becomes a noble celebration of primitive Christianity in a world that lay claims to hastening "the second coming."

It is in this light that Quakers envisage to create a level playing field for all human beings on earth. In this level playing field, "fearing" "doubting" and above all "not belonging" shall forever be banished and only the joys of belonging would characterize mankind.

In short, they strove to inter the idea and practice of otherness. From time immemorial, this perspective, Matson asserts, has been shared by philosophers such as Aristotle, Karl Marx and a host of others (415-16). Edward Coxere's work exhibits both inward and outward scars left by willful and imposed marginalization. As a seaman, Edward Coxere does not limit his spiritual and social warfare to his native Dover, but parades them on whatever port he docks. He takes the reader through a series of eye-opening spiritual and physical journeys by sea on the process of estrangement and otherness. Also, it is worth mentioning that Early Quakers and their ideals were greeted with a chorus of disapproval from every quarter. Yet, they succeeded in spreading their egalitarian doctrine via critical and propaganda pamphlets as well as autobiographical *Journals* like Coxere's. In them, they attacked the society that feeds in a mercenary manner upon the misfortunes of those who espoused contrary views to those of the Establishment. Of this, Adrian Davies reminds us of, "William Thomas, the rector of Ubley in Somerset, [who] was much troubled in 1656 by the dissemination of Quaker books, which he thought assisted the spread of the new religion" (110). Early Quakers, though autodidacts, were very much aware of the oppression meted out to dissidents by the government and the Established Church. They seemed to be creating what Chopra considers a kind of rupture in the harmony thus far enjoyed in England (15).

In *Adventures by Sea,* Edward Coxere carefully documents the effects of a prolonged stay away from home. His story veers to this when he comes back home after a very long sojourn at sea. He makes it evident that this voyage has estranged him to the point that he has difficulty identifying with things English, though an Englishman himself. During his stay at sea, he has had to mingle with Dutch people. He has become "so Dutch" in both language and style that nothing English seems to appeal to his taste. Nonetheless, this estrangement from his English roots turns out to be a saving grace when he is about to be taken captive by a Dutch ship. He tells the reader how he normally escapes captivity:

> ... I was so much of a Dutchman that they took no notice of me more than the rest of the Flemings, for the best English I could then speak was but like Eng[lish], for no man took me to be an Englishman, so that I [e]scaped being carried away. (20)

Again, after this same episode, this "journalist" goes to work on board an English ship. He depicts himself linguistically estranged for he "did not know the names of all the ropes in English, though in Dutch I was not to seek..." (23). This linguistic handicap and fear of alienation are further intensified by the fact that he needs to do what it takes to be well accepted on board the ship in which he now belongs, and this, in spite of his youthful age as he writes, "... also I was young to have such great wages; my fear was that I should not be well accepted of as the rest, I being to seek of many things that was to be done in the ship after the English fashion" (23). Consequently, Coxere's fears and doubts of not belonging transform and become a motivational force that goads him to be pleasant and forthright as he documents, "I took care to please through my forwardness, as also the rest of the officers, that thereby if anything was wanting on one hand it might be made up on the other through my diligence" (23). With all of these elements of estrangement notwithstanding, Edward Coxere regains his mother tongue little by little. He expresses his joys of being part of the present crew and esteems himself worthy and deserving of his wages. These joys are made evident when he becomes coxswain at Plymouth on his way to Newfoundland. Not only does the master take a liking to Coxere, but he has beaten the linguistic odds at the origin of his sense of estrangement and fear of it by naturally acquiring his mother tongue. Now his inclusiveness is manifested by the fact that he can get the names of ropes and sea-phrases to the purpose as he "... grew hardy, and thought [he] could deserve [his] wages..." (23).

Conscious of the ills of estrangement and alienation, this Quaker writer with firsthand knowledge and experience of being estranged while in captivity, understands that the easiest way to war and overcome any form of estrangement is to avoid and/or escape captivity. Early on in *Adventures by Sea*, Coxere gives a hint on the miserable nature of sea-life that leaves him with no other option but the thoughts that "if ever [he] got ashore he should look for a prentice, for [he] did not like such kind of sea-tricks; for when it was foul weather [he] was sick, and when fair they scared [him] with a rope's end" (7). Albeit, having thus acquainted himself with sea-life, Coxere still finds life at home uncomfortable. This leads to a change of heart from his previous stance and determination to stay away from the sea. Coxere has recourse to the idea of wanting to avoid the loneliness of home life while his brother, John, is away. He chooses to ship on board the O*ld St. George* for two reasons: it tells of his desire to combat estrangement and be free of its constraints. Other reasons include the fact that he associates the lieutenant of the ship to his playmate. He is his playmate's father. Also evoked is the idea that his brother was a seaman on this ship. Thus, he substantiates his change of heart.

Furthermore, it is on board of this ship that Coxere brings to the fore the grip of estrangement on every human being in the face of danger. Dramatizing this serious happening (Aristotle), Coxere depicts a struggle that rends not only his whole being but that of the rest of the crew. The *Old Saint George* explodes and leaves all amidst chaos at the mercy of drowning or burning: "two bad masters" (9). This danger levels the Captain, Master and seamen, for, as Coxere writes, "... my life lay at stake and it was `Everyone shift for himself'; the captain was then no more regarded than the cook" (9). Here, Coxere's greatest concern is for his brother, one of the reasons he came to sea. Upon inquiring about his brother, John, he finds out that he also looked for him and even refused to board to safety without him. Coxere writes:

> My care was then for my brother; I asked one in the boat if he did not see him. He told me he saw him on the top of the stern in the ship and that he looked for me. In that he showed natural affection, for he returned back again and refused to get in the boat without me. Those that were left aboard were forced to bestir themselves. (9)

In another early episode, the writer is acquainted with a profound sense of estrangement when he ships with Captain Tilly. En route to Cadiz, he illustrates his clear understanding of the emotions that feelings of estrangement and otherness provoke. In this case, he gives it a positive spin. They constitute a spur to new endeavors and enterprise. As Coxere gets aboard the ship bound for Cadiz, he captures and sheds light on the moment:

> I was sent aboard, and finding myself to be amongst Dutchmen and strangers to me, it did something discourage me; but there was no remedy, I was then fast enough. There were several merchants, who ate in the cabin with the captain, which I tended and two other boys. The master was a very severe man and kept me notably to my business, which did me no hurt at all. I did my endeavour to the utmost to please him, but much out of fear. (10)

This finally pays off. He has a keen understanding of the very sharp experience of alienation which is found among seamen and what it takes to ward off this Damocles' sword hovering over human beings.

Homesickness, a manifestation of estrangement, seems to be omnipresent in Coxere's universe. This manifestation of Coxere's discourse is exactly what Peter Collins describes in reference to Quaker discourse as "absolutely unique" (289). Coxere always seems to have a means of countering estrangement. As he grows hardy, he begins to lose the feelings of being away from home and consequently not being estranged. Coxere expresses his joys of belonging to this corps of seafaring men and intimates that in order to be at home on board a ship with strangers, it is necessary to add the strangers' language to one's linguistic repertoire. In one instance, he points out why he has to acquire the Dutch tongue. Inasmuch as he makes it evident that it is "to understand those I was withal…" (11), one cannot help but conjecture that from Coxere's earlier experiences as an exchange pupil in France, he really felt the pinch of estrangement in not being able to communicate but by signs. Now, he fears a repeat of history and would do just everything it takes to avoid the inability to communicate, which Mandel in "Causes of Alienation" highlights as one of its major causes. It constitutes the worst form of alienation. Therefore, Coxere must become an integral part of his new seafaring family in any circumstance through language acquisition.

Striking a chord on the note of religious practices of seafarers, Coxere continues to show and tell the reader the effective ways of combating estrangement and/or the fears and doubts of not belonging. As they lay cruising in *Pasages* by San Sabastian, Coxere recalls how he kept the trinkets of the friar who said Mass for his Catholic Captain. He makes of his participation in that religious ceremony, an act of inclusion which leaves him with more questions than answers. He thus wonders why they let him handle the trinkets:

> I kept all the trinkets aboard that covered the altar in a trunk, I being the chief cabin boy. The altar was the cupboard, which I covered, where on stood the picture of Christ, which since I wonder they would let me handle their Mass-tools, I being the captain's boy, I suppose it was not minded, for sometimes I was on my knees with them, as I remember. (12)

From the above, Coxere involuntarily kneels down with the rest of the crew. This is rather egged on by fears that he might be cast out and treated as such, coupled with doubts of the eventuality of his non-participation than by the joys of not belonging and/or belonging. Coxere's attitude is explained by Bakhtin's argument that the social world consists of centripetal (official) and centrifugal (unofficial) forces (Collins 289).

Having highlighted this, he makes known how business was carried out at sea. It is done on the basis of religious and/or linguistic affiliation. He paints a glaring picture of business transactions that all point to the process of alienation and/or exclusion engendered by acts of linguistic and religious affiliation. He writes:

> Everyone had a sign whereby the boats might know the ships they were to put their goods aboard. Our captain was so well beloved by the boatmen that when they came to sea to us, though they saw the ship they were to go to, yet they would come and put their goods aboard of us and, being discharged of their goods, would go ashore and tell the merchants they could find none but Captain John Tilly. Our captain being an Irishman and a Roman Catholic, and had the Spanish tongue, and not only so but he was very generous and kept open house for these boatmen. (14-15)

Besides religion and language, another factor responsible for determining inclusion or exclusion in the seafaring arena is age. Depicting himself as a young, diligent and dynamic seaman who has mastered the art of seafaring, Coxere shows how his young age slows his professional progress, his experience and expertise notwithstanding. He cannot be made master on board a ship. The only excuse for this refusal to make him shipmaster is his young age. This is the powerlessness version of alienation which has been also the most studied (Seeman). Coxere has neither the ability to influence the employment policies nor the control over the conditions of employment.

Also, Coxere lacks control over the immediate work process. He glaringly states this when narrating his dealings with a skipper to whom he had offered his services to free himself from estrangement and later required wages. As the skipper is unwilling to accept that arrangement, so is he when Coxere wishes to seize an opportunity of advancing himself with another offer from another skipper. Coxere writes, "Now as this skipper at first was unwilling to allow me wages, now he was unwilling to part from me, but he did consent at last, but not with a willing mind..." (52). This unwilling skipper takes this stance in spite of the estranging conditions in which Coxere finds himself as he describes, "I was poor, and no clothes to shift myself, nor money but the pistole I got ashore..." (52). The present condition in which Coxere finds himself makes his estrangement an act of total exclusion. This exclusion of the laborer from the immediate work process is backed by Stephen Innes who, in a study entitled *Work and Labor in Early America,* stipulates that "the global deployment of thousands of seamen… was predicated upon the broad and uneven process of proletarianization" (255).

Furthermore, though not an anthropologist *stricto sensus,* Coxere observes through his journeys and adventures in Moorish lands the mores and customs of their inhabitants. He elucidates their gestures of friendship, describes their clothing and what they are made of. He details how in their language, the Moors call their clothing. This may come across as a footnote in the whole narrative, but the reader cannot forget that all along, Coxere in his adventures has highlighted language as an instrument of war against alienation and estrangement. Language becomes, as such, a factor of inclusion or exclusion. This, therefore, explicates why Coxere's fear of being estranged pushes him to acquaint himself with the language of every people he comes across.

Coxere underlines further aspects of alienation and estrangement when he is held captive by the Turks. These Turks are not satisfied with overworking him. They give him a bad name as the proverbial "give your dog a bad name to hang it." They call him *Cania Sinsa Featha*, i.e. a dog without faith. Since he does not share their religious beliefs, he is treated with no consideration as a human being. He is thus made to know that he does not belong. This only aggravates his fears and doubts. Nonetheless, he has their language, the lack of which would have called for total exclusion. His possession of the language becomes a factor for desired inclusion. He is courted to become a Muslim with further promises of him being able to take a wife and bear children. However, Coxere sees in this a snare to further alienate him from his wife and children in England. Consequently, he points out to the Turks that he cannot become a Muslim and cannot take a wife for reasons that he already has a wife and children. He is told "that was nothing" (60). Yet the reader understands that Coxere is keenly aware of the troubling consequences of estrangement, for he is always showing concern for his wife and children, most especially when he is away. In one instance, he writes, "... I grew very brisk in hopes to get something for my wife also, who I left bare enough at home, and had been but seven weeks married to her before I came out of this troublesome voyage" (52).

Coxere articulates his work into two marked phases. They are, on the one hand, events and happenings before his conversion, and on the other hand, those occurring after his conversion. Coxere evidentially portrays his struggles as an ungodly brute fighting his fears and doubts of not belonging. After his conversion, he belongs to the Quaker movement. His battle shifts to that of a spiritualist fighting not because of the fears or doubts of not belonging, but because of his belonging to a movement which society is bent on pushing to the margins and crushing. Davies points out that The Society of Friends (i.e. the Quaker movement) to which Coxere now belongs had been persistently denounced as "the sect in the 1650s, [whose] followers [were] 'more dangerous than the most intestine or foreign enemies.'" Again he makes known that they were also seen as those who "condemn your magistracy and ministry, and trample it under their feet" (22). Before digging deep into this observation, it is worthwhile recalling that Davies draws attention to the fact that "the depth of Quaker conviction guaranteed disruption to religious and social life in the parish" (22). Consequently, the circumstances of the birth of the Quaker movement and the ideas Quakers disseminated make estrangement and hostility perfect alibis for inflicting trials, tribulations and travails of alienation and marginalization upon these Quakers. They shared the views that "there was no reason why the church and its authority should be permitted respect" (22). This Quaker perspective suggests a counter view to the Western one purporting that only religion is the 'cement of society' as noted by the historian G.N. Clark in the following terms: "It was not uncommonly a rational and ethical rather than a 'mysterious' religion; but the belief was ... 'no community ever was or can be maintained, but upon a basis of Religion, the 'cement of Society'...'" (xvi). The above quote implies that any thought challenging the current or generally accepted religious beliefs was doomed to be vehemently disapproved of.

The foundation upon which Quakerism was laid is one of equality, unity and inclusiveness. It was as Clark points out, "a new secular philosophy of public and private morality... independent of Christianity or only loosely attached to it" (xvi). Given the said historical basis upon which 17th century English society functioned, it is evidently clear that Quakers, with their challenging and novel approach towards the status quo, were to become an easy target for all kinds of persecution and alienation. Quakers' whole idea of warring estrangement tirelessly stemmed from their successes in spite of the odds erected against them. It is this, amongst other reasons, that motivated Davies in his study of Quakers and the wider English society to consider these early Quakers "as a group of sober

Victorian nonconformists who were renowned for their enterprise in industry, concern for the poor, and an enlightened attitude to pacifism" (22).

Pacifism is a fundamental principle of Quakerism. Upon the basis of this principle, Quakers refuse to fight in wars, to bear arms, to take oaths, to doff their hats to any and to pay tithes amongst many others. They contested the legitimacy of all of these within the status quo. This refusal was bound to flare up suspicion and, sometimes, outright hostility towards and hatred of the Quakers. It was also the fuel of the estrangement suffered by Quakers in both England and the New World from the inception of the movement. This explains why historians of the period, such as G. N. Clark, rightly underline the idea:

> The witness in law courts took an oath. So did the soldier, the statesman, the judge, the king. Parliaments, armies, and fleets, trading posts, hospitals and colleges had their chaplains and prayers. These were not mere survivals; it was impossible to carry on the world's work without them. (xvii)

Emphasizing the impossibility of not functioning without taking oath, tells of the fate awaiting Quakers who postured against oath taking. In cases of war, the nation compulsorily drafted young individuals i.e. *Press Gang*. This was done without due consideration for the individual's personal or religious conviction. In *Adventures by Sea*, Coxere reveals a deep sense of estrangement provoked by his fear of being press-ganged i.e. drafted to belong to a corps of warring seamen doing just what his personal conviction and religion fight against. At the end of a tumultuous journey, Coxere finds himself at home. He is unemployed, yet terrified by the idea of being recruited by force into the navy for war. He "could not walk the streets without danger, nor sleep in safety" (27). Caught between Scylla and Charybdis, Coxere and his older brother, John, keep to their chambers, estranged as prisoners deprived of any form of freedom. However, to overcome this insurmountable fear of belonging and/or not belonging as well as the perpetual sense of privation these two brothers suffer, they choose to ship themselves as volunteers on board a man-of-war. He writes:

> We keeping our chamber like prisoners, though we knew we could keep any from coming up the stairs to us, yet it was too much like a prisoner's life, so that, we being weary of it, we agreed together to ship ourselves volunteers on board of a man-of-war then in harbour. (27)

During these warring expeditions, Coxere is intent on avoiding being made a captive hence being estranged. As a consequence he changes his masters and nationality as circumstances warrant. It is in this light that the labor historian Stephen Innes appraises Coxere: "Coxere was truly an international workingman finally refusing to participate in nationalistic violence of the era of trade wars and becoming, instead a pacifist and Quaker" (255). Amidst the changing of his master, Coxere does not mince his words as he tells his readers:

> I served several masters in the wars between King and Parliament at sea. Next I served the Spaniards against the French, then the Hollanders against the English; then I was taken by the English out of a Dunkirker; and then I served the English against the Hollanders; and last I was taken by the Turks, where I was forced to serve then against English, French, Dutch, and Spaniards, and all Christendom. Then, when I was released from them, I was got in a man-of-war against the Spaniards, till at last I was taken prisoner by the Spaniards. (28)

Again, in another instance in which Coxere is willing to avoid captivity, he paints the cowardly attitude of his captain that dashes his hopes of remaining free of estrangement. He is finally made prisoner. However, Coxere still finds an opportunity not to suffer the unbearable consequences of being sidelined and shifted to the margins. It is as a result of this that Coxere informs the reader:

> I understood, that they did intend to make a man-of-war of our ship and that I should a been' gunner, for English gunners are in esteem with them, and I, being so fit for their purpose, having the language, I, finding such good entertainment, was not willing to shew any dislike to frustrate their hopes, lest I should a been stripped and abused. (45)

Coxere's primal survival instinct gets him to think how any such opportunity to be free of estrangement could have been jeopardized. He makes evident that in the midst of these thoughts, he strikes a fellow captive, a cook to the merchant, who spoke ill of England to humor the Spaniards. Little does he know that his action would be taken for an affront from a prisoner. Just when he is about to be abandoned at the mercy of soldiers who are ready to strip him bare, he is taken into safety to the gunroom. The gunroom crew being all French, Coxere finds himself quite at home with nothing to worry about since he has the French tongue. He thus escapes being alienated as he says: "I having the French tongue stood me in good stead" (46).

It is worth noting that Coxere's linguistic skills have on several occasions spared him the trouble of being made captive. On one occasion, upon being seized by the Spaniards, Coxere ventures a daring escape on board a Spanish man-of-war. Here again, thanks to his linguistic skills in French, Dutch and Spanish, he prevails and is carried aboard another ship. This ploy is recurrent in Coxere's universe. He acquaints the reader with the fact that his fear of estrangement or further estrangement (when already taken captive and estranged) underlies his guise. Taken captive in the Bay of Cadiz and left as bare as a beggar, Coxere tells of the job he has at hand. It is that of battling the dreadful consequences of captivity. He writes:

> My next work was to put all the ingenies I had to work how to cheat the proud Spaniards of a prisoner the second time, for once I did effect the like design and made my escape at Malaga, when I was there prisoner (80).

Once again, he shows the reader how he pulls his feats. He takes advantage of the fact that a boatman on the ship in which he is taken captive does not know him. He uses his linguistic ruse or expertise in Spanish to have this boatman cheat his own king of a prisoner. So to avoid being made prisoner of war, Coxere writes:

> I speaking Spanish, yet I was forced to be as private as I could from being discovered, as well from the boatman, that he might not know me to be an Englishman and a prisoner, as from the man-a-war's men. This design took effect, though in the daytime, for I went into the boat and was carried away undiscovered aboard of the Hollander, where I paid the boatman, and he went about his business, not knowing he had cheated his king of a prisoner. (80)

As Coxere details the conditions ashore thereafter, he demonstrates his keen understanding of the alienating conditions in Spanish prisons. He would be "half starved" (81) if sent ashore. Thus, he pleads with the steersman to speak on his behalf to the skipper. Coxere's chilling accounts of estranging conditions in Spanish prisons as well as his fears of being estranged seize the skipper's heart and he cannot but take pity on Coxere and help him. In this instance, the linguistic weapon which Coxere has hitherto used to free himself from estrangement almost becomes a handicap. His exquisite linguistic knowledge of the Dutch language almost deters the skipper from helping him. However, he still prevails and discovers with joy that the boat's crew is composed of "half Dutch, half French" (82). This mention is important as it is his linguistic skills in both the Dutch and the French languages that lend credence to his being accepted on board and as he states, "… that suited very well with a hungry belly after the Spaniards have so pinched [him]" (82). Coxere concludes this voyage marked by instances of estrangement with these lines:

> This voyage I had been from England a year and a half, in which time I had been a slave with the Turks, a prisoner with the Spaniards, as being taken by them, and came home only my clothes to my back to my poor wife, but poor and penniless yet glad to see each other in health again after these troubles. My son Robert died, whilst I was a slave, and Elizabeth was born. I was pitied by many, but counted unfortunate. (83)

For Coxere, every means possible to combat estrangement as a seaman is welcomed. When taken prisoner on one occasion by the Spaniards, Coxere shares his experience and that of an Englishman, Humphrey Mantell, who had also been taken captive prior. The interest of this episode in the story and in this discussion on estrangement stems from the fact that Mantell, just like Coxere, resorts to freeing himself from the burdens of estrangement whenever the occasion arises. It should, therefore, come as no surprise that "… for his liberty [Humphrey Mantell] entered himself as one of their company, and fought against us, so came aboard to plunder" (78). This is also an occasion for Coxere to expose the Spaniards in their greed and quest for gold. This leads them to inhumanely strip fellow human beings and leave them abjectly miserable. Dispossession as a process of estranging is Coxere's acerbic critique here. It is a sharp trial for Coxere, and he thinks it can only be combated by what he needed the most at the time: "patience" (80).

Most of the adventures and struggles against estrangement predate Coxere's conversion, "Convincement in Quaker parlance," into Quakerism. It is a period he describes as one of prosperity which could have blinded him from deeper spiritual quests. However, "had not the Lord happily prevented it" (89), it is certain that Coxere would have continued on this path. Coxere's tale of conversion and its aftermath reflect that of most, if not all those who before or after him became Quakers. His tale of becoming a Quaker is one marked by curiosity. The consequence of this is overwhelming with alienation. He chooses to go and listen, with keen interest, to a debate between two Quakers (Edward Burroughs and Samuel Fisher) and a Anglican Priest. It is through this unconscious process of becoming and belonging that Coxere's world will soon be turned upside-down. He will experience estrangement where he least expected it.

Coxere starts making up his mind against shameless dishonesty, ambition, greed, cruelty and hypocrisy when during the debate most of the listeners (who are some of the rudest people he knows) heap all their support on the priest. They all deride the Quakers and their position. This makes Coxere more convinced by the message of the Quakers. He starts by questioning, as do the Quakers, not only the lawfulness or unlawfulness "of fighting and killing enemies" but also its religious basis. It is this questioning that spurs Coxere to attempt to meet Burroughs and Fisher. This kind of success made by Quaker evangelists worried the authorities (Davies 13).

Upon meeting with Burroughs and Fisher, Coxere notes that even though he is a stranger to them, they answer with words that "did not encourage [him] ~~me~~ to fight but left [him] ~~me~~ to the working of the power of the Lord in [his] ~~my~~ own heart..." (90). This highlights what Davies considers "a more accommodating attitude on the part of Friends to outsiders" (11). The narration of the voyages following this meeting is marked by a change in tone, mood, style and characterization. Having embraced the Quaker idea of letting the Lord wrought in the heart that which he should hearken, Coxere starts by taking his distance from the general religious practice at sea.

The distance he takes serves as a factor of estrangement. In describing the manner of devotion at sea, Coxere makes known his earlier participation. Before, he would join the rest of the crew for worship. However, after his convincement, his joys of belonging to this creed of worshipers at sea become a heavy burden of estrangement. Where he previously had celebrated, sang and cheered with other seamen, he now has only the need to weep. The hypocrisy of these worshippers on board occasions his self-estrangement. When Coxere realizes that his fellow seamen "are so estranged that they lose most of their awareness and self-knowledge [as well as] self-doing" (Churchich 119), he starts by stopping to sing, fellowship and pray with the rest. This self-ostracism is just a preamble, foreshadowing societal estrangement to come as he writes,

> [S]o that I sat by them and did not dare open my mouth to sing, neither at last to join with them in prayer, the prayers of the wicked being abomination to the Lord, but would walk on the deck by myself, which was no small cross, I having command over between thirty or forty men under the master, where the master and men's eyes were all at me to see me so much altered as not to come to prayer among them. (91)

This shift in attitude becomes a cause for concern for both master and the thirty or forty men under Coxere. Coxere is far removed from every other activity he has participated in prior. He captures one of such instances in the lines that follow:

> As also we had a feast aboard, [...], where many guns were fired off at healths. I walking at such a time like a stranger, where

before I used to be active in firing off the guns, I had a check from the master, as if nothing were minded. (92)

Coxere, also on this occasion, highlights one of the fundamental attributes of the Early Quaker movement that made Quakers an easy target for societal estrangement. In their attempt to level the society, Quakers spited the idea of taking oaths, doffing hats, using "you" (plural form) in place of the singular "thee" or "thou" for a single individual. They consider "youing" and "thouing" as markers of social inequality and pillars of estrangement. They resented all outward behavior of complimenting which they considered societal indicators of rank, class distinction and false respectability, giving one group or individual the sense of superiority or inferiority over the other. It is against this background that during his voyage to Malaga, Coxere refuses to put off his hat in answer to complimenting from greeting Spaniards as he notes:

I being among the complimenting Spaniards, so that I could not pull off my hat in answer to their complimentings, I found a daily cross as to outward behaviours, customs, and manners, beside the Enemy's workings within, that in this time the Lord let me see that fighting, killing, and destroying one another was of the Devil and not of Himself. (92)

Coxere's autobiography exhibits the paroxysm of estrangement. His espousal of the Quaker peace principle of non-violence, not fighting and killing of enemies, refusal to take oaths and to bear arms render his finding a job extremely difficult. There is no better way of estranging a person than by refusing him/her a source of employment. He succinctly points out his travails. He has been lying at home for several months, out of employment, not because of the lack thereof but as he states, "the name of a Quaker and not fighting shut me quite out of esteem with them" (93). This traumatic spell is corroborated by Davies who makes evident how "... isolation was traumatic, since the community they relied upon for worship and the bulk of their social relationships was no longer welcoming" (104).

However, Coxere finds a willing Edmund Tiddeman ready to ship with him. Rumours soon spread that Tiddeman is about to ship with a Quaker. The whole of his family and in-laws, pushed by fears and doubts of one of their own switching camps to belong to a movement that paid neither attention nor respect to the Established Church and societal forms of respectability as well as their belligerence, fervently opposed Tiddeman's employment of Coxere. Tiddeman's fearful mother in-law, most especially, requests of Coxere to "... promise her not to go with her son, lest he should become a Quaker, and then what merchants would employ him?" (93) Her fears and doubts as well as those of the entire family and society are based upon such unfounded claims as "it was noised abroad as a dangerous thing to carry a Quaker to sea, fearing he should also become one too" (93). It is certainly because of this that "[his] wife and relations were wholly set against it, endeavouring to prevent it, so that [Coxere] became as one not fit to be suffered in a ship" (93-94). Yet, by accepting to employ Coxere, Tiddeman strains his relations with his wife and his wife's family forever. No doubt upon his wife's death, her mother boldly states her position vis-à-vis Tiddeman, saying that "now he might take whom he would; she would not concern herself no more as touching me or his turning Quaker" (95). This concerted persecution of Quakers from the outset has its origin in Quaker advocacy for a creedless religion and the priesthood of all its believers.

This journey with Tiddeman holds a central position in Coxere's narrative, *Adventures by Sea*. It sheds light on the estrangement Quakers suffered in England. Again, it gives Coxere the opportunity to depict the harsh realities of estrangement and hostilities seventeenth century Quakers were exposed to both nationally and internationally. It is also the occasion for him to elucidate how

Quakers could have survived these harsh realities of human degradation and estrangement to which they were exposed. Upon arrival in Faro Portugal, Coxere does not mince words when highlighting the danger he unavoidably runs of being stabbed. In these Portuguese adventures, Coxere sees and humorously describes the Portuguese with a tinge of sarcasm as a ceremonious people walking with their hats in their hand. Conscious of this, Coxere still goes about his business, not minding them. One captivating instance is his presence at the Custom's House where he has to do business. In a typical Coxerian humoristic shift, he probes into the psyche of the custom officials to expose their views on Quakers and reckons, "they looked on us but to be a parcel of clownish seamen without breeding..." (96). He escapes this danger and sums up the adventures with the international views on those of his creedless Quaker religion in the following words:

> [In] the year 1662, we were hardly known to be a people amongst many abroad, so that they knew nothing, but all to be done in contempt by us, and the more, they counting all heretics who are not Papist, so no sin to kill a heretic. (97)

So, upon embracing Quakerism, besides the humiliation from Tiddeman's in-laws and family, and their willingness to ostracize Coxere, he has to deal with ruthless employers. These potential employers understand Coxere's dire straits and would exploit both his experience and linguistic competency to the fullest. They offer to pay him exceedingly low wages on board a ship they were fitting to send to trade in the straits of Gibraltar. Upon negotiating his wages, Coxere realizes the alienating and degrading act of proffering a job seeker wages that are incommensurate to his or her experience. In short, Coxere in his case would have scorned any such offer in the past. Nonetheless, Coxere is compelled to cheaply sell his labor to this ruthless employer in order to keep body and soul together. Thus, they reach an agreement.

From thence, Coxere's narrative brings to light a series of imprisonments suffered by Coxere and his Friends in belief. These imprisonments fanned the flames of Quaker estrangement. Edward Burroughs, one of the earliest itinerant Quaker preachers and reputed as the Quaker politician, notes the ill use made of the people called Quaker:

> And in all these counties we had much opposition, sufferings and cruel dealings of men of all sorts. Every gaol may witness, how seldom any of them were without some of us imprisoned these six years; and scarcely one steeplehouse or market may witness. (36)

Coxere's testimony, like Burroughs', is one of state-orchestrated alienation against a people whose only crime is their belonging to a group of people in quest of freedom of worship, especially to worship God in their own way. Coxere is first picked at Yamouth. He gives details of this arrest and the mistreatment he and his religious acolytes receive thereafter in the hands of their persecutors: the bailiffs and the jailors. They are all willing to estrange Coxere and his co-religionists. They would coerce them to eat only what the jailor and his wife provided them. This fails and the jailors make further unreasonable demands with the goal of starving the prisoners.

In a twist of faith, Coxere, like his fellow Quakers, makes of this fight a spiritual warfare in which the oppressed, the dispossessed, the displaced and the alienated are thus treated for their conscience's sake and their love for God, while their adversaries work for the devil. Given that both initial and the unreasonable demands failed to have the detainees feel the real pinch of estrangement, these detainees are removed from the public jail and secured in a hall on the top floor of the Town Hall. The detainees are left with nothing but water for several days. They are not allowed visits or contacts with the outside world. This dispossession is a sharp trial for Coxere and his Friends. He expresses his frustration at "not having liberty to go out..." (103). This estrangement in his home country is what goads Coxere to have recourse to a flashback in which he portrays his life as a slave in the hands of the Turks. He proceeds in a comparative juxtaposition of estranging conditions in the hands of the Turks and in those of the English. He then overtly states in caustic terms his harsh treatment:

> Such unkind usage I never had when I was a slave under the hands of Turks, such as the Christians call Infidels, that though I was chained a-nights with a great iron chain, and was made to work a-days, and sometimes beat, yet they gave me my bellyful of bread to eat with my water; but here, among my countrymen and such as called Christians, they gave me not the privilege as they gave their dogs, for they would not deny anyone to give them a crust of bread. (103)

By and large, in warring estrangement, Coxere has skillfully probed into both the psyche of individual human beings and those he came across in his adventures by sea as well as the psyche of the society in general to highlight the toll that the plague of estrangement can take on humans and on the society. He also shows how this plague can be fought and overcome. He further takes into account what Bakhtin in the twentieth century considered as the authoritative utterances that set the tone for "each epoch, social circles, small world of family, friends, acquaintances and comrades" (88-89). Over and above, in spite of the fact that Coxere, like most seventeenth century Early Quakers, is an autodidact, his rhetorical skills in exploring issues of integration, affiliation and alienation had long been recognized and highlighted by the first editor of *Adventures by Sea,* E.H.W. Meyerstein. He writes, "In matters of humour, variety and description of self-portrait, Edward Coxere belongs to the great heroes of adventure fictions which would stimulate youths and easily make one to forget old age" (xix). From the foregoing, it is clear that Coxere seriously takes to crushing any endeavor to subjugate and alienate another human being. This had become customary with Early Quakers. However, unlike Bourdieu's claim of the class-generated nature of *habitus*, the Quaker case of warring estrangement as illustrated by Coxere becomes what Peter Collins calls in "Discipline: The Codification of Quakerism as Orthopraxy, 1650-1738" "a code of discipline that not only emerges from religion but does so through practice preceding belief" (88). It is in this vein that Harold Loukes, to sum up this Quaker endeavor, points out that "the Quaker way leads us to think of men and women the world over as parts of the family of God" (119). Consequently, none, irrespective of circumstance, race, creed, gender, sexuality or sexual orientation should be left out of the human family circle.

Works Cited

Coxere, Edward. *Adventures by Sea*. Trans. Bill F. Ndi. Mankon-Bamenda : Langaa, 2012. Print.

Bakhtin, M.M. *Speech Genres and Other Late Essays*. Trans. Vern W. McGee. Austin : U of Texas P, 1986. Print.

Brockbank, Elizabeth. *Edward Burrough of Underbarrow 1634-1662*, London: The Bannisdale Press, 1949. Print.

Chopra, Ramesh. *Dictionary of Philosophy*, New Delhi: Isha Books, 2005. Print.

Collins, Peter. "Both Independent and Interconnected Voices: Bakhtin among the Quakers" in Nigel Rapport. (Ed.) *British Subjects: An Anthropology of Britain*, Oxford: Berg, 2002. Print.

_____. "Discipline: The Codification of Quakerism as Orthopraxy, 1650-1738." *History & Anthropology* 13.2 (2002): 79-92, Print.

Churchich, Nicholas. *Marxism and Alienation,* Madison, NJ: FDU, 1990. Print.

Clark, G.N. *The Seventeenth Century.* Oxford: Clarendon, 1957 - Print.

Davies, Adrian. *The Quakers in the English Society 1655-1725.* Oxford: Clarendon, 2000. Print.

Fox, George. *The Journal,* ed. Nigel Smith. London: Penguin, 1998. Print.

Hill, Christopher. *The World Turned Upside Down.* London: Penguin, 1991. Print.

Innes, Stephen. *Work and Labor in Early America.* Chapel Hill: U of North Carolina P, 1988. Print.

Kotchnig, Elined P. "Quakerism and Analytical Psychology" *Inward Light 49* (1955): 1-13. Print.

Kotchnig, Elined P. "Quakers and C.G. Jung" *Inward Light 49* (1955): 14-27. Print.

Loukes, Harold. *The Quaker Contribution*, New York: Macmillan, 1965. Print.

Mandel, Ernest. "Causes of Alienation." *in The Marxist Theory of Alienation: International Socialist Review* 31.3 (1971): 19-23 50-59. Print.

Matson, I Wallace. *A History of Philosophy.* Orlando: Harcourt Brace, 1987. Print.

Rapport, Nigel. (Ed.) *British Subjects: An Anthropology of Britain,* Oxford: Berg, 2002. Print.

Seeman, Melvin. "Alienation Studies" *in Annual Review of Sociology* 1 (1975): 91-123. Print.

Section II:
Outside Looking in

Chapter 4

Out of the Circle: United Marginals in Francis B. Nyamnjoh's *The Travail of Dieudonné*

By
Adaku T. Ankumah

Alienation has been a topic of interest in the literature of the twentieth century. Haakayoo Zoggyie notes in his recent publication on the same topic that though the reasons for alienation may be different, alienation is found in people in the "deepest recesses of the Amazon forest to the most sophisticated city on our planet" (9). Indeed, the pages of literary texts reveal characters whose alienation comes from their abject poverty to E.A. Robinson's character Richard Cory who is "richer than a king" and who "glittered" as he walked by to make onlookers envious, but went home one night and "put a bullet through his head." In Cory's case here mentioned, one may question if his final act is the result of his fears, doubts or joys of not belonging and/or belonging. However, researchers and theorists who write on alienation tend to focus much attention on its negative psychological effects—the powerless, meaningless, isolationist existence of those on the outside looking in, distanced by their "lacks." Richard Schmitt, professor emeritus of Philosophy in *Alienation and Freedom*, describes the life of the alienated thus: "One day follows another, often boring and repetitive, sometimes utterly catastrophic, but always incomprehensible and not under anyone's control at all." He concludes that "[a]lienated lives lack intelligibility" (77).

The powerlessness of the alienated has been defined by Melvin Seeman as "the expectancy or probability held by the individual that his own behavior cannot determine the occurrence of the outcomes, or reinforcements, he seeks" (784). He accounts for this powerlessness from Marx's explanation of the worker not being a contributing factor in production. Thus though he is involved in production, he has no decision-making role. Based on Seeman's definition, it stands to reason that on a continent where people's lives have been determined by outside forces, alienation will feature prominently in the literature produced in Africa. However, critics have challenged this notion of alienation located from the outside and impacting the lives of another group. For instance, in his published inaugural lecture at the University of Ibadan in 1982, "In Praise of Alienation," a title that appears oxymoronic, the Nigerian professor and critic Abiola Irele challenges what he refers to as the "pathology of alienation as inscribed in our [Africans'] experience as a colonized people" (202). Generally, proponents of the alienated African position suggest that in the traditional past, citizens enjoyed an edenic relationship with their culture, before the intrusion of colonialism, when "things fell apart." Irele contends that instead of viewing alienation negatively, Africans could reverse the negativity by seeing Western civilization as providing "the paradigm of modernity to which we aspire" (202). In other words, Africans must use the tension which exists between themselves and Western culture and civilization brought by colonialism in order to catch up with the rest of the world (224). Obviously, this capitulation to "modernism" and the former colonial masters has drawn much criticism both inside and outside of the continent, given the fact that Irele at one point championed the cause of Negritude in Anglophone Africa. However, some contemporary African writers reject this path to "disalienation," which again suggests that Africans cannot solve their problems unless they look to the West for a solution. Writers like Cameroonian-born author Francis B. Nyamnjoh have chosen a different approach to address the problem of otherness, alienation and dispossession of the masses in many African countries.

Recognized in March 2013 as the African Hero of the Year for 2013 by the African Student Union of Ohio University, Francis B. Nyamnjoh wears many hats, including that of a social anthropologist and a novelist. In *The Travail of Dieudonné,* Nyamnjoh's protagonist, Dieudonné, an elderly man who initially works as a houseboy for a white couple in an African country, drowns his woes in alcohol. He does not, however, allow his exclusionary status as a "nouveau pauvre," one marginalized by class, birth, race, ethnicity, religion, etc. render him voiceless and powerless in a society where the leaders and the "nouveau rich" exploit them. Far from feeling estranged from himself or his community, Dieudonné and others disenfranchised in his community, subvert the negativity of exclusion, alienation and marginalization, by empowering themselves and taking control of their lives.

Dieudonné's alienation comes from different aspects of his life, all of which are intertwined. A product of colonialism, Dieudonné's Warzone is caught between the wars fought for control of his part of the country. These wars are "fuelled by the Muzungulander merchants of death" (34). This is a reference to the French colonial masters and local warlords fighting over minerals and other natural resources of the region. The colonial experience itself, that encounter between the colonial master and the colonized, results in alienation. One cannot discuss alienation especially in postcolonial Africa without a reference to the psychiatrist and activist Frantz Fanon, who wrote extensively on the effects of alienation on the colonized. Frantz Fanon, the Martinique-born psychiatrist and Algerian freedom fighter, talks about the compartmentalized world of colonialism which produces a Manichean world of superiors and inferiors, oppressor and oppressed, etc. The dualism manifests itself in the socio-economic realities of both sides, producing a sense of powerlessness in the colonized as they undertake manual work to produce raw materials to sustain the colonial powers (37). In turn, the language and culture of the colonized, deemed inferior, give way to those of the colonial giants who wield power. Colonial aggression experienced by the native turns into inward terror for them and manifests itself in acts of aggression on each other, since they are unable to pour out their frustrations on the colonizer, who uses violence to maintain power. Thus in the worlds Fanon portrays in his works, the mark of separation is whether one belongs to the world of the colonizer or one does not belong to it. Violence becomes the method for maintaining the separation or fighting it (38).

Dieudonné's state of being an outsider begins when his father, an ordinary man in their village, a devout Muslim with the aim of raising a devout son, is conscripted into the colonial army to defend the interests of the mother country. The only son in a family of four girls, Dieudonné is taken into the war by his father who had hopes of his son getting an education. He doesn't get the education, and after seven years, father and son return to Warzone. Dieudonné's alienation intensifies after his return. The village has changed dramatically, as he has too. He sees firsthand the devastating effects of another country's war on his own village. Almost all the young men of fighting age have been swept away to fight in a foreign war and most of the young women of marriageable age are without men to marry them, including his four sisters. All of them have become, in his own words, "victims of war" (58). Even his own female relatives—mother and sisters—have changed, with his mother especially aging and suffering from approaching blindness. With the village decimated of young men, the women and elders are planning to boycott growing cotton, a crop which does not serve as food but fuels the industrial machine of the West. The females left behind by war are sadly aware of the incongruity of their situation that they barely have enough to eat, yet they are enriching others in far-away places. Having been gone from home for several years, Dieudonné's isolation from his family is so pronounced after his return that he feels he no longer belongs. "Alienation," Richard Schmitt notes,[...]refers to a growing estrangement between individual persons, to cooling affections, and to a loss of trust" (1). Three short days after a seven-year absence, he leaves his family, not knowing where he is heading. He will much rather go anywhere than stay with people who have become strangers to him. Home is no longer a place of belonging.

Alienation follows him even in his love life. His first wife, Amina, an Arab woman, runs away from him. Due to his constant abuse, the second wife, Fatimata, from his ethnic group, waits for him to finish paying the bride price; then she elopes with a young man from another ethnic group. His third woman, Tsanga, disappears one day, leaving no trace, after taking Dieudonné's savings stashed underneath the mattress. As a woman who has had six husbands, Tsanga seems to care for her husband. This explains why Dieudonné weeps like a child abandoned by a foster mother when he discovers that she is gone (17). Tsanga, who believes that variety is the essence of life, is willing to settle down with Dieudonné, but she is overwhelmed by his "childish irresponsibility" (10) especially after drinking bouts. He attributes his estrangement from these women to his economic status: "Perhaps because I'm poor and know nothing" (96). His low-class status and its attendant problems are destroying not just his own life but his relationships. However, he compounds his problem with alcoholism and, in the case of his first wife, with physical abuse.

As he finds his way through many adventures to the fictional Mimboland, he is arrested by the police because he is an illegal alien, subject to deportation for not having documentation to be in the country (74). The irony is that with his irregular status he needs the help of a white friend of the policeman to hire him as a garden boy. Afterwards, the white man is himself deported to Muzunguland for some unspecified crime. Irony, as it becomes apparent in Dieudonné's narrative of his past, becomes a major tool for him to articulate his alienation.

In "Language, Mobility, African Writers and Pan-Africanism," co-authored by Nyamnjoh and Katleho Shoro, the authors deal with the so-called language problem in African literatures, with writers like Ngugi wa Thiong'o parting ways with colonial languages to write in endogenous languages like Gikuyu and Swahili and others like Achebe, Okot P'Bitek, and Soyinka who Africanize colonial languages to underscore the "multiculturalism and complexity involved in the lives of colonised [sic] peoples" (43-44). Nyamnjoh belongs to the latter group that believes the colonial languages cannot be expunged from Africa, but they can be "creatively" blended with the endogenous languages to produce an "amazing and constantly changing linguistic landscape in Africa," the type of linguistic blend heard on the streets of townships like Soweto (13). Mimboland as a fictional Cameroon, Nyamnjoh's country of birth, is a place of multiple languages: Muzugulandish, Tougalish, pidgin, and endogenous languages. At times in a couple of sentences, Nyamnjoh is able to pull several languages together, as in this passage where Dieudonné reminisces about the loss of his wife Tsanga:

> His thoughts would turn to his beloved Tsanga. "*Mi Yeewnii* Tsanga—'missing you badly Tsanga'" he would add in his mother tongue, as if hoping to reach his ex-wife by telepathy. "Wherever she is, I'm warning every man to keep his hands of her. Ne la piratez pas. C'est ma femme. (158)

The linguistic Babel created by the multiplicity of tongues, as demonstrated in the above quotation, is another source of alienation in the novel. Dieudonné, who speaks different languages from those spoken around him, finds himself linguistically alienated in the different areas of his country. In his migration from home to nowhere in particular, Dieudonné sojourns in Lola, in West Mimboland. Here unskilled plantation labor is needed for the banana, palm oil, rubber, coffee plantations, all catering to the colonizers. Thus agents try to recruit cheap labor in Dieudonné, but they discover that he can only speak Muzungulandish, which they don't understand. His inability to speak their Tougalish earns him the nickname "useless frog," for the agents are convinced that "anyone worth his place in their world needed to prove himself in Tougalish" (65). Dieudonné surmises about his treatment and his nickname and concludes that his alienation stems from these agents perceiving him to be a threat since they don't understand him: "Perhaps from some unpleasant past experiences, they had come to consider Muzungulandish as the language of troublemakers, crooks, spies, dissemblers, noisemakers and weaklings" (65). Again, Dieudonné finds himself estranged from others not only because of his linguistic difference but also because of the work he does.

The alienation Dieudonné and his fellow citizens experience at work follows a classic Marxist definition of alienation of labor. In his writings, Marx notes that work, especially the modern variety in factories, is external to the worker in that he is not the owner or the one who benefits from his labor. Given his separation from the work he is doing and the fact that he has needs to meet, the worker feels compelled to work, more from necessity than from the love of work. Thus without any compulsion to work, the worker will not work. This is the case of plantation workers in Warzone and Lola who know that growing cotton is not for their own welfare but for that of their white masters. Ever the perceptive observer, Dieudonné poses a question to his audience and provides answers:

> Do you know that a farmer can flourish in such strange crops as cotton, cocoa, and coffee, yet die of famine. If you don't, let me tell you that these crops have no immediate value as food. You can't eat cotton, can you? They are meant to inflame with hunger. (63)

Not only are these plantation crops labor intensive; they are also low-paying jobs, given the energy expended. The little money the farmers make is "swept away by taxes, medicines and school fees for children" (63). Dieudonné would rather die than work in a plantation; however, not all his country folk arrive at this conclusion since his fellow Warzoners still continue to work in the cotton plantation.

Dieudonné feels this alienation with all the foreign people (Muzungulanders, as Nyamnjoh refers to them) he has worked for as houseboy all his life. His worst experience is with the Toubaabys who treat him "like a lifeless tool, a machine of sorts that relieved Madame of her household chores, a zombie" (18). The narrator's word choice of "zombie" underscores the way his bosses regard him—lifeless, like an automaton, someone who acts without thinking. Heartbroken after his wife Tsanga packed out of their dilapidated home and left with his small savings hidden under the mattress, Dieudonné expects at least some sympathy from the couple. However, he is told to leave his personal affairs "outside the confines of their secluded residence" (18). His treatment at the hands of these masters on a day that he loses the love of his life sends him weeping all the more.

To worsen his already very bad situation, he has no control over his wages since his previous white masters pass him on to the new master with information about his wages. He, the worker, has no say in how much he will be paid; the boss dictates the terms. Dieudonné reaches the conclusion that the more he toiled the less money he made, so he names himself "Payless" (85). After working for various employers for forty years, he has no money to show for it. He is still confined to the margins of society as he still lives in a rat-infested shack in a neighborhood which is an open sewer. In fact, the inside of his shack can be seen from the outside because of cracks in the wall. This description of Dieudonné's neighborhood and shack follows Fanon's classic description of the native town, medina, or reservation as a "place of ill fame . . . a world without spaciousness" (38). The poor man is at a loss as to what to call his services to the various whites he has served: "labour of love, love of labour, labour of hope, hope of labor" (87). He sees a "bit of everything" in what he does, so the pun is not for amusement. The "hope of labor" is certainly a pressing and evocative issue since Monsieur Toubaaby constantly reminds him that "Nyamandem is crowded with hundreds of thousands seeking employment as domestics" (19). Thus he is replaceable as a worker. Unfortunately, Dieudonné does not help to secure his job with his lateness and alcoholism; eventually, after failing to show up one Saturday morning to cater for a big party given by the Toubaabys, his hope for labor is gone.

Dieudonné's marginalization at work is further highlighted by the fact that the "darling children" of the Toubaabys, the one dog and eight cats he cooks for, are worth more than human beings. Compared to the meager MIM 6,000 he makes a month, the pets get MIM100,000 spent on them, in addition to having their own medical doctors in a foreign land. Dieudonné's audience finds this information about veterinarians for animals incredulous. As human beings, they can't afford to see the few doctors available to the entire population. How do animals get flown out of the country for consultation over loss of appetite? Madame cries over one animal staying with a friend, and yet does not care about the human being working for her.

Perhaps his second-class status becomes even more obvious in his religious background which alienates him from the dominant religion and requires re-naming, a process that disregards his Muslim background, undermines his person and re-invents his identity as a Catholic. Born into a Muslim family, his father, a practicing Muslim who raised him on the teachings of the Koran, named him Allah-Go'onga, meaning God Almighty, in hopes that greatness will be his future. His second employer, a "staunch Catholic," will not hire anyone with a "pagan" name to work for her. The irony of her position is that Dieudonné's name is not a pagan name. His previous name and the name given by his mistress both begin with "God": God Almighty and God given (or given by God). The difference is that his original name is Muslim, but the name given by his boss is Christian French and therefore not "pagan." Desperate for a job that will provide for his sustenance and not concerned about names, he allows himself to be re-named, though the negative impact on his identity and selfhood does not escape him, as he tells his audience: "And that is how Dieudonné took over Allah-Go'onga, and has over the years imposed himself with an arbitrariness that shatters whatever sense of self that my inner self has been trying to cultivate" (75). Due to his religious estrangement, Dieudonné has little to no knowledge about the practices of his newly-acquired faith, including not eating meat on Good Friday. Thus when he violates this practice, the priest is disappointed, especially with Dieudonné's logic for the violation. He claims the meat is made fish by sprinkling water on it, just as the priest did to change him from being Allah-Go'onga to Dieudonné (75-6). After two years of service to his mistress, he loses his job for not following the dominant religious practices of his boss. For Dieudonné, then, religion does not offer a way out of his alienation. It actually contributes to his plight.

Being confined to the margins of society definitely affects Dieudonné and his sense of worth. Characteristically, he manifests typical traits of the alienated. He navigates between sadness and joy, never able to enjoy happiness without reliving some aspect of his harsh existence. The narrator tells us that "[s]udden bouts of depression were a characteristic of his" (110). When the Toubaabys treat him like a little boy, he is moved to tears or even worse contemplates suicide. His lowest point with the Toubaabys comes after one of their visits to their home country when Dieudonné is left in their home to take care of their animals. This same period a coup d'état occurs in Mimboland, with rebels seizing power for three days and cutting off electricity and other supplies, especially to the rich area, Beverly Hills. For three days, Dieudonné is more concerned about his survival than that of the animals under his care since he barely has food and drink himself. To his surprise, Madame Toubaaby is not concerned about what happened and how he survived: she is concerned about her expensive wine which has disappeared. The incongruity of the question given the dire situation makes Dieudonné think death is better than living, but as he notes, sometimes, even one's "application to die is rejected for no apparent reason" (118). As a result, it is worthwhile interrogating and exploring the coping mechanisms one like Dieudonné, caught in the grip of alienation, develops to be able to survive his fears, doubts and joys of not belonging and/or belonging.

Human beings have taken different approaches to coping with alienation. Some argue in favor of acceptance or resignation in the face of cosmic forces beyond human control. Alienation, others believe, informs human existence as existential philosophers posit and thus cannot be overcome. Overall, the estranged have tried to use various means to at least cope with alienation. In Nyamnjoh's novel, as in real-life experiences of those outside the margins of society, alcohol becomes one of the coping mechanisms. In exploring the reasons for alcoholism in this particular group, Melvin Seeman and Carolyn Anderson resort to Marxist theory tying work to self-identity. Though there are other factors which lead to serious drinking, such as lack of education, social isolation, etc., when work is less than satisfying, making the workers sense their powerlessness, the tendency to rely on alcohol increases (61-62). Dieudonné, "a committed drinker," finds friendship in the bottle, for human beings have failed him (2). To loosen up and tell his story, he needs a drink. Even the names of the beer promise to deliver some joy or comfort: "the friend of friends," "refreshingly smooth enigma of darkness powered by Guinness" (2-3). In the warmth and friendship alcohol offers, Dieudonné is never bored. In fact, when inebriated, he temporarily forgets his poverty and misery and gains a "strange feeling of well-being, of freedom, and even of belonging" (4).

Alcohol, however, is not used just by individuals to solve personal problems; Dieudonné is convinced it is used by the government to solve political, social and economic problems as well. In response to Dieumerci's question as to what he would do if the government banned alcohol, Dieudonné reasons that it will be foolish for the government to do so because those saddled with financial, domestic and other problems use alcohol to avoid suicide or political violence (101). Moreover, government officials, including the President of the country, own the most prosperous breweries and will not like to cut off their source of wealth. In that respect, the government makes it easier to get permits for businesses involving alcohol than to get permits for other businesses. The brewing companies also offer promotional gifts which include free beers to free cars; thus like the lottery, people keep buying, hoping to win something big and in the process, they get more addicted to drinking. It appears the government is interested in people drowning their problems in alcohol than in challenging the mismanagement of the country's resources; thus its goal is to have a bar in every corner of Mimboland to numb citizens into inaction about mounting problems (102). As a disillusioned civil servant notes,

> We no longer have the means to feed our children and grandchildren, to send them to school or to attend to their health needs. . . . Our situation is critical. We live [in] a world of words not a world of miracles. (30)

Indeed, instead of "miracles," Dieumerci, a graduate student, has found that in under two years, the number of licensed bars went from 3, 002 to 4,500 (103).

This praise of alcohol may be disturbing to some, especially in Dieudonné's situation, for when soaked, he is unable to get up to go to work on time. His eventually losing his job can be traced to his alcoholism. Dieudonné is also aware of the dangers of alcohol, which he sees as a legacy of the colonial days. He notes that alcohol makes "ash of manhood and nonsense of women who dare smile its way." Hence he drinks but fears the bottle at the same time (90). His operating principle in drinking is to drink without drowning his integrity (91), a position that many who drink are unable to reach.

Writers on alienation have noted the "threat" it poses to humans since people feel their condition beyond their control. Whether it is family, mind, emotions, etc. to cope with the situation, the alienated adopt various strategies to protect themselves from succumbing to its power. As Schmitt notes, some try to fight the ambiguities of life alone; others resign to it, while some imitate others (50). The marginalized in *The Travail of Dieudonné* resort to other means that marginalized people have used beside alcohol to deal with their situation: solidarity with others. For Dieudonné and his group of friends, a united front as the oppressed offers hope in dealing with their various challenges in life. This motley group consists of people from different walks of life. There is Dieudonné, the protagonist, whose life story forms the basis for the novel. Dieumerci Aphrika is the intellectual of the group, the scholar, researcher whose desire is to fill in the gaps of his mini-dissertation on cotton production in Warzone, Dieudonné's homeland. This intellectual curiosity prompts Dieumerci to ask Dieudonné a few questions about his life. However, he does not have the final word on voicing the woes of the oppressed as intellectuals normally do. The consensus about the underclass is that they are not intellectually capable of understanding their plight in the larger scheme of events; and even in novels like Ngugi's *Petals of Blood* there is an activist like Karega with some education to rally the people. Nyamnjoh does not abrogate the rights of the downtrodden to articulate their issues. Dieumerci, who has read about the postcolonial situation of Warzone and even uses the vast library in the Toubaaby home, knows very little about the colonial period itself. Thus Dieudonné becomes his "advisor and professor": he has a whole range of questions to ask Dieudonné that he can't ask his academic advisor.

The questions Dieumerci cannot ask in the classroom, he is able to pose to Dieudonné in the friendly atmosphere of the neighborhood bar, Le Grand Canari Bar, where he and others drown their problems. Located at "Le-carrefour-de-la-joie," the "crossroads of joy," the name addresses their hopes and expectations for frequenting that place, offering clients the "therapeutic potions" they are looking for. In fact, the bar's influence is described using religious language, for it offers a "ministry of enjoyment" and offers everyone "what they came to seek" (2). In contrast to other bars in the neighborhood, the Grand Canari, according to Dieudonné, is "exceptionally friendly" (42), though the scholar is skeptical about a drinking place with a cordial atmosphere. Dieumerci is thus surprised to find the ambiance pleasant, with clients affable, courteous to each other, some even calling Dieudonné nicknames, a sign of their affection and familiarity with each other. Dieudonné is well liked by this company as they applaud his sayings and are ready to buy him drinks and food. Should the purveyors of doom and gloom for the alienated enter this dilapidated bar located in the slums, they will be surprised by the camaraderie of this new-found "family" that has its individual challenges but also value community over the isolation found at the margin of society. In the company of other disillusioned, there is shared comfort as they resist the forces that harass them.

Music plays an important role in this bar too. Many writers have noted the impact of music on the oppressed. Amiri Baraka notes in *Dutchman* that without music, Black musicians like Bessie Smith would have committed murder (35). Other African American writers and critics have discussed the therapeutic role of music like Blues to life's challenges African Americans have encountered in their experience in America. In "Signifying the Blues," author Robert Switzer draws on the words of a blues song by John Lee Hooker that "[t]he blues is healing" to elaborate on this music's impact:

> The blues somehow touches us at the core of our inner-most suffering and hurt—whether from betrayal or a sense of powerlessness, or at the loss of a friend who had become, in

some measure, like the mirror of one's own soul. . . . But the healing power of the blues is not so much about feeling better, if by this one means that a weight is lifted, that one feels "happy" instead of "blue." Doubtless it is part of the captivating mystery of the blues experience that it feels good to sing the blues, and to listen; that one is feeling bad, but somehow feeling good about it (25).

At the Grand Canari, Madame has set up a "permanent all-purpose, all-night, all-day band" (154) to cash in on people's misery. However, the local Bikutsi tune offers therapy for those "trapped as they are in misery and constant death. It offers them an opportunity to scream with their feet" (155). Pédale, a new variation of the popular Bikutsi, is gaining popularity. The narrator gives a detailed description not only about the dance but also its impact on the people's psyche as they pedal away on the dance floor:

[D]ancers crush together on the circular floor at the center of the gigantic wooden block, shaking in frenzied trances, intoxicated with physical and emotional pleasure, yearning to purge themselves of the frustrations of life at the margins. Under the threat of death induced by poverty, plagues, disasters and the indifference of those in positions to make a difference, the accelerated beat does the trick, and with each vibrant song, the accumulated uncertainties and insecurities seem to melt away and are even forgotten, as Mimbolanders cycle away intensely. In this sense, Pédale is proving quite empowering as it offers the forgotten the chance to deride those who have made it a habit of poking fun at ordinary lives. (155)

Thus the significance of this music is not its aesthetic quality, though it certainly has that quality. Neither is it an "anesthetic" to deaden pain and numb fears, as Switzer notes in his essay. This music offers this marginalized group a chance to respond to their varying degrees of challenges and assert their humanity by refusing to succumb to their hopelessness. It is music that is "deliciously raw, meant as it is, to shock the dead and dying out of silence and compliance" (155). It has the power to transform dancers as they participate, but it does not alter their scorn of their ruthless leaders, for they regain power to disparage them. For a short period, they reverse roles as they are not the smeared but the ones who smear. With their feet they trod on the high and mighty.

The purveyor of this "deliciously raw" music is none other than Precious, the barmaid, singer and partner of the "yet-to-find-a-job Dieumerci," who is provocative on stage. Her sensual music, with erotic undertones, makes Dieudonné uncomfortable, unless he takes it in with his King Size beer. One may ask why this overt sexuality among a group struggling to survive the failure of their postcolonial state. The narrator makes it clear that Bikutsi music offers social commentary on a gamut of issues which are projected into public space: "[F]rustrations, sex and relationships, and the private lives of prominent individuals" (154). In its voluptuous nature, this music epitomizes the ills of society, the rape of the country in the past and its present exploitation by the ruling elite. Even at Dieumerci's defense of his mini-dissertation, when Precious "insisted on entertaining" those present with her "suggestive voice and luring wriggles" (156), the illustrious Monsieur Toubaaby could not resist the dance floor. Even the "high and mighty" who have banned her lead song on her debut album, still enjoy her music in the privacy of their homes and gyms.

Thus the irony of this music is that it resonates with the powerful elite too—but only to advance their exploitation, especially of females who are reduced to objects of desire for powerful men. The pot-bellied president of the jury that evaluated Dieumerci could not resist making a sexually explicit comment after Precious sings, comparing her music to Dieumerci's mini-dissertation: "A good mini-dissertation is like a good mini skirt," he laughed, "sufficiently short to arouse interest but long enough to cover the subject" (156). Not only with his words, but also with his eyes, this old man strips

Precious, scrutinizing every part of her body and arousing himself to the extent that he is afraid he may get a heart attack. Dieumerci does not appreciate this open flirtation with his girlfriend.

However, this music does not focus simply on the negative; it also taps into the rich traditions of the people with its message "of hope and faith in traditional values and dignity," a message that the "sidestepped bulk of the ghettoes and beyond" (156) still respect. These values, which their rulers have rejected for the values of their colonial masters, become a magnet bonding the disenfranchised.

The group gathered at the Grand Canari uses its marginalized position to forge solidarity, providing support in the form of drink and food for people like Dieudonné, a worker who barely earns enough to sustain himself. The hospitality shown among the group is contagious. In choosing the location as the place to narrate his woes instead of telling his story in the very house of his oppressors, Dieudonné notes the uniqueness of this venue as compared to other drinking joints: "the Grand Canari is an exceptionally friendly place, quite generous to the likes of me... It's a jolly bar, the one and only. I think you are going to like the atmosphere" (42). True to his predictions, Dieudonné is warmly welcomed by the patrons, and the civil servant in the group, Chopngomna, sees to it that Dieudonné and other members of their party have enough to drink. Even Margarita, Chopngomna's latest girlfriend, insists on paying for two more bottles of beer for Dieudonné (88). After supplying Dieudonné with more drinks than he can afford to buy, Margarita provides him with meat to satisfy his hunger. Dieumerci also reaches out to Dieudonné as a grown son looks to the welfare of an aged parent. He parts with his own meager earnings to provide him with clothing and food. In addition, he and his girlfriend Precious begin a savings account to raise enough money to reunite Dieudonné and his wife Tsanga and to eventually send the "exile" back to be re-acquainted with his homeland and family. The operating principle among these people is provided by Dieudonné: "Ordinary people just want to be happy. All they want is to feel close to life once in a while" (164). They accomplish this goal not only with their solidarity, music, dance and drinking but also with humor.

Perhaps the most important function of this group is the way they give agency to their plight. Different people handle alienation in different ways: some choose silence to handle their alienation; others may voice their frustrations, lamenting their condition. This group, with Dieudonné and not the scholar Dieumerci as the spokesperson, vocalizes its marginalization but not in a defeatist manner. Analyzing the conversation in the Grand Canari, one may agree with Salvatore Attardo that it qualifies as "working class humor" which he defines as "humor produced by members of the working class for other members of the working class." He describes this type of humor as not "politically correct" most often and at times could be considered "offensive" (121), as it deals with various issues involving race, women, sex, etc. Indeed, Dieumerci is attracted to Dieudonné due to his sense of humor. He gives credit to the two Jesuit priests he served before changing masters to the Toubaabys, who left him with a "basket of jokes." Given the situation Dieudonné is in, the student expected to encounter a morose person, withdrawn, and definitely not laughing, but Dieudonné is not silent. Some of his jokes target his white bosses and their conduct. Dieudonné overhears Mr. Toubaaby refer to himself as an "academic polygamist" because he failed to become a polygamist in real life. Dieudonné will use this to note that the Muzungulander is focused on whatever s/he does, unlike the Africans: "When a Muzungulander decides to study books, he eats and sleeps books, he sleeps books, he celebrates books" (27). With this statement, Dieudonné implies that Africans don't immerse themselves deeply into solving the pressing issues they face. Contrastingly, the colonial bosses are consumed by their activities that they don't have time for other things. Could this implied sarcasm or irony be directed at the group's inability to be consumed by their desire to extricate themselves from alienation? Or is it just aimed at making those around him laugh?

Nyamnjoh skillfully turns his humor into irony. On this score, Gloria Onyeoziri, in *Shaken Wisdom*, notes that irony "can be a response to an oppressor convinced of his superior wisdom" (1) just as it can be used by the oppressor to reinforce his domination. Though she notes that there is no particular type of irony that can be identified as uniquely African, African writers like Chinua Achebe, Ahmadou Kourouma, and Calixthe Beyala have used irony in various novels. Irony, Onyeoziri observes, is present in oral tradition, but in postcolonial writing, it informs the texts of many writers. The author of *Shaken Wisdom* draws from Laura Rice's work *Of Irony and Empire* to underscore irony's power to be a liberating force in the lives of the oppressed:

> Irony is strongly associated with freedom because of its liberating potentials—not the least of which is laughter. Irony is apotropaic; through mockery, it helps the oppressed resist internalizing the evils of injustice. (qtd. in Onyeoziri 36)

Certainly in Nyamnjoh's novel, the marginalized group, with Dieudonné as its spokesperson, uses irony to deal with their chronic struggle with the rich and powerful oppressors.

Dieudonné's ability to articulate his own pain and suffering becomes the means for this man who describes himself as a "nothing man" (71) to liberate himself from depression, disillusionment and exclusion. Using verbal irony, sometimes pungent and caustic, Dieudonné denounces the oppressive practices of his white bosses, the exploitation of their workers and the tragic conditions under which the workers live. In his bitterness, he alludes to the horrible treatment he and others have received at the hands of the white bosses: "When you see a Muzungulander with a snake, you first kill the Muzungulader and then kill the snake" (71). The implication does not escape his audience that the colonial masters are more dangerous than snakes. The "venom" they have poured on society and which is destroying their lives is worse than the snake's. Dieudonné recognizes the bitterness of his statement as he balances it immediately by acknowledging that there are thousands of good Muzungulanders. Next, he takes aim at missionaries. In one of his favorite jokes, he talks of a missionary who meets a hungry lion and prays to God to inspire Christian sentiments in this lion so he won't become dinner for the king of the forest. The lion, in turn, asks God to bless the food he is about to receive and prays for everyone to get his or her share of missionaries (85). The audience falls down in laughter at this joke.

Sometimes the joke is on Africans, leaving his audience, who revel in the jokes about their colonial bosses, disgusted. Dieudonné pokes fun at African soldiers who barely know their left from right and must have straw put in one boot and bread in the other to ensure they go in the right direction (84). Neither does his audience like another joke about African soldiers in Europe who think toothpicks are meant to be eaten because very little of the sticks are served at the end of their meals. The audience sees this joke as "racist" because of the way it mocks African soldiers who fought for the Europeans but were treated more like grown children ("les grands enfants") than grown-ups. What the audience fails to note is that Dieudonné uses this joke also to comment on the small serving sizes in European restaurants, leaving African soldiers underfed at the end of their meal that they are ready to take their forks to eat the toothpicks! As noted earlier by Onyeoziri, irony gets complex since it can go both ways: at the oppressor and the oppressed.

Another way Dieudonné extends the power of words is through the use of aphorisms. The novel is seasoned with these terse, pithy sayings drawn from popular sayings and expressed using either pidgin English, English or French. The theme of his presentation is based on one of these sayings that "no condition is permanent," and it is itself a powerful testament of the tenacity and fortitude of the alienated.

Through the power of language, Dieudonné reclaims his voice. His purpose in agreeing to tell his story is that no one knows his story; he and only he knows. In addition, he hopes Dieumerci will write it down so that "posterity might also know about those of us whom history books and writers constantly fail to mention, because they have never bothered to see us as flesh and blood" (47).

Novels like Francis Nyamnjoh's *The Travail of Dieudonné* bring to light a move by some contemporary African writers to claim the voice of the powerless and not allow them to succumb to feelings of helplessness, isolation and meaninglessness. These innovative texts are not using the standard Marxist approach of using intellectuals to articulate the ills of society, especially the plight of the working class. Instead, in a postmodern twist, they engage the very people greatly affected to challenge the status quo. The ending of the novel reveals the resiliency of the people. Dieudonné explains: "The more I try and fail in my attempt to shape my life, the more I realise [sic] how my will is but a tiny little bit of Allah's grand design. [. . .] He is sad, deeply sad, but doggedly devoted" (163). The fact that there are obstacles in changing his life does not deter Dieudonné from trying. In a frenzy after acknowledging the vicissitudes of his life, he "gets up, takes a shaky step forward . . . [and] screams violently" (164), braving all fears and doubts, and challenging the invisible forces that seem to mock all his efforts. Dieumerci delivers the closing words of the novel by reiterating the importance of these "little people" like Dieudonné: "Those who say little things don't matter should know how the lion feels when a fly enters its nostrils" (164). The Dieudonnés of society cannot be ignored forever. They have a major role to play to bring about change. The high and mighty cannot continue to ignore them, just as the lion cannot ignore the tiny fly in its nostril. In the words of Zoggyie, these people make an attempt to "disalienate" themselves, to "reverse or subvert" (2) those conditions in society which attempts to silence and subdue them. They reclaim their voice through the use of language and joyfully insert themselves with neither fears nor doubts into the master narrative of their "superiors." Thus, they reject the minority status imposed on them and the resultant social failure for which they are programed.

Works Cited

Attardo, Salvatore. "Working Class Humor." *Humor: International Journal of Humor Research*." 23.2 (May 2010): 121+. *Literature Resource Center*. Web. 9 Apr. 2013.

Fanon, Frantz. *The Wretched of the Earth*. Trans. Constance Farrington. New York: Grove Weidenfeld. Web. 12 July, 2013.

Irele, Abiola. "In Praise of Alienation." In *The Surreptitious Speech: Présence Africaine and the Politics of Otherness 1947-1987*. Ed. V. Y. Mudimbe. Chicago: The U of Chicago P, 1992. Print.

Jones, LeRoi (Amiri Baraka). *Dutchman & the Slave*. New York: Morrow Quill Paperbacks, 1964. Print.

Marx, Karl. *The Economic and Philosophic Manuscripts of 1844*. "Estranged Labour." *Karl Marx Internet Archive*. Web. 27 Aug. 2013.

Nyamnjoh, Francis B. *The Travail of Dieudonné*. Nairobi: East African Educational, 2008. Print.

Nyamnjoh, Francis B., and Katleho Shoro. "Language, Mobility, African Writers and Pan-Africanism." *African Communication Research* 4.1 (2011): 35-62. Web. 9 Sept. 2013.

Onyeoziri, Gloria Nne. *Shaken Wisdom: Irony and Meaning in Postcolonial African Fiction*. Charlottesville: U of Virginia P, 2011. Print.

Schmitt, Richard. *Alienation and Freedom*. Boulder, CO: Westview, 2003. Print. Seeman, Melvin, and Carolyn S. Anderson. "Alienation and Alcohol: The Role of Work, Mastery, and Community in Drinking Behavior.

American Sociological Review 48.1 (1983): 60-77. *JSTOR.* 5 Apr. 2013.

Seeman, Melvin. "On the Meaning of Alienation." *American Sociological Review* 24.6 (1959): 783-791. *JSTOR.* 5 Apr. 2013.

Switzer, Robert. "Signifying the Blues." *Alif: Journal of Comparative Poetics* (2001): 25+. *Literature Resource Center.* Web. 9 Apr. 2013

Zoggyie, Haakayoo N. *In Search of the Fathers: The Poetics of Disalienation in theNarrative of Two Contemporary Afro-Hispanic Writer.* New Orleans: UP of the South, 2003. Print.

Chapter 5

F. Scott Fitzgerald and the Pain of Exclusion

By
Benjamin Hart Fishkin

For all his elegance and talent as a social critic, F. Scott Fitzgerald's literature is about deterioration. He intimately laid bare a loss of heart and a breaking of confidence. In reverse proportion to the Hollywood films he wrote for or at MGM his search for love and success were not realized. The nation and women did not deliver the fulfillment he had hoped for. The details of Fitzgerald's life would read and sound like a Blues song if not for the worried eloquence and the depleted complexity of the teller.

Fitzgerald's alienation stemmed from not knowing where he belonged. In a letter to his younger sister Anabel he stated, "You've got to find your type," but I am not certain Fitzgerald ever did (Bruccoli, *A Life in Letters* 9). His stories about young love and the search for a genuine career were almost always disappointing. The reality of America was not nearly as pleasing as the theory. As a young man, Fitzgerald stated that "the public loves to find out the workings of active minds in their personal problems" (Bruccoli, *A Life in Letters* 35). Literature, all too often, is about the psychological challenges of living and accepting what we, and others like us, cannot rise above. The psychological penalty of willful or imposed exclusion creates incalculable damage. It shapes and molds the recipient who is not genuinely welcomed. Though talented, Fitzgerald remained an unwelcomed guest who could not solve what was troubling him. Prolonged alienation changes the way individuals view the world and the manner in which they comment upon it. These are questions not only about wealth and power, but also about borders and boundaries that are translucent and the failed attempt to cross them.

F. Scott Fitzgerald was haunted by rejection from high-class families more than by anything else, and this included bad literary reviews in the New York press. High-class families were people who, from the outside, seemed to have no problems. His active mind was tortured because he was largely walled off from them. He suffered by not belonging. If America tends to luxuriate in the romance of the self-made man, Fitzgerald would have loved to have watched someone else struggle with his/her environment while he luxuriated in a comfortable chair with a warm drink. The development of his art and the existence of his satire were indelibly shaped during his brief life by his status as an outsider. The smooth effortless prose snugly covered a much more serious and evil concern beneath the text. He was an uncomfortable, unhappy and angry man who was not measured or well-adjusted in his day-to-day affairs. The far more difficult question to answer is whether a more measured and well-adjusted Fitzgerald in his day to day affairs would have yielded the same sort of sensitive and vulnerable author. Would he have the willingness, the desire and the ability to detail the exploits of the youth of the 1920s? If one subscribes to the philosophy that only those who suffer have any worthwhile observations to write about, would the removal of Fitzgerald's perpetual winter of discontent have also removed the awareness and experience that was the Jazz Age from his psychoanalytically obsessed and thinly veiled autobiography? The purpose of this study is to examine whether alienation and exclusion are the bit of sand that acts as the irritant that results in the smooth pearl that is his literature of the 1920s. If this is, indeed, the problem, why didn't his sudden acclaim at twenty-four, with the instant success of *This Side of Paradise*, make him feel better and enable him to move on?

From the moment "The Diamond as Big as the Ritz" first appeared in *The Smart Set* in June of 1922, it was clear that Fitzgerald had a craving for acceptance. He was not getting his needs met. His literature, and this was true of his debut two years earlier in 1920, presented people who were weary and unhappy. *This Side of Paradise* is a novel of descent. The author presents an idle culture with a sharp and incisive analysis. Early on, it is revealed that John T. Unger "came from a family that was well known in Hades" (Bruccoli, *The Short Stories* 182). Such a classical reference is neither very promising for Fitzgerald himself nor for the existence of a stable family in The Jazz Age that he was to chronicle. There is more than a touch of Dante at work and tellingly the protagonist's mother in *This Side of Paradise* is named Beatrice. "The Diamond as Big as the Ritz" is a test. The semi-autobiographical Mr. Unger has his thought process poisoned before he even knows that he begins to think. Hades, which is literally the underworld in Greek mythology, is a place for departed souls. To get there, one must cross a river of pain (what the Greeks referred to as the Acheron). The text here is a weighing machine of spiritual and cultural values. This is important because Fitzgerald is denied easy access to the respect and privilege he yearns for. This society is a sophisticated one erected as a gated community—a housing complex of identical structures where people do not wish to interact with others. People who live in the author's Hades "have been so long out of the world" that they no longer know (if they have ever known) what goes on within it (Bruccoli, *The Short Stories* 183). Major American cities like Chicago and New York have become communities and groups of people with impenetrable boundaries between them despite the nation's promise to the country.

 Fitzgerald has always been out of the world he wishes to be a part of. In an early letter, composed shortly after she consented to marrying him, Zelda Sayre said, "I hate to say this, but I don't *think* I had much confidence in you at first" (qtd. in Turnbull 102). This displays the lingering doubt that she had in him and that which he possessed in himself. It also reveals marriage to be an exchange meriting more of a shaking of hands than a romantic embrace. The relationship had all sorts of problems. It is possible that all men have doubts, but Fitzgerald was one of the few that lay them bare for all to see. His literature, which always contains sober realism, reflects this lack of self-assurance. Things did not get better with age. The overly fanciful nightlife he experienced as a newlywed celebrity, I would argue, indicated that something is missing. Romance, in this setting, was unfulfilling. There was stimulation to the point of excess. In the early twenties, Alexander McKaig, one of Fitzgerald's close friends, wrote in his diary about the latter's "success complex" (qtd. in Turnball 113), a behavior that involves placing oneself upon a pedestal to compensate for a nagging lack of security. Selling books was not enough, and as he got older, there was pressure to write them faster and sell more of them. Fitzgerald's confidence in his earlier years was largely a facade papered over by alcohol and conspicuous consumption. According to Robert Sklar, in *F. Scott Fitzgerald: The Last Laocoon*, the twenties were remembered for their "high living, audacious young people" and it was F. Scott Fitzgerald who led this movement and was its spokesperson. This meant speakeasies, parties, restaurants and travel in the then glamorous era of the ocean liner. The charm and realism of his literature conceal an insoluble problem. Beneath the high living was a fragile and frightened out-of-control personality whose loneliness was exacerbated by a lack of safety in his marriage and how he and Zelda conducted their affairs. To escape, he withdrew into his creative writing where attractive and compelling people were optimistic and never had to breathe the unpleasant city air that surrounded him. There was never a traffic jam, and well-polished cars never honked their horns. In addition, Fitzgerald's characters never had to consume because they already had everything. This enthusiastic desire to not have to worry about the fine print, to be daringly unconventional and to spend without anguished deliberation was an emotional wish, not one based on fact. Style was everything. It covered up gaps and flaws that would otherwise remained uncovered. When John T. Unger in "The Diamond as Big as the Ritz" arrives at Saint Midas' School in Massachusetts, everyone has "pocket change." A student at "the most expensive and the most exclusive boys' preparatory school in the world" already unknowingly has what Zelda and Scott are chasing (Bruccoli, *The Short Stories* 183). The clientele are not there because they are intellectually precocious youths. One's presence there is a self-fulfilling prophecy. Wealth obscures all else and ensures the best possible outcome, and it does so without making a sound.

Fitzgerald's flaw is that he wants so desperately to glide beyond the velvet ropes into this world that only a fraction occupies. This is, at first glance, a critique of capitalism—the structure in which assets are privately owned in a free-price system that only has room for a select few at the very top. That was where Fitzgerald wanted to be and his unwillingness to bend left him broken. Society would not permit him to be economically independent, let alone privileged. This idea to transcend class, obtain power and *keep* that power—a commodity which everyone wants--is a reach or leap that great authors have grappled with. First they see a new alleged paradise; then they want to make it their own. He is almost a male Emma Bovary whose actions belie his original environment—even one as frothy and as speculative as the roaring twenties. If Flaubert's heroine uses extravagances to cover up her boredom, Fitzgerald uses expenditures to conceal his fear. One year into marriage, the Fitzgeralds moved near New York's Plaza Hotel solely so they could order room service. The nightmare is that they will be forgotten or replaced by a ravenous public who suddenly wants to read about someone else whose new exploits seem more entertaining. This outlandish behavior depicts an unhealthy, irrational eagerness. These pleas, an accelerated attempt to keep up with and surpass the Joneses, cut no ice with the actual Joneses. Not only did they not respect him; they did not know him. He was beneath competing with. Edith Wharton, whose maiden name was Jones, like Fitzgerald wrote for

Scribner. Unlike Fitzgerald, she had a pedigree which opened doors that for him, remained shut. There is more than a bit of a teenager's alcohol induced rage directed at this world of extremes in his over-the-top behavior. Beneath the smooth surface, there is anger and rebellion, what his Southern debutante wife might call a "hot mess." His wife, at first, did not consider him to be a successful suitor. This negative evaluation of Fitzgerald as a petitioner was a financial decision by a beautiful, yet erratic, woman whose values and mores come from her place and position in society as an Alabama State Supreme Court Justice's daughter. His desire for her clashed with her family's desire for a very different type of boy —not a university dropout who was both poor and not from the South. He had become, as he described the people of Fish in "A Diamond as Big as the Ritz," "a race apart" even though this separation had no biological categorization (Bruccoli, *The Short Stories* 185). This gap, an ambiguity about where he belonged, created a persistent longing to short circuit the Social Darwinism that bleeds into his literature. This is what makes "The Diamond as Big as the Ritz" so special. Something is broken. The less fortunate are "some species developed by an early whim of nature, which on second thought has abandoned them to struggle and extermination" (Bruccoli, *The Short Stories* 185). This great divide has national implications that cannot be mended. This is why the story has its roots in the embers and ashes of the Civil War.

The Montana estate of Percy Washington's direct antecedents could only have been conjured by F. Scott Fitzgerald. The home, which is literally "not going to be anything like you ever saw before," a structure that is next door to an entire mountain that is one large perfect diamond, reveals his depleted psychological condition (Bruccoli, *The Short Stories* 186). At times the fearful eat too much, shop too much and take prescription medication too much. This is an attempt, or a series of attempts, to cover some deep-seated fear. No single entity will serve as a solution. A bank account that is well funded does not do the trick. The money must be seen as a physical entity that embodies security. It must be displayed. To do this the author creates a world in which he does not live. If in real life, Fitzgerald was a poor boy from Saint Paul; in the story he has access to a solid diamond. It can be touched, it can be seen, but it is a secret and cannot be talked about. The anxiety that produces empty bottles of liquor, silver trays of food no one can finish and what Federico Fellini called the "sweet life" in his film *La Dolce Vita* is based on a fear that one day the wealth and acceptance that is so addictive can be taken away. The attention paid can be withdrawn. Even more essential to this study is what happens when something vital to one's happiness is taken away and one will never again be as he or she were before? This is the calamity of the Great Depression of the early 1930s where a once pleasant excess quickly recedes and becomes, in retrospect, a subject of ridicule. If someone with Wharton's wealth owns a place at the banquet by birth, Fitzgerald terminally and tenuously rents one. The former's is irrevocable—not even the scandal of Edith Wharton's divorce damaged her standing. The latter is temporary—only book sales can keep F. Scott Fitzgerald before the public eye.

Americans, both in the 1920s and to a lesser extent right now, are considered to be idealistic. Instead of basing things on a firm and sturdy construction, there is a tendency to create "castles in the air" without paying any attention to intrinsic value. This tendency to see things not as they are, but as they should be and hope for the best, creates frenzied agitation when these two worlds collide like taxicabs on lower Broadway seeking the very same fare. The housing bubble of 2008 and the resultant crisis is evidence of this. To some degree this is a positive, but Fitzgerald willfully (almost naively) crossed over in his narrative into a world of illusion. He was a man who was not interested in the concrete. Fitzgerald rejected or ignored what William James referred to as pragmatism, and he was purposely not practical in either his thinking or his art (Gillin 38). He reveled in delusion much like a man who looks for his pocket watch under a gas lamp in the street because the light there is better than the light in the location where he had lost it. Characters become reliant on conditions and outcomes that can't possibly be so. Upon closer look, the language of "The Diamond as Big as the Ritz" is foreboding. The sky is "poisoned," the sunset "like a gigantic bruise," the people of the town "abandoned...to struggle and extermination" (Bruccoli, *The Short Stories* 185). Things are so luxurious for the passengers on the Transcontinental Express from Chicago that they somehow seem "above it all" in a warm haze of opium. The lotus flower that produces this is a financial status that can "fix" any problem, and this is our author's unique territory. The boys do not care at all about the men who live in the town, those on the train or the servants—nearly all of whom are African Americans from the South. This is a racial split as well as an economic one. Frederick Wegener in "The 'Two Civil Wars' of F. Scott Fitzgerald" speaks of "the failure of such developments to obliterate the historical past..." (249). Life in the South is not as carefree as the passengers. The material wealth that Zelda needs and the effect this money seems to have on character propels Fitzgerald into the imaginative world in which he is most comfortable. I hesitate to use the word classist because the boys in question are so enveloped in "honeyed luxury" that they cannot think of any class other than their own (Bruccoli, *The Short Stories* 190). Furthermore, people born to this comfort, unlike Fitzgerald but not unlike Zelda, would have no concept of what it was like to work for a living, to pay bills or to do without anything they desired. The car that ferries Percy and John to the Washingtons exquisite chateau has...

> upholstery consisted of a thousand minute and exquisite tapestries of silk woven with jewels and embroideries, and set upon a background cloth of gold. The two armchair seats in which the boys luxuriated were covered with stuff that resembled

duvetyn, but seemed woven in numberless colors of the ends of ostrich feathers (Bruccoli, *The Short Stories* 186).

Worthy of note is the closing reference to the ostrich who, when frightened, literally places its head in the sand. All of this fantasy, surely reflective of the twenties which produced it, plays out as madness in light of the great stock market crash that is only a few years away.

This excess of ambition in "The Diamond as Big as the Ritz" functions as a character in and of itself. The Swiss hotelier Cesar Ritz provided accommodation to royalty. When the Hotel Ritz opened in 1898 in Paris, it redefined prestige. The adjective "ritzy" literally is derived from this string of hotels. All of this glitter has a direct proportional relationship to the Fitzgeralds and how they lived their lives. "Oh Charlie," Fitzgerald said to a Minnesota friend who was also a writer, "…how wonderful it is to be young and beautiful and a success!" (qtd. in Turnball 126). If this was a success, it was not a permanent success, for it did not last. It is one thing to be blessed with good fortune if in fact that was the case. It is quite another to boldly and without modesty call attention to it. There was no sensible reason to maintain such a facade of affluence. It was no more financially responsible than the era he came to embody. Zelda and Scott Fitzgerald simply spent money faster than any wealthy employee could earn it. In October of 1920, they ran through all of their resources despite the fact that Scott had earned $ 20,000 in the previous twelve months (Turnball 114). Even an extremely conservative estimate would place the purchasing power of such a sum at more than $ 200,000.00 today. Ninety-three years ago, this was a fortune. Large families could subsist on a fraction of such an income. There was no planning. For an author whose characters never had to give money a second thought, Fitzgerald easily, and erroneously, thought he was one of them. His inability to manage his own finances connects directly to his creation of a world in which fiscal responsibility is not necessary. Virtually no one really enjoys this privilege. He had to imagine an environment of ease to mimic the actual one he could not enter.

Somehow being a sensitive artist is never enough. The ability to create, which Henry James had explored a generation earlier in *Roderick Hudson*, could grab the attention of a young girl, but it could not win her. Initial optimism was almost always unfounded. As time progressed, it was never realized. The rich, according to Andrew Turnbull, were somehow segregated with "a better seat in life's grandstand, and their existence was somehow more beautiful and intense than that of ordinary mortals" (150). Fitzgerald's people had no idea there *was* a grandstand. The metaphor is that of a race and those without resources, those poor people who worked for a living and aspired for a better life, found themselves up at the starting line tired and out of breath, whereas those with hereditary lineages and connections began the contest rested, well-nourished and with every conceivable preparation. The "No man's land" between the two was a chasm. The biggest of many tragedies is that the two groups so mistrusted and did not know one another or see one another on equal footing. Similarly, to the segregated South, people did not have meaningful contact with people unlike themselves. Towards the very end of his life, Fitzgerald revealed that his literature always emanated from the same experience. I was a "poor boy in a rich town; a poor boy in a rich boy's school; a poor boy in a rich man's club at Princeton...I have never been able to forgive the rich for being rich, and it has colored my entire life and works" (qtd. in Turnball 150). This problem was never resolved. In his fiction, the reader has a great grappling with the unfairness of it all, something that can be incomprehensible to a young reader. When Fitzgerald finally did meet Edith Wharton, at her eighteenth-century villa north of Paris, she was entertaining an American-born Cambridge don who was everything Fitzgerald, a drop out, was not. The new guest was so nervous and plied with alcohol that everyone was uncomfortable (Turnball 154).

The meeting ended abruptly and Ms. Wharton marked in her diary that he never be invited again.

If doors did not literally close in his face, the message was clear: this was a crash or collision that he could not fix. As a Midwesterner, Fitzgerald revealed that popularity was not enough. F. Scott Fitzgerald lacked a comfortable birth. Like an actual biblical scar upon the skin, this hurt would forever remain. While the vestiges of America's lack of meritocracy do still exist today, they are comparatively unimportant and much more subtle than they once were. Film Critic David Denby stated in May of 2013 in *The New Yorker* that "no great writer hit the skids so publicly," and I would add no great writer told a recurring story that so many people did not want to hear. People did not want to identify with an author who felt he was peering through a thick glass much as a prisoner does on visiting day. The party sailed calmly on without him, for the most part indifferent to a social disaster that was not of his own making. If a standard literary figure like Daisy Miller had a comfortable birth and no knowledge, which in itself was a tragedy, Fitzgerald was the contrary. The pain and poignancy of his writing is that the ultimate goal, no matter how much we would like to pretend otherwise, involves tragic suffering and almost never comes within our grasp and stays there.

"The Diamond as Big as the Ritz" torpedoes "the genteel romantic ideals that pervaded late nineteenth-century American culture…" (Bruccoli, "The Last of the Novelists" 9). America's fascination with the individual who, like John T. Unger, finds himself in new circumstances and adapts, starts out well, but does not deliver. When the story was first published in *The Smart Set,* our youthful hero finds himself in an intoxicating fantasy.

> A large negro in a white uniform stood beside his bed.
> "Good-evening," muttered John, summoning his brains from the wild places.

"Good-morning, sir. Are you ready for your bath, sir? Oh, Don't get up—I'll put you in, if you'll just unbutton your pajamas— There. Thank you, sir."

John lay quietly as his pajamas were removed—he was amused and delighted; he expected to be lifted like a child by this black Gargantua who was tending him, but nothing of the sort happened; instead he felt the bed tilt up slowly on its side—he began to roll, startled at first, in the direction of the wall, but when he reached the wall its drapery gave way, and sliding two yards farther down a fleecy incline he plumped gently into water the same temperature as his body (Bruccoli, *The Short Stories* 190 - 191).

Is the boy welcomed into this nonparallel universe by those who wish to help him, or is he a lobster waiting to be boiled and served up with melted butter for others' consumption? The proverbial "hug" he receives is really an attempt not to embrace, but a calculated and Machiavellian move of cunning and duplicity designed to strangle him into compliance. The values of the United States are not (in the aggregate) about helping those who need assistance, and they certainly are not about including those without the means to survive an economic downturn into their neighborhoods, schools and clubs when one occurs. Were that the case the class studies of Fitzgerald would not have been written. There would be no social visibility and girls could seek love matches rather than the calculated business decisions which dominated the previous century. If there were no social visibility the youthful debutante at elaborate parties in fancy Southern hotels would not be in a rush to wed and could afford to be patient rather than be reconciled to being yesterday's news. She would have a value that transcended her age, beauty and bloodline.

The American Dream of home-ownership and stability, once professed by John Steinbeck in the 1930s, eventually succumbed to the idea of being wealthy. The roots of this problem, and it is a peculiarly American problem, go back to the years following World War I and, as a culture, we have never learned from them. Fitzgerald needed the stability that both he and his era so prominently lacked. He needed an actual home and instead opted for a series of sterile hotel rooms. The people in the culture needed to quietly enjoy their families and instead opted for a never-ending party comprised of guests that they did not necessarily like. There was no measured thought. There were no routines, and there were no conventions to break from. Not only was money spent in the twenties without any responsibility, but also it was spent on things that were superfluous and showy cinema items that had no practical value. The desire of wealth comes from a reality that it is both hard to obtain and even harder to retain. Those who do have it wish to preserve it. The use of the word "preserve" here, does not mean merely allocating funds into the safety and security of a trusted bank prior to the creation of the Federal Deposit Insurance Corporation in 1933. The host family in "The Diamond as Big as the Ritz" will kill to preserve its wealth and the secret that surrounds it in a dichotomy that is not dissimilar to the gangland violence of this very era. The Arnold Rothstein based character in *The Great Gatsby* is likely a gangster because he is shut out of more acceptable career pursuits during prohibition. If money yields power then power, according to Fitzgerald, is used to exclude. The fact that Percy's grandfather is a "direct descendent of George Washington" indicates that this is not a setup that has emerged by accident (Bruccoli, *The Short Stories* 192). This is not an aberration. Americans can be corrupt and bereft of morality, and despite more palatable stories to the contrary, they can be just as practiced at the art of deception and just as stratified in terms of class as the ancient European nations we spring from.

While it is easy to surrender to the nostalgia of American life before the 1929 stock market crash, the hope that we can somehow retreat and "go back" to the lives of those who came before us, the unsettling conclusion is that we are longing for an era that was not nearly as pleasant as the dream. It is the outsider, the character of John T. Unger, who must try to sort out this revision. This means not sharing the fantasy, but shattering it. Veronica Makowski refers to this as "remoteness from real human concerns" (196). I would say this is simply callousness. Although Percy and John can be excused because of their youth, the same cannot be said of the system that produced them. Surely the servants had real concerns, but to emphasize them or even name them would disavow the fantasy. Class, race, and money--what Makowski calls the "plantation" system (even though there are no actual plantations in New York--exists because those in power are able to fool themselves into thinking that those who have no power also have no objections (191). It takes a series of complex mental maneuvers and verbal gymnastics to arrive at the conclusion that exclusion does not hurt. The assumption is that the poor are mindless, or worse still, somehow swayed to believe against their better judgment that the unearned suffering of the system will be redemptive within their own lifetime. This is a fallacy. The Blues singer who has a quarrel he cannot give voice to with his slave owner adeptly substitutes the name of a nonexistent girl into the subject line of his song. This maneuver exists to cover up a problem—to make things go easier not by confronting a contentious problem, but by pretending it does not exist. Fitzgerald rejects this reflex action to sweep dissent under the carpet, but he is so smooth and so graceful in his technique that one must read very carefully between the lines or he/she will miss his description of a world in utter free fall.

The depicted disillusionment is subtle, but much like a cartoon whose witty dialogue entertains adults while children enjoy the colorful pictures, there is meaning beneath the surface. The short story has subtext. Fitzgerald wishes us to delve beneath the glittering prizes that the American Dream professes to have created. Why did the United States expand its territories westward? Was the philosophy of "Manifest Destiny" anything other than a push for territory with racist implications—just like the decision of Colonel Fritz-Norman Culpepper Washington to travel to Montana? Did the writings of Henry David Thoreau, who objected to military conflict and to slavery, both part of the very framework of "The Diamond as Big as the Ritz", simply disappear from our national consciousness? A more probing question is how much thinking on the subject did the populous exert on the topic in the first place? By being such a stylish writer, Fitzgerald is telling us what we have left behind, that our definition of worth and merit has been seized by threat of force. It is a story about more than merely money, if the two words can be placed together; it is about the politics that produces it, makes it grow and keeps it in the hands of a select few. Literary critic William E. Rand tells us that the Unger family, "while comfortable financially, is definitely not part of the power and money elite" (233). The resultant question is how do the elite, in terms of money rather than philosophy, get to be that way? They send what Rand terms their "lower end" kids to Saint Midas Preparatory School which is a thinly veiled name for the Newman School, a New Jersey prep school Fitzgerald attended before enrolling at Princeton (234). The outsider is a *tabula rasa* who knows nothing, is introduced to a world he is attracted to (John says, "I like very rich people. The richer a fella is, the better I like him.") and is then told he does not belong (Bruccoli, *The Short Stories* 184). The purpose here is to tantalize, to play with poorer people for the purpose of amusement, something an American of the revolutionary era (if the myth were true) would never dream of. In a very real sense the nation is a tease.

…And so," cried John accusingly, "and so you were letting me make love to you and pretending to return it, and talking about marriage, all the time knowing perfectly well that I'd never get out of here alive…If you haven't any more pride and decency than to have an affair with a fellow that you know isn't much better than a corpse, I don't want to have any more to do with you!" (Bruccoli, *The Short Stories* 205)

The promise of happiness is aroused in vain. Kismine is not a real girl. She is initially and purposely misleading. The imagination presents itself not as something healthy, but as something that is dangerous and obsessive to the temperament—an element of brain chemistry that is like a sports car with a powerful engine that can easily get out from under a driver who is new to the road. John's "imagined future" of flowers, girls, gold and stars is never set right (Bruccoli, *The Short Stories* 195). There is no true friend or family member to help him. He is alienated by geography, prestige and wealth in an environment that is vastly different from where he grew up, where the female has all the power.

As a boy, John is isolated and dependent. Not only must he deal with being institutionalized in a prison with all the amenities of a five-star hotel; there is a gender studies component here as well. The motif of the self-assured male and the female who cannot survive without him is flipped around so that their biological traits have little to do with their circumstances. Kismine is in a position to grant him love and to withhold it. She, the female, rather than he, the male, has all of the answers. She represents both the means and the attributes a "girl" like Zelda Fitzgerald would want. But John is not a girl. She approaches him when he is lying down in a patch of moss—prostrate. This is assuredly not the way most courtships in the 1920s commenced. The main character is an antihero, passive and clueless. Without any sort of forewarning, he is forced to grapple with the country's old problems—but no one in the country comes to his aid when cracks appear in the narrative of the American Dream. John must not only combat the ample problems of being in love; he must step into a myth where he has no weaponry and wrestle with problems of the psyche that not even a silver bullet can kill. The dream of American uniqueness is dangerous, and Kismine is equally false because it/ she is produced by isolation (Makowski 196). As a boy coming of age, he must confront a change in the atmosphere that no one has prepared him for. This sort of a disturbance of normal conditions, a storm of conflict within his own thought process, is every bit as dangerous and as painful as physical warfare. This kind of suffering, an acute bodily disorder, undercuts his own Southern upbringing and leaves him longing for an ideal that was never there and was never innocent. This marks F. Scott Fitzgerald's endeavor to break into a circle out of which he has been pushed and left on the margins.

Works Cited

Bruccoli, Mathew J. "The Last of the Novelists." *F. Scott Fitzgerald and The indent Last Tycoon.* Carbondale and Edwardsville: Southern Illinois UP, 1977. Print.

_____. *F. Scott Fitzgerald: A Life.* New York: Scribner, 1994. Print.

_____. ed. *The Short Stories of F. Scott Fitzgerald.* New York: Scribner, 1989. Print.

Bryer, Jackson R., Ruth Prigozy, and Milton R. Stern, eds. *F. Scott Fitzgerald in the Twenty-first Century.* Tuscaloosa: The U of Alabama P, 2003. Print

Denby, David. "All That Jazz." Rev. of *'The Great Gatsby*" dir. Baz Luhrmann. *The New Yorker* 13 May 2013: 78 – 79. Print.

Gillin, Edward. "Princeton, Pragmatism, and Fitzgerald's Sentimental Journey." Bryer, Prigozy, and Stern 38-53.

Makowski, Veronica. "Noxious Nostalgia: Fitzgerald, Faulkner, and the Legacy of Plantation Fiction." Byer, Prigozy, and Stern 190 - 201.

Rand, William E. "The Structure of the Outsider in the Short Fiction of Richard Wright and F. Scott Fitzgerald." *CLA Journal* 40 (December 1996): 230-245. Print.

Turnbull, Andrew. *Scott Fitzgerald*. New York: Scribner, 1962. Print.

Wegener, Frederick. "The 'Two Civil Wars' of F. Scott Fitzgerald." Bryer, Prigozy, and Stern. 238 – 266.

Chapter 6

Minority Identity and the Question of Social Failure in John N. Nkengasong's *Across the Mongolo*

By
Blossom Fondo

Introduction

Fiction from formerly colonized societies still continues to engage passionately with the question of their colonization. This is not so because colonization constitutes the only reality for these societies. Rather it testifies to the enduring legacies of the colonial experience, which decades after its formal end are still felt in these societies provoking some critics to opine that colonialism has always succeeded in staying on despite its formal end (Nyamnjoh 8). Simon Gikandi in "African Literature and the Colonial Factor" has noted that;

> But what is now considered to be the heart of literary scholarship on the continent could not have acquired its current identity or function if the traumatic encounter between Africa and Europe had not taken place. (379)

Going further he quotes George Balladier whose 1955 study of the colonial situation observed that despite changes that had occurred in the era of colonization, "the colonial problem remains one of the main issues with which specialists in the social sciences have to deal. Indeed the pressures of a new nationalism and the reactions resulting from decolonization give this problem an immediacy and a topicality that cannot be treated with indifference" (qtd. in Gikandi 119). This, to Gikandi, underlines the conjunction between African literature and the colonial situation. He asserts that

> Colonialism, especially its radical transformation of African societies, remains one of the central problems with which writers and intellectuals in Africa have to deal. The tradition of African writing [...] was built and consolidated when African writers began to take stock of the colonial situation and its impact on the African psyche. Even the African writing that emerged in the postcolonial era, a literature shaped by the pressures of 'arrested decolonization', and the 'pitfalls of national consciousness' can be said to have been driven by the same imperative as writing under colonialism, the desire to understand that consequences of the colonial moment." (379/380)

Gikandi therefore opines that the political and cultural force of colonialism was so enduring that writers concerned with the nature of African society could not avoid the trauma and drama that accompanied the imposition of European rule on the continent.

Besides the gross exploitation and the imposition of foreign values on the colonized, another persisting trauma was the forging of pseudo-alliances among the colonized. This was done through the bringing together of disparate communities under the umbrella of one nation. John McLeod in "Nations and Nationalisms" has noted that "the national borders of most (once-) colonized countries have been imagined and imposed by European powers, who reorganized and violated indigenous mappings of terrain" (102). This often resulted in questionable nation-states characterized by internal ruptures, mutual suspicion and hatred. As concerns Cameroon, Britain and France received the country as mandated trust territories from the League of Nations after they defeated the Germans. France received the Eastern part of Cameroon, known as *République du*

Cameroun while Britain received the Northern and the Southern Cameroons. Worse than these divisions was the class system that succeeded the colonial administration. Based on varying degrees of perceived or imagined differences, the succeeding bourgeoisie schooled in the colonial education system and therefore wired to "naturally" emulate the colonizers proceeded with the erection of a rigid system of discrimination. McLeod concurs with this when he underscores that,

> in the decades since colonialism formally ended in many Third World locations, it has seemed as if the worries of writers such as Fanon and Armah, about the emergence of exploitative forms of national authority have proved too true. (114)

The consequence of this was a deeply hierarchized society where groups in the society were accorded the status of the subaltern with little or no access to opportunities for self-improvement.

John N. Nkengasong's *Across the Mongolo* captures just such a situation. In this novel, he dwells on the question of marginalization of one group by another based on cultural and linguistic differences. In the fictional postcolonial state of Kamangola, which is not unlike the Cameroon of Nkengasong's origins, he presents the tensions ensuing from such a troubled relationship. In this chapter, I intend to explore Nkengasong's portrayal of this discriminatory practice based on identity and how this results in social failure for the marginalized, who in spite of their struggles, are doomed to fail in the realization of their legitimate dreams.

Identity, Power Politics and Marginality

Across the Mongolo presents two groups in the postcolonial nation of Kamangola. These groups are distinguished one from the other based especially on their linguistic backgrounds which are the consequence of their colonial past. There are the minority Anglophones to whom the protagonist Ngwe belongs and the Francophones who constitute the majority and are the wielders of power. Ngwe is a young intelligent boy who is forced to travel to the French-speaking part of the nation to pursue university education in the lone University of Besaadi. It is when he gets there that he comes face to face with the reality of his minority status and its implications in Kamangola.

However, before pursuing this discussion, it is important to define the aspect of Anglophone identity as this would give insight into the novel. In a general sense, the term Anglophone refers to an individual who speaks English but is not part of the British Isles. These are mostly former British colonies, who by virtue of the colonization by the British inherited the language especially through the colonial school. Within the nation of Cameroon, the notion of Anglophone has different connotations. Basically it refers to those from the regions of Cameroon who express themselves officially in the English language. Joyce B. Ashuntantang in *Landscaping Postcoloniality* defines Anglophone identity with regards to the English language. She holds that "just like the literature, the identity of individuals in this region has crystallized around English because of their minority status within a dominantly Francophone Cameroon" (1). She therefore adds that "English in Cameroon […] has come to be a marker of identity for Anglophone Cameroon"(1). Nontheless, Ashuntantang underscores the fact that although other former British colonies in Africa speak English, the term Anglophone rarely comes into play; unlike in Cameroon where "a certain energy has been injected into the term […] because it lives in opposition with the term 'Francophone' (17). From another perspective, Simo Bobda cited by Ashuntantang defines Anglophone from an ethnic point of view. He holds that

> The term Anglophone, as is understood in Cameroon, has mostly an ethnic connotation. It refers to a member of an ethnic group

in North West and South West Provinces which were formally part of British Cameroons[...] the term Anglophone has very little to do with knowledge of the English language; indeed, an Anglophone in the Cameroon sense does not need to know a word of English. (18)

Ashuntatang therefore concludes that "As a result, Anglophone ethnic identity goes beyond language to embrace the sociocultural" (18). The apparent oppositionality between the Anglophone and Francophone cultures and the poor political system instituted by the ruling majority Francophone has reduced the Anglophones in this country to underdogs. Anglophone identity therefore signals not only a sociocultural or linguistic category, but especially indicates the marginalization often attributed to minorities in ineffective systems.

This discussion of minority identity is guided by postcolonial theory for a number of reasons. This is mainly due to the fact that the circumstances encountered in the novel are a consequence of its colonial past. The two identities found in the text; the Anglophone and Francophone identities are material effects of colonialism. When Ngwe leaves his village to travel to Ngola for University education, he travels across the river Mongolo which divides both sections of the nation. These two states are as a consequence of their colonial experience as explained by one of the passengers in Ngwe's bus to him:

The River Mongolo. It is the great River, the boundary between the English colony of Kama and the French colony of Ngola, the two federated states that gave birth to the Federal Republic of Kamangola. (37)

In this colonial creation, the vestiges of the colonial relationship are so strongly present that the same power relations are at work as the minority Kamans are subjugated by the majority Ngolans, in a manner not unlike the colonialist subjugation of the colonized. The nation of Kamangola is therefore a colonial creation and the union seems to be a forced one seen in the description Ngwe gives of the bridge that connects but also divides the two states: "As soon as the vast expanse of the plantations ended, a huge arched structure appeared before us. It seemed that it chained two worlds together and below was a deep dark abyss" (37). This situation is what Ashcroft, Griffiths and Tiffin in *Post-colonial Studies: The Key Concepts*, have underscored as:

> Recognition of the fact that most of the world has been affected to some degree by nineteenth –century European imperialism has not always led to an understanding of the continuing effects of colonial and neo-colonial analysis increasingly makes clear the nature and impact of inherited power relations, and their continuing effects on modern global culture and politics. Political questions usually approached from the standpoints of nation-state relations, race, class, economics and gender are made clearer when we consider them in context of their relations with the colonialist past. This is because the structures of power established by the colonizing process remain pervasive, though often hidden in cultural relations throughout the world. (1)

It is therefore clear that the fictional nation in the novel results from its colonial past. Unfortunately, this seems to have brought together two groups of people who cannot get along by virtue of their stark differences at many levels. Also, postcolonial theory appears to be well-suited in handling issues of identity and marginality. Both constitute important concepts in postcolonial studies and their interplay is almost redundant since people especially within abusive systems such as colonialism have always been accepted or rejected based on their identities. Stephen Morton has intimated that "marginality is one of the privileged metaphors of postcolonial studies" (162). Postcolonial theory is that form of cultural criticism which uncovers the artifacts of the colonial encounter in works of arts from the formerly colonized societies. Bill Ashcroft, Gareth Griffiths and Helen Tiffin underscore that

> post-colonial theory involves discussion about experience of various kinds: resistance, representation, slavery, suppression, resistance, representation, difference, race, gender, place, and the responses to the influential master discourses of imperial Europe such as history, philosophy and linguistics, and the fundamental experiences of speaking and writing by which all these come into being. (2)

They add that it is "based in the 'historical fact' of European colonialism, and the diverse material effects to which this phenomenon gave rise" (2). Rumina Sethi in *The Politics of Postcolonialism* has added that "studies in postcolonialism became preoccupied with all minority cultures- including [...] literature of the diaspora and the dispossessed of the countries of Asia, Africa, Latin America, Australia, Canada, the Caribbean and New Zealand" (2). This aspect of postcolonial theory is particularly useful in the treatment of minority identity and the question of marginality as the minority in the text is dispossessed of their rights to a dignified existence.

The history of mankind has often pointed to the ways in which identity determines whether one wields power or is abused by power. For example, blacks worldwide have suffered some of the worst forms of abuse due to their blackness, just like the Jews suffered untold abuses as a consequence of their identity. Similarly, women have for a long time experienced discriminatory treatment as a result of their gender. Also, in many societies, homosexuals still occupy outsider status by virtue of their sexual orientation. What is clear in all of this is that when one group controls power in the society, its identity becomes normative and everyone else is expected to somehow strive to meet up with what is considered normal while some do this so as to benefit from those in power. It is generally a situation of resistance leading to rejection or one of assimilation leading to some kind of acceptance or what Edward Saïd terms "conscious affiliation proceeding under the guise of filiation"(qtd. in Ashcroft, Griffiths and Tiffin; 4). Ashcroft Griffiths and Tiffin further explain that this is"mimicry of the centre proceeding from the desire not only to be accepted but to be adopted and absorbed" (4).

Returning to the text, one reads how Ngwe's sense of self and personhood becomes shattered once he crosses over to the Francophone part of the nation. There, he suddenly ceases to be a native of Nweh, but rather becomes an Anglophone and he is shortly to learn the implications of this. Although African nationalism justified its political claims through the invocation of the "essential humanity of the colonized" (Gikandi 387), the succeeding bourgeoisie ironically denied the minority groups this right to their humanity. They were relegated to the same secondary status accorded the Africans by the Europeans during the peak of colonialism. They therefore experienced a second colonization at the hands of fellow compatriots. This is the "development of internal divisions based on racial, linguistic or religious discriminations" (Ashcroft, Griffith and Tiffin; 2) which also constitute important legacies of colonialism.

The forced union created by the colonizers can be seen as having seriously distorted the sense of self of the minority groups who are forced to exist in their nation as outsiders. The idea of a forced union is further brought to light when the bus ferrying Ngwe is stopped by Gendarme officers at the Mongolo Bridge. Ngwe steps out to observe the river and reflects on his knowledge of the history of his country:

> I walked toward the bridge I had heard much about this historic river when we studied civics in Wysdom College. We were taught

about the Plebiscite that brought the two colonies to function as federated states in one nation. Later in high school, our history teacher [...] always talked about the plebiscite, the functioning of the federated states and their transformation later into a United Republic with a lot of disappointment. (39)

This disappointment is doubtlessly explained by the unequal power relations that came to characterize the union. Whereas the union was meant to be between two states with equal rights, the majority Francophone state of Ngola quickly adjudicated several powers unto itself including the right to push the minority Anglophones to the fringes of society. Nkengasong's choice of words, speaks of what awaits Ngwe and other Anglophone who go across the river Mongolo. The use of words such as "abyss", "muddy water" is illuminating as it is indicative of what Ngwe as an Anglophone will encounter once across the Mongolo. Contrary to his expectations of brighter horizons, he is in effect stepping into an abyss, he is moving into muddy waters. This is further emphasized by the vivid description given of the bridge

The bridge was a masterpiece of metal engineering. It looked like the giant sample of manacles and the shackles around the necks of slaves that were pulled by the slave masters such as I had seen in pictures in history books. [...]. The images of slaves floated in the consciousness. Dark, bare-breasted mothers, hungry children and men trailing miserably and unconditionally in a queue, the stiff stubborn shackles tagged with iron collars rattling on their necks, the large beads of chains on their feet jingling as they moved unconditionally to some unknown suffering. The waist-coated white man, their master, skinning their bodies with copper whips under the searing tropical sun (39/40).

This is an allusion to the slave trade. While it may sound like an overstatement when compared to the marginalization suffered by the Anglophones in Ngola, it shows nonetheless the same mindset at work. That by which individuals and groups are judged unworthy by virtue of the difference in identity and their status as minority and consequently treated as sub-humans. This comes forcefully to light when while still ruminating about the Mongolo bridge, Ngwe is seriously ill-treated by the Francophone Gendarmes, simply because he is English speaking. Thus by virtue of his linguistic minority and Anglophone status, Ngwe's movement to Ngola is a movement into some kind of slavery. This is so because not only will he be considered an inferior being but he is treated with little consideration. Ngwe will be denied his basic rights and he seems doomed to fail in such a system. But at this moment, Ngwe is completely ignorant of what awaits him at Ngola. His expectations are rather on the high where he imagines that,

> [...] the university was certainly going to be a great world of high virtues, a place where people behaved themselves and there were explanations ready for any handicap. The superb air, the dignifying gentleness and cultured manners of the top executive that pervaded the atmosphere of the college of arts were certainly more seriously and maturely executed at the university. (48)

Ngwe strongly believes that he was going to meet elegance, excellence and respect at the university (49).

When Ngwe has to begin the arduous task of processing documents for his registration at the university, the reality of his Anglophone identity comes to light. When he goes to the *prefecture* where his documents awaiting legalization have been lying for ages, he is turned off by the lady he finds there who states matter-of-factly "ne m'annouille [sic] pas! Je ne suis pas la pour les Anglophones" [17](57). She expresses such hostility because he is an Anglophone, which within the state of Kamangola is synonymous with being a second-class citizen. This trend continues when he goes to complete

---

[17] don't bother me, I am not here for Anglophones"

his enrolment at the university. The worker in charge, who does not understand the English Language, rejects his file on the grounds that he did not present his transcripts. When he is proved wrong, instead of showing remorse, he heaps insults on Ngwe for being an Anglophone "les anglos aiment toujours les annouilles" [18](61) and the other francophone students jeer at him: "pauvre anglo! Anglo for Kromba. Tu ne pouvez pas rester chez vous a Kromba, Anglo"[19] (60)

Ngwe's minority status here serves as a platform for his humiliation by the francophone majority. Instead of one's identity serving as a means of identification and self-definition, what is witnessed here, is one's identity becomes an excuse for marginalization, for *othering* and ultimately for defining him/her as an unwanted outsider who cannot – must not – be treated with equal consideration. The unequal treatment meted on Ngwe can only lead him to begin developing fears, angst and doubts of his belonging. So he poses questions as to the implications of being an Anglophone. Thus, although he finally succeeds in registering in the university, it is at the cost of the gross humiliation he receives from those who give the impression that "we were compatriots" (62). The fact that they only give an impression shows the falsehood and hypocrisy that lies at the heart of the Federated United Republic of Kamangola. From all the evidence, the nation is neither federated nor united, and much less, a republic as seen through the xenophobic language used against the Anglophones just for the sake of their inherited colonial language.

Furthermore, although this republic is supposed to be officially bilingual with both the English and French languages receiving equal status, what comes across in the novel is a state wherein the French language overwhelmingly dominated at the detriment of the English

---

[18] Anglophones are always a nuisance
[19] Poor Anglophone from Kromba, why couldn't you stay at home? By this the francophones imply that Ngwe ought to have stayed in the Anglophone region instead of coming over to the Francophone region. This shows the disdain and scorn for the Anglophones in the nation of Kamangola.

Language. Not only this, but by virtue of the Francophone majority status, French has become positioned as the norm and as a consequence, whatever falls short of it is considered as an aberration and treated accordingly. This becomes glaringly clear when Ngwe after a class taught exclusively in French dares to ask to be clarified in English. This provokes a torrent of booing which humiliates him considerably. He recounts how his encounter with Dr Ambo, the lone Anglophone lecturer in the university opens his eyes to the gross marginalization of the English language, its users, the people from the region where the English language is spoken and by extension the Anglophone identity. Ngwe captures this situation in the following passage:

> All my lecturers were Francophones except Dr Ambo [...] at times he gathered a few of us Anglophones to discuss with us and most often regretted that the country did not use him effectively because he was English speaking. He told us that since it was government policy to eliminate the Anglophone culture in the country using the university as one of its weapons, we had no choice but to give in to complete assimilation into the francophone culture. (64)

This assimilation or attempt thereof becomes apparent when Ngwe recounts that in the University, they had been asked to obligatorily answer all their questions in French and not English. He relates his bitter experience:

> On one occasion I gathered courage to ask to be explained a notion in constitutional law I did not understand. Soon as I started the first words in English, the lecture hall broke into a tremor of booing and jeering *'Anglofou', 'Anglobete'*. Cat-calls and screaming came out from all directions. Twisted papers and

assorted objects flew from every direction and landed on me. (64/65)

Ngwe's language of expression- English- marks him out as an Anglophone of the minority identity and holds him up as an outsider. Although he is supposedly a full citizen of Kamangola, his linguistic difference makes him a second-class citizen who is subsequently subjected to such a humiliating treatment. McLeod has noted that "language was the most important ways in which the national people's commonality as well as its exclusive limits were defined" (101). Here although it is supposedly one nation, Ngwe still suffers exclusion as a result of his linguistic difference. He explains his plight thus:

> I stood transfixed, bemused, dumbfounded as though the ritual of disorder has hypnotized me and transformed me into a worthless object. For the rest of the two hour lecture, I thought deeply over the humiliation I faced from my countrymen [...] I decided to go into my shell to avoid speaking English in public places, during lectures or on campus. (65)

This goes in line with Ashuntantang's assertion thus

> Therefore, the value of English as an official language for the Anglophone carries other responsibilities. It is tied with their collective identity, the only weapon of unity they have for fighting against the Francophone majority. In contrast, and true to majority-minority dynamics, the Francophones do not rally around French as an identity symbol. Thus fighting for the equality of English language vis-à-vis the French language in Cameroon has become synonymous with fighting for the rights of Anglophones within Cameroon. (18)

So, Anglophone identity refers not only to a category but also to a kind of treatment and the fight against the English language is a fight against the Anglophone personhood.

This treatment of Ngwe based on his status as minority ties in with David Richards who quotes Sartre underscoring that "identity is neither natural nor essential, but constructed from discourses of difference and inequality" (11). So, Ngwe's identity as an Anglophone in Kamangola is not a mere description of who or what he is, but a further indication of what this identity represents in Kamangola. It defines Ngwe's *outsidedness*, marginality, as well as his lack of access to equal treatment and opportunities as his francophone counterpart. Thus identity in his universe is both a state and a state of being. It is not just self-defining but also defines what role one is made to play in the society. Therefore, for Ngwe, his minority status renders him a social outcast. Consequently, Richards talking of Edward Saïd and the question of identity intimates thus:

> First and foremost Saïd embedded a process of questioning which postcolonialism shares with many other forms of poststructuralist analysis of the "essential" of "natural" of "commonsense" categories by which identity is constructed. Fanon and after Saïd, postcolonialism sees identities not as fixed and rooted but as products of a world in constant motion. Although "race", ethnicity and nationality may appear to be the solid bedrock upon which we shape a sense of ourselves, those are not nor have they ever been stable but are always being formed and reformed in different patterns and combinations in a process of constant interaction and change shaped by historical circumstances. As a consequence, identities are also in a constant state of flux. Colonialism has been a major engine driving an accelerated pace of change, forcing different cultures into new forms, 'unfixing' what was thought to be solid and creating new identities. The postcolonial project is therefore concerned to

deconstruct the older language of identity founded upon notion of impermeable entities such as the nation, culture, and selfhood and to reconstruct the debate around hybrid and porous formations such as displacement, dislocation and migrancy. (19)

Ngwe's minority identity results from the colonial encounter which transformed him from a Nweh citizen to an Anglophone in Kamangola. Prior to the colonial encounter Ngwe was not an Anglophone, but colonialism has bestowed upon him another feature of identity which unfortunately defines him as a minority or an inferior person. Unlike the Francophone students of the University of Besaadi, Ngwe has no access to knowledge. The French language which occupies the position of power has been positioned as the language of instruction and so he cannot be expected to understand his lessons. The result of this is his continuous failure in the university although he is a brilliant student.

In the world of *Across the Mongolo*, the question of identity takes up a significant position because of what it is meant to serve. The Anglophone minority is subjected to all sorts of humiliations, but worse than these; the English speaking Kamangolans are denied access to opportunities for self-advancement and success. At the University of Besaadi, the total exclusion of the English Language implies that students of English expression cannot acquire the knowledge necessary for their becoming. Yet, it is the lone University in the nation. Here the concept of subalternity comes forcefully to play where; Ngwe is not given a piece of the national cake. The concept of subalternity occupies an important place in postcolonial discourse. Ashcroft, Griffith and Tiffin define subaltern as someone "of an interior rank" and that "it is a term adopted by Antonio Gramsci to refer to those groups in the society who are subject to the hegemony of the ruling class. Subaltern classes may include peasants, workers and other groups denied access to 'hegemonic' power" (198). His identity as Anglophone singles him out for the worst forms of marginalization such as social exclusion and dehumanization. He is ascribed an inferior citizenship which deprives him of the same rights as his francophone Kamangolan counterpart. Although he is a Kamangolan and duly enrolled at the University, he cannot participate in the lessons nor can he understand them. The lone Anglophone lecturer, Dr Ambo, cannot teach a main course, first of all because he refuses to do so in French and moreover, the crushing francophone system of Kamangola has refused to recognize his certificates from Anglo-Saxon universities. Although Kamangola is a multilingual and multicultural society, it is the francophone culture that dominates. In this light, Couze Venn has underlined that

> Cultures are heterogeneous and polyglot, the result of appropriations, borrowing, grafting and reconfiguration that are proccessual are dynamic, responding to a field of force that includes diasporic displacements, material and symbolic exchanges of all kinds, power relations determining forms of exclusion and inclusion. (77)

Accordingly, the francophones have adopted the same posture as the colonizers who in their unequal relationship with the colonized came to present themselves as the

> model of the normal or ideal-type subject as the 'developed', rational, autonomous, unitary, being who is ideally meant to be white, male, Western; a model that has been established and become normative or dominant in the course of colonialism and modernity." (Venn 77)

What we therefore witness in this novel is an inextricable relationship between identity and subjectivity. Ngwe as an Anglophone is given a specific treatment. This is because his identity is not of the "norm" so he is constantly subjected to a myriad of abuses. He cannot participate as a full citizen in his nation. Identity therefore ceases to be a mere category or description but extends to an indication of a case of exclusion. In Kamangola, identity defines the state of belonging and / or not belonging. For the Anglophone minority they are made aliens in their own country and therefore cannot be said to belong.

Consequently, in the aftermath of Ngwe's humiliation in class, he concurs that "I felt my head reeling with shame and dejection" (73). He stops participating in class and resolves to keep "a low profile for the rest of the year avoiding any linguistic confrontation with any of my superior brothers with conscious consideration" (73). The gaze of the francophone majority has succeeded in inscribing the inferiority feeling in Ngwe, causing him to move to the periphery of campus life. In such a system where one's identity plays such an important role, Ngwe seems doomed to fail.

Ngwe's Existentialist Nightmare or the Failure of Becoming

At the opening of *Across the Mongolo*, the reader is made to understand that Ngwe who left his village to acquire knowledge in Ngola has returned mad. It is when the healers of the village are called upon to try and restore him to sanity that the full story of his tribulations is told. It is during Ngwe's "talking cure[20]" that one comes to understand that his dementia is the result of the hostile environment of the University of Besaadi, where he had suffered because of his Anglophone identity. This mental disintegration which results from the traumas he experienced in Ngola, is similar to the type of neurosis Frantz Fanon highlighted in his treatment of colonial racism in *Black Skin, White Masks*. Talking of the Negro child he stipulates that "a normal negro child, having grown up within a normal family, will become abnormal on the slightest contact with

---

[20] A treatment for different psychological disorders which involves getting patients (sometimes under hypnosis) to talk about their inner lives with professionals.

the white world" (111). This statement captures Ngwe's plight whereby his transition from a Nweh to an Anglophone boy ushers him into a world of diverse traumas. So, Fanon holds that "It could not be stated more positively; every neurosis has its origins in specific *Erlebnisse*" (111).

Ngwe's status as a minority in the discriminatory nation of Kamangola seems to have programmed him for failure. When he understands that he cannot speak the English language in class and resolves therefore to keep a low profile, his fate seems to have been sealed. The first tragedy to befall him is the fact that he fails to move to the next class. He bemoans "most grieving was the fact that I had to repeat the class at the end of the year" (95). Although Ngwe initially blames the failure on the abject poverty in which the Anglophone students live, his friend, Nwolefeck, soon clarifies by vehemently contradicting him, saying:

> besides, who told you that it is poverty that made both of us fail to go to year two? You cannot blame any Anglophone who does not succeed here. It is the system. Not that we do not work hard. We do not know French and we do not answer our questions during exams in French. How do you expect to succeed? We have no alternative. (100)

Nwolefeck's response holds to ridicule a nation which is supposedly bilingual but where incidentally, those in the minority are expected to subsume their identity into the majority system without which their failure is inevitable. An intelligent boy, like Ngwe, who has practically sailed through his prior education is now failing to move to the second year in the University because, by virtue of his identity, he has been judged unworthy by the system in place. Ngwe's dream of elevation through the university is rapidly being transformed into an existentialist nightmare, where no matter how hard he tries, it seems only failure awaits him.

When eventually Ngwe's situation experiences a slight change through his success in moving to the second year, his hopes are raised and he believes that things might yet improve for him and the fellow Anglophones. He states thus:

> I was beginning to see my ailing dream rejuvenate: my dream to see myself live with some impact in my society, in my country: my dream to attain status and influence and solve the problems of the ailing society which tortured me: my dream to stop the injustices done on those of us that we the minority English colony shared one nation with the majority French colony. (125)

All of Ngwe's bitter experiences as an Anglophone, spur him to create the Young Anglophone Movement (YAM) at the university in a bid to improve their lot. He explains that by driving home this message:

> I was either going to be a man, a full man or nothing. A full citizen and not an assistant citizen. The movement was the only available means by which young Anglophones could fight for their rights and merits, without which my quest for knowledge was going to be in vain. Without this, I was never to get to the position of my dream, I was never to attain my childhood ambition, and all my education would have been naught. (142)

Ngwe realizes that success in his society is not determined by merits. The system in place, rather designates who succeeds and who fails. For Anglophones like Ngwe, the mark of failure has already been branded on them. His only hope therefore is to fight for the right to succeed like his Francophone brothers. He has come to understand the tragic situation whereby "no matter how educated an Anglophone was, he was never to enjoy his full rights and merits of citizenship put side by side with his Francophone masters" (142). So on the day of the launching of YAM, he tells the other Anglophones that "we had the right to be full citizens and not second-class citizens, to be full ministers and Directors and not second-class ministers and directors" (143). Ngwe's efforts to reclaim his full personhood and be able to pursue his dreams are laudable, unfortunately though the system in place will not accept this. This therefore provokes a violent crackdown, ruthless torture and detention by the police force. Tipped of an imminent arrest of the leaders of this movement, Ngwe is forced to flee to his village. This results in his missing his exams and therefore having to repeat the second year. The university system does not allow anyone to repeat the same class twice, thus Ngwe has to obligatorily succeed or lose all the years spent so far in the university. When he fails the June session, all his hopes rest on the re-sit September session as he narrates: "[…] if I did not succeed, that was going to be the end of my *mandat* in the faculty and possibly in the university. That was going to be the end of all hopes and ambitions" (160). Faced with this dilemma, he invests his all towards succeeding. Tragically, he fails at the end. This implies that his studies at the Faculty of Law have come to an end. He reflects on the years spent and states: "[…] four years squandered in an intellectual wilderness, in the turbulence of an undefined visionless existence, of lawlessness and anguish. All hopes and aspirations crushed" (161). Once again the reasons for Ngwe's failure are linked to his minority Anglophone identity which is treated with spite and accorded no significance in the nation. He decries this situation: "I wrote my examinations in the English Language against the dictates of my lecturers who demonstrated palpable ignorance and bias against the language" (162). Ngwe fails not because he was ill-prepared or incapable of succeeding; it is rather identity politics at work. He carries the "stigma" of his unwanted Anglophone identity. In the throes of distress he laments "why was I born an Anglophone?" (110).

Having fully assimilated the implications of his Anglophone identity, Ngwe can only lament the colonial moment that created an Anglophone identity. In the lines that follow he stipulates:

> Curse that day that the white man first came to Africa and tore our world apart, brought misery to our lives, brought anguish, pain, sorrow and despair, changed me from a Nweh man to an Anglophone and then subjected me, into slavery in the estates of my brothers who were fortunate to be colonized by the French. (123)

This colonial identity has signaled nothing but hardship and sorrow for Ngwe. His failure places him in such a tragic situation that he sees himself as an Anglophone - merely a spectator there to watch others move ahead in life and accomplish their dreams:

> I sat at the edge of the pavement of the faculty, staring unto the vacancy of the mundane universe of a university. The happy ones who spoke the language of my brothers of the other side of the Great River laughed and chatted merrily about the place. The Anglo, the pariah, the slave like me was compelled to escort them in their unsubstantial galore and excellence. (163)

Words like "vacancy", "pariah", and "slave" evoke the emptiness that has characterized Ngwe's life in the University of Besaadi. By reason of his minority status, he is a pariah in the society, treated as a slave with the results being his failure after four years of toiling under hostile circumstances in the university. The system has ensured by a well-calculated mechanism of exclusion, that individuals like Ngwe must necessarily fail. Thus he compares himself to "shit that was thrown at the corner of my Francophone masters" (164). His identity has singled him out in a world where the norm is to be francophone.

Thus he concludes "I was the Anglo incapable of partaking of the galore of high society" (164).

Ngwe starts experiencing the outset of mental disintegration at this juncture. Faced with forces too powerful for him and which have refused him a place on the table of success, because of his identity, his psyche begins fragmenting. He explains as follows:

> my mind became the explosion ground for the tremors of the world. My head pounded like a mortar in which palm nuts were crushed. I became dizzy and weak, talking to people I did not know, people I did not see, voices chattering in my ears voices laughing at jokes that had no humour [sic] in them… (164)

Worth noting is the fact that Ngwe's plight is not singular, but represents the general plight of the Anglophone minority. This is pointed out by his girlfriend Shirila. When she tries to comfort him, she points out that other Anglophones have experienced worse treatment than his at the University of Besaadi. She does so by questioning:

> [...] have you not heard of students, particularly Anglophone students who have spent eleven years in this university? Four years in the Faculty of science, four years in the Faculty of Law and three years in Arts where they finally succeeded to have a degree? (169/170)

Such an outrageous situation highlights the question of social failure where one group is programmed by a discriminatory system to fail. This situation can be well-explained by the marginal status accorded the Anglophone. Ashcroft, Griffiths and Tiffin have defined marginality as indicating a "*postitionality* that is best defined in terms of the limitations of a subject's access to power"(121). They further define it as an indication of "various forms of exclusion and oppression" (121). By marginalizing the English language in the lone university of Besaadi, the Anglophones are excluded from a proper education which implies that failure is inevitable. Eleven years to acquire a B.A. cannot be termed success, especially when the Francophones easily sail through the system which favors them. Thus Shirila adds that "success in this university and in the country as a whole depends on gambling and not merit" (170).

To give himself another chance, Ngwe follows Shirila's advice and moves to the Faculty of Arts. Here, however, the same forces are seen at play as even here Ngwe fails once again "when the results were released a few weeks after writing, I did not find my name on the list. I was shocked, vexed, infuriated. I could not understand. I knew I had done my best during the examinations" (197). In *Across the Mongolo*, the best of the Anglophones is not good enough for the system that has placed them at the margins and has put in place various contrivances to ensure that they remain marginalized. For Ngwe, the result is not only his failure to earn a B.A from the university, but his total social failure which comes about when he, in the aftermath of this academic failure experiences a complete mental breakdown. This as a result of accumulated abuses meted on him by the system. He expatiates thus:

> A dreary feeling invaded my whole being. I did not know on which ground I felt my feet. I left the Dean's office, dreary and drunk. I stood at the balcony and peered at the bizarre world of falsity and viciousness. A knot clicked in my brain; the giant blocks of the Faculty, the concentrated aluminum roofs in the plateau beneath, shadows of invisible persons, voices of drunkards, thousands of pestles pounding in my head [...]. (198)

It is at this point that Ngwe returns to his village; an epitome of social failure. The dreams, aspirations and ambitions which propelled him in his quest for knowledge through which he could improve upon himself have all been thwarted by the system in place. When Ngwe left his village years earlier, the expectation was that he would return having succeeded and possibly made a name for himself. Unfortunately, the society has denied him that possibility. He returns a failure, a social outcast, unfit for mainstream society. All of this because of his identity. He has been refused the right to exist as a full citizen in his own nation. Anglophone identity has not merely served to identify or describe English speaking Kamangolans, but has served to carve out what position they must occupy in the country. Thus whereas Couze Venn has defined identity as "the relational aspects that qualify subjects in terms of categories such as race, gender, class, nation, sexuality, work and occupation" (79), *Across the Mongolo* indicates that it ceases to be mere categorizations but extends to encompass what advantages are accorded to whom. Thus for Ngwe, his identity as Anglophone, as a minority in the society is not a mere sociological category but this also implies that, he is an inferior citizen of the country and as such is not entitled to the same treatment as the Francophone majority. It is as such that Carlson Anyangwe in *Imperialistic Politics in Cameroon* commenting on the unequal union between the Anglophone and Francophone States that resulted in such a social malaise, holds that: "by 1989, it had become clear even to the blind that the relationship between the Southern Cameroons and Cameroun Republic is the type that exists between the horse and the rider, between the hostage and the hijacker, between colonized and colonizer"(159) It is this gross discrimination, caused by the way Anglophone minority identity is perceived, that results in Ngwe's failure. Consequently Anyangwe adds that "marginalization, domination and annexation were words often used to describe the phenomenon of subjugation" (159). This aptly describes the plight of Ngwe and the other Anglophones as the subjugated in the state of Kamangola.

Conclusion

Ngwe's tragic tale mirrors what happens when the society makes victims of other members of the society. Instead of protecting the rights of the minority, the forces of power prey on this minority, denies it its rights to exist on an equal level with the majority. The linguistic and cultural differences have marked both majority and minority out for the worst forms of marginalization which include dehumanization, depersonalization and complete exclusion from opportunities of becoming and self-advancement. By ensuring that the minority does not have access to the same opportunities as the majority, the system has already guaranteed failure for the minority.

Thus, throughout the novel, the reader is left with identity politics being viciously played out to Ngwe's detriment because he is a minority. The young, intelligent and ambitious boy who leaves his village with dreams of becoming a highly successful man of influence in the nation has returned to his village mentally deranged. The perpetual humiliation, frustrations and discrimination means that for the Anglophones in Kamangola, success is more or less a mirage. Ngwe ends up broken, dejected and demented because his identity has cast him as an outsider and he is treated accordingly.

Although Maryse Conde quotes Adele King who wonders if "an identity is not simply a matter of choice, of a personal decision based on the possession of certain inner values" (820), a reading of *Across the Mongolo* shows that an identity can be conferred upon one by the power structure of the society and most often to serve a particular purpose. Thus, whereas Ngwe considers himself before his trip to Ngola as a Nweh boy, once there, he becomes an Anglophone, an identity which he comes to understand as synonymous with subalternity and marginality. As a consequence, Ngwe's dreams, optimism and hopes end up buried under an identity conferred on him by his colonial and neo-colonial heritage.

Works Cited

Anyangwe, Carlson. *Imperialistic Politics in Cameroons: Resistance and the Inception of the Restoration of the Statehood of Southern Cameroons.* Mankon, Bamenda: Langaa Research and Publication CIG, 2009. Print.

Ashcroft, Bill, Gareth Griffiths, and Helen Tiffin. *Postcolonial Studies: The Key Concepts.* London, 2007. Print.

Ashcroft, Bill, Gareth Griffiths, and Helen Tiffin. *The Post-colonial Studies Reader.* London: Routledge, 2005. Print.

Ashuntantang, Joyce B. *Landscaping Postcoloniality: The Dissemination of Cameroon Anglophone Literature.* Mankon, Bamenda: Langaa Research and Publishing CIG. 2009

Chew, Shirley and Richards David. *A Concise Companion to Postcolonial Literature.* West Sussex: John Wiley, 2010. Print.

Fanon, Frantz. *Black Skin, White Masks, New Edition.* Trans. Charles Lam Markham. London: Pluto, 1968. Print.

Gikandi, Simon. "African Literature and the Colonial Factor." in Irele, F. Abiola and Simon Gikandi (eds). *The Cambridge History of African and Caribbean Literature.* Cambridge: CambridgeUP, 2004. 379-397. Print.

King, Adele. "Postcolonial" African and Caribbean Literature." in Irele, F. Abiola and Simon Gikandi (eds). *The Cambridge History of African and Caribbean Literature.* Cambridge: Cambridge UP, 2004. 809-820. Print.

McLeod, John. "Nation and Nationalisms" in *A Concise Companion to Postcolonial Literature.* West Sussex: John Wiley, 2010. 97-119. Print.

Morton, Stephen. "Marginality: Representations of Subalternity, Aborignality and Race" in *A Concise Companion to Postcolonial Literature.* West Sussex: John Wiley, 2010. 177- 192. Print.

Nyamnjoh, Francis B. "Potted Plants in Greenhouses': A Critical Reflection on the Resilience of Colonial Education in Africa." in *Journal of Asian and African Studies* 47.2 (2012): 1-26. Print.

Richards, David. "Framing Identities" in *A Concise Companion to Postcolonial Literature*. West Sussex: John Wiley, 2010. 1-28. Print.

Sethi, Rumina. *The Politics of Postcolonialism: Empire, Nation and Resistance*. London: Pluto, 2011. Print.

Venn, Couze. *The Postcolonial Challenge: Towards Alternative Worlds*. London: Sage. 2006. Print.

Chapter 7

Changing the Status Quo from the Margins in Bill F. Ndi's *Gods in the Ivory Towers*

By
Adaku T. Ankumah

The performing arts in oral tradition had a functional role and was relevant to the concerns of society. Though the entertainment component was present, the stories, poems, proverbs, riddles were not simply told merely as art for art's sake; they were also used to pass on the mores of society and to reinforce behavior deemed acceptable by the standards of moral ethics in the community. These stories were passed down from one generation to the next, but they were never static, were not stuck in the past nor irrelevant to society. Thus the focus was on the here and now. Deviant behaviors in contemporary society were subject to ridicule and even to songs of insult. With the emergence of written literature, the African writer has not deviated from this commitment to literature. As Christopher D. Roy mentions in his introduction to a collection of African art, "[i]n Africa there is little 'art for art's sake' but a great deal of 'art for life's sake'" (Introduction). The levels of commitment, though, may differ, i.e. anywhere from "reactionary through liberal to radical," as Nigerian playwright and critic Femi Ojo-Ade notes. He characterizes the liberals as those who want to demolish the colonial power structures to replace them with new ones that will promote their interests. The liberals, he maintains, want to "play it safe, spitting words of revolution even while wining and dining with the reactionary powers that be" (10). The radicals, those who want to bring effective change, in Ojo-Ade's mind, are in the minority, and their work is effective because they go beyond mere words to collective action between the writer-activist and the masses. Ngugi wa Thiong'o, Ojo-Ade's choice as an exemplar of this level of commitment, applies Marxist interpretation to history and change in an undertaking that unites intellectuals in the "ivory towers" with the masses.

One contemporary writer who falls into this category of radical commitment using literature is Bill F. Ndi, a Cameroonian author who has published several collections of poetry but is versatile with other genres, such as drama and essays. Though his play *Gods in the Ivory Towers* does not necessarily espouse Marxism, this terse, one-act play touches on various issues confronting characters whose location evokes Ndi's Cameroon. The setting is on a hill called Ngoa situated in a village that goes by the same name but has not lived to the expectations of its people. A protagonist with a similar sounding name, Ngwa, refuses to yield to the discouragement, despair, disillusionment of the villagers and from the margins, challenges the status quo. Ndi adopts a minimalist approach in terms of setting, character description, development, and dialogue. There is an omniscient Narrator, the protagonist Ngwa, the two academics and a couple of young people who interact with Ngwa. However, in terms of effect, Ndi uses this one-act play to examine the alienation produced in this neo-colonial country by members of the ruling elite and their acolytes. Ngwa finds himself on the margins of society due to his name, his linguistic difference, and lack of pedigree. However, his isolation does not lead to capitulation. Instead he turns his alienation into resistance. Through his protagonist Ngwa, Ndi notes that any radical change in this society must begin with a rejection of the status quo, since its acceptance convincingly leads to a fatalistic view that this is how life will be. It is incumbent on the disenfranchised to believe that each one holds within himself or herself the seeds of change.

From the very beginning of this one-act play, the site of alienation is situated in the very setting of the play—a hilly country, a desert wasteland that frustrates the goals and aspirations of its people, especially its youth. The Narrator refers to himself as the traditional town crier, "just a seer and a crier," crying for his village, Ngoa, for "wasted youth" (4). With four appearances in the course of this one-act play, the Narrator is lucid in his understanding of the plight of his hometown of Ngoa, especially the plight of the youth. This hill inspires fear in all, both young and old, and yet there is no avoiding it if one hopes to succeed in the "village college," a college that is a microcosm of what happens within the macrocosm that is Cameroon. Indeed, symbolically, the hill represents the unattainable for the people of Ngoa, for try as they do, the youth, especially those whose language differs from the language spoken by the majority, find themselves unable to make it to the top figuratively, imprisoned and isolated from success. The name itself contributes to their fears, for as the Narrator tells the reader, the name of the village is not derived from the lush green landscape of the surrounding. A city with a welcoming name tends to inspire its citizens, but Ngoa "scares the villagers" so much so that the name is more of a taboo, the unmentionable (4). It appears young people born in this barren land come into the world with several strikes against them. A place which does not have a good reputation for progress, Ngoa brings to mind the ancient city of Nazareth, Jesus' hometown. When Philip, one of Jesus' disciples found another follower, Nathaniel, to introduce to the Master, Nathaniel asked, "Can anything good come out of Nazareth?" (John 1: 46). Indeed, one may pose the same question about Ngoa since its location and name suggest that it is a place from which nothing good may come, a rugged wilderness.

To compound the estrangement of the protagonist Ngwa, his father names him after the very hills that have become synonymous with the mediocrity and failure that tie his people down. His name is a homonym of Ngoa, the hill that frustrates the efforts of its citizenry. Mballa, Ngwa's peer, actually questions the wisdom of Ngwa's father, Pa Mbeh, in choosing his son's name, a name that almost matches the name of their languishing city in spelling and pronunciation, a name synonymous with deterioration, decay, decline and even defeat, especially among the youth: "Do you think your father did justice in choosing your name?" (6). Mballa is skeptical that any amelioration will come to a village that appears forsaken by God Himself. He reminds Ngwa: "Just remember God willed them there, the hill, Ngoa, here and equally did not want us to reach there. He deprived us the strength and power to climb up Ngoa or that to use in bringing them down!" (8). Indeed, Mballa's resignation in the face of challenges appears to reflect the attitude of the whole community towards the challenges they face. This "culture of silence" has contributed to the negative environment because the people do not reconstruct a future for themselves except what they have received, and their silence empowers their oppressors and further increases their marginalization. Mballa invokes a variation of the philosophy of determinism/fatalism: "It is [a] fact that everybody as well as everything is nothing but toys and puppets in the hands of the gods. . . . You shall never be what your old man willed but that which God and the gods have willed" (9). This recapitulation reflects what Francis Nyamnjoh, a Cameroonian writer, critic and anthropologist, describes about attitudes in Cameroon, a country he notes is the "burial ground" for different theories or generalizations. He refers to Cameroon as a "peculiar case," a place where citizens are inured to hardships, with very little protest or any action of substance to change the situation (102). This nonchalance about their situation plays an important role in their subjugation, just like the greed of their political leaders has contributed to their not belonging to their own country. Ngwa has to battle this fatalistic approach to life throughout the play, for his peers have been paralyzed by it, making them impotent to solve their own problems.

One man who tries to reverse the negativity associated with the hill is Pa Mbeh, referred to as a "lunatic" for naming his son Ngwa after the hill. However, Mbeh's madness may actually be prophetic, the insight of a man whose actions baffle the rest of his compatriots. As one critic notes, madness in African literature is often "stripped of its negative connotations for satirical purposes" and the mad person takes on the "trappings of a hero, a prophet, a sage, the custodian of communal morality, the irrepressible conscience of the community" (Asaah 502). Mbeh is very much aware of the situation and by choosing to name his son after the hills, he is very much deliberate about what he hopes to achieve. "Much madness," penned Emily Dickinson, "is divinest sense," for Mbeh, aware of the challenges facing society, has rejected the taciturn behavior of the rest of society and has decided to challenge the status quo by naming his son after the very mountains that pose as obstacles to their advancement. His hope in so naming his son is to "[imbue] this child with the strength which will permit him to untie the fate the gods have tied and dropped in front of his fellow villagers" (4-5). Clearly, this deliberate act of naming, therefore, is not the action of a "madman" but of a man who has not retrenched from society and is seeking means to change their bleak future by confronting the issue head on. In that sense, Mbeh is a lone visionary, for the rest of his countrymen are satisfied with maintaining the existing hierarchies in society which keep them constantly frustrated and incapable of action. In his harsh criticism of the system, Francis Nyamnjoh attributes the desire to maintain the status quo from all segments of society to the idea that directly or indirectly, Cameroonians benefit from the system and so have no interest in changing it, for "the system's 'undoing' will be their own undoing" (112). Indeed, the apathy of the citizens is such that Nyamnjoh views the entire country as the "victim of a hypnotic spell [cast] by the sorcerer state" (102). Thus the alienated reinforce their alienation by their indifference to their situation and their resistance to change, even the small one Mbeh made in naming his child.

The "culture of corruption," as Nyamnjoh describes the situation in a country that once found itself at the top of the 1998 Transparency International's ignoble list of most corrupt country in the world, manifests itself in various ways in the play, and the group most vulnerable is the youth since corruption threatens the future of young people in this country. The majority like Mballa has accepted the corrupt system, looking for ways to make it in the system instead of fighting and resisting corruption. Thus their fears of not belonging and their uncertainty about their future make them vulnerable to corrupt ways of belonging with the powerful. One way for them to attain success is through "bottom power," selling sexual favors for advancement as the young men Ngwa and Ojong discover. Ojong is sent to the police station to sign papers, and the older woman who is supposed to sign the papers advises Ojong not to look at women advanced in age "as if they were rags or filth, good-for-nothing but the incinerator" but to be valued "like cattle would value an area of more greener pastures" (15); otherwise he would never succeed. The statement by the woman reinforces the malfunction of the country and, therefore, the need for the powerless to find means other than hard work to survive.

Ngwa does not allow his dissatisfaction with the corrupt system to lead him to inertia, as has happened to the rest of the citizens of Ngoa. He could have sat down and lamented his unfortunate circumstances or could have spent a good portion of his life having idealistic dreams, dreams that are impossible to fulfill. Instead, with determination to live up to his name and the aspirations of his "infamous" father, Ngwa decides to chart a different course from that of his community to climb to the top of the hill. As the Narrator tell us, "His determination [is] to unteach that which has been taught from generations to generations" (11), and this determination leads him not just to develop the physical muscles needed to climb, but also his intellectual muscles so he can read well and find himself at the top. He does not want to be godfathered to the top; he wants to reach the top with his intelligence.

However, when he enrolls at the village college to pursue postgraduate studies in Sociology, he realizes that his climb to the intellectual summit will not be easy. Nnomo, the female sociologist he hopes to work with as his advisor, is not interested in purely academic work: "How come you're calling me madam? You're making me old" (21). She queries Ngwa because he hasn't used "an even lovelier word" to address her. After calculated delays to meet her advisee in her office as scheduled several times, Nnomo finally suggests a meeting in her apartment—what she has hoped Ngwa would suggest after all her excuses of not keeping their appointments. When Ngwa finally makes the visit, what meets his eyes has nothing to do with research. The author does not disguise her intentions as she lies in a settee, dressed in a "transparent sexy nightgown" reading *Nous Deux*" (32). Sexual exploitation of students on university campuses in African is something which has been referred to in works by other African writers. Francis Nyamnjoh, in *Intimate Strangers* refers to a Dr. John-Strong Long Bottom, a professor of Environmental Sciences at the Diamond University of Science and Technology (DUST for short), a married man who spends most of his evenings and nights with Evodia Skatta, a female student at DUST. His wife, very much aware of the activities of her philandering husband, turns to the Roman Catholic priest, to at least ban her husband from the Eucharist. The priest's non-compliance with her request leads her to quit the Catholic Church for a Pentecostal one. Though normally female students are the victims of such acts, male students are becoming targets as females increase in the professoriate. On the surface, it appears insidious since the relationships are maintained in inconspicuous ways, but given the serious consequences on marriages and diseases like HIV/AIDS, these extra-marital affairs can be dangerous.

Communication experts tell us that for a meaningful exchange to take place, speakers as well as listeners must be on the same page, but Ngwa and Nnomo as locators do not stay on the same page with the same meanings behind their words. While the student wants to proceed with his work, the professor thinks the living room is not conducive to work and so she spreads her naked body on her bed, to the dismay of the student. When Ngwa finally understands the intentions of his advisor, he flees the apartment in disgust. Casting herself as the primeval mother, Eve, Nnomo is at a loss why Adam will resist her advances. Rejection evokes bitterness and revenge in her: "He will learn the hard way! I have been here for years! He came and met me here so shall he go and leave me here. I am the stone of the river bed. An idiot from nowhere can't change the status quo!" (38). From her metaphor, Nnomo indicates that change is not going to come soon, for such abuses are entrenched in the system as a stone is in the river.

In presenting her case before her lover/Head of Department (HOD), Nnomo casts Ngwa as the criminal, "the devil that came to [her] house under the pretext of work" (40). Given his intellectualism, Ngwa appears before HOD, "*determined as ever*" to be heard, to ask questions and receive answers. In his determination not to be deterred, he reminds one of Edward Saïd's description of the role the intellectual must play as a "dissenter" in society. Published under the title *Representations of the Intellectual*, the article is part of the 1993 Reith Lectures, a series of lectures on contemporary issues delivered by a prominent person in that area on BBC Radio. Saïd takes a critical look at the role the intellectual should play in society:

> [T]he intellectual is an individual endowed with a faculty for representing, embodying, articulating a message, a view, an attitude, philosophy or opinion to, as well as for, a public. And this role has an edge to it, and cannot be played without a sense of being someone whose place it is publicly to raise embarrassing questions, to confront orthodoxy and dogma. . .

. The intellectual does so on the basis of universal principles: that all human beings are entitled to expect decent standards of behaviour [sic] concerning freedom and justice . . . and that deliberate or inadvertent violations of these standards need to be testified and fought against courageously. (11-12)

Ngwa clearly qualifies as the intellectual in this play, for whether he is debating another college student Mballa, who ridicules his dreams as "ephemeral illusions" and challenges his dream of succeeding in the future, or talking with the other college student Ojong just looking for a "willing listener" to help him sort out his problems, Ngwa presents the progressive way he embodies to both of his listeners. Mballa especially represents the reactionary force in the play, ridiculing Ngwa and his future plans as unrealistic. He questions Ngwa's convictions: "By common nomenclature, you figure yourself a lion in the midst of goats. . . .Maybe you will end up imprisoned between some laps someday! One never knows . . . !" (9). He predicts the very pathway to success, sexual favors, that Ngwa rejects as he questions what he perceives to be Ngwa's arrogance in seeing himself as a man of great strength, power, and courage to change the status quo and the rest of them as useless, inferior. Sadly, Ngwa cannot change Mballa's perception of things, so after calling him "ignorant," he abandons his friend to pursue his vision.

Even in dealing with the powers that be, Ngwa is not perturbed. He boldly confronts the professor/mistress-HOD/lover duo; when Nnomo calls him "bad," he responds, "Who is bad? Is it you or me?" (44). When the HOD, annoyed that Ngwa dares to call his mistress bad, informs him that he will be thrown away from this bastion of civilization to the primitive place where he belongs, he gives a lengthy speech:

You are not ejecting me from here because I have committed a crime or an offence but because you rogues don't want honest intelligent people here in Ngoa! . . . how did you ever become a professor if objectivity was not anywhere in your lexicon? Too bad. . . ! your professorship, I believe, was from the gutter picked like that of most of your colleagues in this village college! (44)

It is along this line that Nyamnjoh, indeed, concurs that some academic positions are obtained by "conceptual rhetoric" used to shore up the government rather than by academic credentials, leading a university group to lament the "misère intellectuelle" [intellectual misery] in Cameroon (107).

Ngwa learns that he has to contend with more than just sexual harassment to advance; he has to face the language barrier. Cameroon has been recognized as the only country in West Africa that uses as official languages the two dominating colonial languages, French and English,. The Eastern part (Republic of Cameroon), which used to be a mandated trust territory of France speaks French and the Western part (West Cameroon or Southern Cameroons), a British mandated trust territory, speaks English. This colonial heritage, dating from 1919 when the French and British, at the end of World War 1, were given the mandate to govern Cameroon after the defeat of the previous colonial power, Germany, still presents challenges for the country. In fact, one Cameroonian writer calls the language problem the "thorniest" of all the problems facing the country (Vakunta), with French dominating the national television and radio stations. Theoretically, bilingualism makes Cameroon appealing, for in the legal document proclaiming the two languages as official languages, these words are included: "both languages having the same status" (qtd. in Echu). However, within the country, the dominant language, French, has become the new shibboleth for advancing in society, including academia. As Echu adds, "The domination of French is due to the demographic factor, the fact that Francophones have continued to occupy top ranking positions in government and the civil service, and also because there is no effective language policy that guarantees the rights of minorities" ("The Language Question"). Another bonus to the preferential treatment given to French is that there are two "separate but not equal" systems of education, with the French system doing a better job at preparing students for post-secondary education than the Anglophone system (Echu). When Ngwa goes to the HOD's office with Nnomo to sign his academic advisor's papers for the Admission's Office, the second clarification the HOD seeks is simple: "But may I ask if he is from our part of the .... Er! I mean, is he Francophone?" (23). The hesitation in HOD's voice is momentous. HOD seems to be aware that the question is out of place in a bilingual country where it should not matter whether one speaks French or English. Most importantly, when Ngwa responds that he is a polyglot, it should not matter whether he is "French enough" or not. Ngwa, stunned by the language requirement, asks, "[H]ow can Language be a barrier to any in this bilingual village!" (25). The irony of the situation is obvious, and by capitalizing *Language*, Ngwa draws attention to the all-important, dominant language, French, which has subsumed English. Thus *bilingualism* has become a big joke since what matters is French: "Let me tell you: this village and its school were not meant for English speakers. . . !" HOD states categorically (25). The Anglophones don't belong since their language and culture are consistently degraded by the majority.

Another irony that Ngwa draws out for the biased professor is that both French and English are part of the colonial legacy, borrowings from Europe, and both languages have influenced each other (23). Thus the two sides should not be arguing over what doesn't belong to both of them, for what belongs to them, the endogenous languages of Cameroon, have been neglected in the ascendancy of the European languages over them. Later in the play when Nnomo turns the table on Ngwa and reports him to HOD as the instigator of the amorous relationship, she uses "Anglophone" as if it is an insult, a derogatory label for a person: "Yes! That Anglophone! He has begun fomenting trouble...." (40). For HOD, there is a reason for calling these "English speakers" *les gauchers"* in their "tongue," French. The word, which in French also refers to left-handed people, connotes lack of social graces and sophistication, clumsiness, uncultured, uncouth, rustic, even crude. Thus Ndi shows through this brief scene, the challenges young Anglophone students face in advancing in a society where French is the passe-partout or master key that opens the door of success and English is the language of inferiority and backwardness.

Apart from speaking the correct "tongue" to advance in this society, parentage and pedigree also play a huge part in belonging in Ngoa. The familiar saying that success is not based on what you know but on whom you know holds so true in Ngoa, as it does in many countries around the globe. To come from a good stock connects one to the right people and therefore to opportunities. Two questions HOD asks Nnomo when she introduces the graduate student to him are whether Ngwa is from her neighborhood and whether Ngwa's parents were "friends of a kind" (40). These questions invariably align with class, similar to questions about which side of the rail road tracks one lives on or whether one lives in the East, West, North or South side of some cities in America. For Ngwa, he may have been born on the wrong side of town and his father, Mbeh, may have been a lunatic as the people think, but that father's vision in naming his son will not perish. As Ngwa challenges his peer Mballa, though his father may not be alive to see the product of his imagination, he will not be disappointed with the results: "The iron with which he moulded [sic] me, now mustering like troops on hills, shall crack down this small hillock. And that is the justice he did and to me too, justice done! Done to all the people of Ngoa!" (7).

One may ask why HOD's questions are critical to the admission process and not the more obvious one of his academic performance as an undergraduate. The simple answer is that exclusion from opportunities is justified by one belonging to a group deemed inferior by another deeming itself superior. The rest of Ngwa's townspeople have accepted their position of inferiority and the existing hierarchies without challenging the system. However, for Ngwa, alienation fuels revolution, a clamor for change. He views himself and his people as "architects of the mammoth task" they have in front of them (7). They cannot choose their parentage or pedigree, but they can choose their response to the challenges in their lives. He is fully aware of the nature of the challenge; it is immensely huge, not just from the opposition but even from people like Mballa who are so steeped in fear and superstition about existing structures. But as he questions Mballa, "If they [the handful of people who control the majority] why not everybody?" (7). He makes this last statement as he hits his chest with the pointing finger and with pride. His prediction is that one day the villagers would move up that hill "as if they were sailing on a smooth river or skating on ice" (8). This prophecy will be fulfilled after he goes to prepare himself for the fight ahead. Ngwa knows that he is unprepared to face the mountain at this time, but with preparation he will be back. Then, as he says, "I will stand up and Ngoa will tell me if he is stronger that Ngwa!" (9). Like Dr. Martin Luther King, Jr., Ngwa has been to the mountaintop and has seen the "promised land" where his fellow citizens will no longer have to face imposing problems that threaten their very existence. He is very certain that he is capable to change the destiny of his whole village, given his father's faith in his name.

Thus Ngwa is not alienated by his alienation; on the contrary, his limited opportunity to advance in this corrupt society motivates him to fight to eliminate the sources of his estrangement. The powers that be are determined that a nonentity like Ngwa will not challenge the existing structures and escape with his life. As HOD threatens him, when he and his colleague have finished with Ngwa, there will be "[n]othing to make people remember your passage here!" (41). Those who dare to expose and confront corrupt leadership and their power to hurt the disadvantaged must be ready for the opposition to mount their own full-blown assault as they do not want to cede an inch of their gains and share with people the spoils looted from them.

Fighting courageously for the intellectual has a price tag, and sometimes it is an expensive one. In some African countries, the intellectual who challenges the status quo must be prepared to go to jail, be exiled from his or her country or be executed, as it happened to the writer and environmental activist Ken Saro-Wiwa of Nigeria, who protested oil spills in the Delta region of Nigeria. Even the author of *Gods in the Ivory Towers*, like other Anglophone writers from Cameroon, is very much aware that to articulate one's views on various issues carries with it the possibilities of exile and not belonging. Ngwa's challenge of the center from the margin of society leads to his ejection from both the college and the town.

Those in the center do not abdicate power easily, as Ngwa discovers. Even after exposing Nnomo's illicit relationship with him to HOD, he and his mistress react angrily to him, calling him "bad," not deserving a place around "smart civilised [sic] people" but belonging to "primitive non-natives" (44). Nnomo is glad that she is staying and Ngwa is expelled! The ones who see clearly in this society are the ones who do not belong, for they threaten to expose the evils of the powerful elite. Ngwa's reward is expulsion from society, and he has more than the academics to deal with. The king of Ngoa charges Ngwa with "triple crimes": "Hustling with the gods of Ngoa, attempting to change the status quo, and insulting state institutions" (46). At this point, Ngwa's options are limited after he is left at the foot of a higher peak than Ngoa. His one option is to climb Gerinah Heights, more elevated than Ngoa, or to perish. His peers may have given up with this new challenge, but not Ngwa who chooses to confront his problems head-on and create a viable future for himself. He may have lost a battle, but the war is not over. After being jostled and manhandled by HOD, Ngwa stands his ground: he promises to meet them again and confront Ngoa a second time.

It may appear oxymoronic, but Ngwa needs this exclusion from society to pursue progress and advancement. So long as he is stuck in this physical and mental rut, he cannot see his way out to help others.

Richard Bjornson succinctly brings out the paradoxical statement that there is no progress without alienation, and that is, indeed, the joy of not belonging:

> In fact, it might well be argued that alienation in one form *is a prerequisite* (italics mine) to the human mind's movement towards knowledge. To achieve new insights, people must at least momentarily distance themselves from their present state of consciousness. If they refuse to do so, they will remain imprisoned in a static configuration of ideas and assumptions. . . . Viewed in this way, alienation is one stage in a process that makes progress and heightened awareness possible. (148)

Ngwa certainly subscribes to this view about alienation and progress, for he has to be kicked out to figure out his next step. However, what about the rest of the youth in the play? How do young people advance in such a society? Do they join in an "if-you-can't-beat-them-join-them" mentality or do they challenge the inequities in their society? Do they get discouraged by the realities of succeeding to the top as another college student Ojong gets and wants to retreat downhill? Ndi suggests through his protagonist Ngwa that a paradigm shift is needed: one is from a negative mindset to a positive one and another from the ignorance that the elders want the youth to live under so they will continue to believe that everything is good; therefore, there is no need for change to enlightenment about their problems and the ways to address these. A society that accepts the status quo without critically examining issues cannot experience change. Sadly, even a young man like the college student Mballa is locked into the mindset of accepting and not questioning things. His derisive comments when Ngwa expresses optimism about his future reveals this mindset: "[Y]ou better not think yourself better than any of those grasses or rocks that constitute Ngoa. You may be dreaming thinking as the village myth holds that you are a god or His image, but . . . Myths are myths. . . !

(9). People like Mballa have not been able to distance themselves from this paralyzing way of thinking. In the words of Bjornson, they need to "estrange themselves from themselves" (148), to break away from the past and its way of prescribing the boundaries of what is acceptable or not acceptable. Lasting change must come from within, not from without. As Ngwa tells the disheartened Ojong, the secret to making it is within each person: "(Emphatically). You and only you have the solution to your problem and not me! All I might help you do is to identify that solution you have in you and with you!" (14). In other words, Ngoa citizens hold within themselves this power to change, and it takes likeminded people like Ngwa and Ojong alienating themselves from their narrow mindedness to increase their capacity to think outside the limits of their society.

Ngwa certainly experiences this change with his positive mindset, but unfortunately for the reader, the author leaves us in the dark about the specifics of the change except for the announcement from the Narrator that after months and years, Ngwa makes it to the summit of success, just as Ojong has informed him earlier that he is popular in Ngoa: "Ngwa, you are the one every tongue in the village talks of as being the messiah to undo Ngoa and his numerous ups and downs!" (13). What did he do exactly to make it there? We are left to conjecture; after all, it is a one-act play and so it is more challenging to elaborate on all issues. The Narrator's enigmatic parting words, though, raise questions whether this change is possible. In the closing pages of the play, the events of years are crowded in about three-quarters of a page. Ngwa returns in a position of pre-eminence, just as his father has hoped when he named him, with his people looking up to him "to drop them his bread crumbs" (47). He is gracious enough to help them, hoping they have learnt their lesson about coming out of their shells and assuming responsibility for their own survival. They cannot expect the powers that be to act on their behalf. Before leaving the stage, the Narrator addresses the audience: "Only you can now tell me if the gene of the insane fell in the abyss and if I should continue crying for the village, sadly or joyfully!" [*Remains on the stage mute*] (47). Why should he cry *sadly* if Ngwa's return signifies hope? Why is the Narrator unable to utter a word at the end of the play? Is he uncertain about the nature of the change Ngwa brings? Certainly, the gene of Pa Mbeh does not fall into the abyss, for his offspring returns and fulfills the hopes and aspirations his father had in naming him after Ngoa, the seemingly insurmountable hills. In the prophetic words of Ojong, Ngwa remains "the first to have topped our hill within such a short space of time, and with such brilliance and intelligence!" (13). Returning to Ojo-Ade's comments about committed writing, could it be that the Narrator senses that only one person changes; the rest of society remains the same. Ngwa has empowered himself through his not belonging, but have the rest of his people done the same? Where are the young people like Mballa and Ojong? Ngwa is happy to drop a few crumbs for his people "in the hope that they did learn their lesson" (47). However, do the people learn their lesson or, like Ojong, will they heave sighs and curses, dreaming about the future, but never realizing that dream? As Ngwa tells Ojong,

> To dream is one of the best things one can do. Live an experience in a dream and tell me if it were not really exciting! Dream and put it into practice. You shall realise [sic] imagination is experience already lived in that part of the world where she is born. (18)

What the people need is to move from the intangible world of dreams to the concrete world where these dreams can materialize. At the end of the play, one man's uncompromising quest to bring about change has worked, so the Narrator can be joyful about that achievement. The rest of the people may be slow to move, which brings the Narrator sadness, but change of such magnitude comes about slowly.

A telling moment in the play is the silence which terminates the speech of the Narrator. Why does he remain incapable of speech, mute, at the end? Has he exhausted himself, with nothing more to add to what has already been said? In a 1966 article on silence, Susan Sontag, an American writer, filmmaker, academic, political activist, notes the significance of silence to modern art: "Silence remains, inescapably, a form of speech (in many instances, of complaint or indictment) and an element in a dialogue" (5). The Narrator's silence, thus, is pregnant with meaning. He has been talking in different places throughout the play, but his message remains unheard. By breaking communication, he indicts his audience and the characters, especially those who are inclined to inaction. Yet silence can also offer the audience a chance to process the information received from a work of art or as Sontag phrases it, "[s]ilence keeps things 'open'" (11). In keeping quiet, the Narrator gives the audience the chance to digest what has been said.

In *Gods in the Ivory Tower*, Ndi uses his protagonist's isolation at the margins of society to reveal the constructive use of alienation. What to others may be undesirable and lead to anxiety becomes for Ngwa the very means of liberation—thanks to the foresight of his father. Thus not belonging does not have to incite fear and apprehension about the future. As Bjornson and Irele note, alienation, then, becomes indispensable to change, giving those who take the opportunity to rethink their options a chance to chart a new course, as Ngwa does in the play. The rest of society, though, must be willing to make a break with the past, or they will be imprisoned by their fears of not belonging. This paralysis at the hands of their environment exacts a tremendous cost which imposes on the African nothing but estrangement.

Works Cited

Asaah, Augustine H. "To Speak or Not to Speak With the Whole Mouth: Textualization of Taboo Subjects in Europhone African Literature." *Journal of Black Studies* (March 2006): 497-514. Web. 7 Jan. 2013.

Bjornson, Richard. "Alienation and Disalienation: Themes of Yesterday, Promises of Tomorrow." Mudimbe 147-156.

Echu, George. "The Language Question in Cameroon." *Linguistik Online* 18.1 (2004). Web. 6 Aug. 2013.

Irele, Abiola. "In Praise of Alienation." Mudimbe 201-224.

Mudimbe, V. Y. ed. *The Surreptitious Speech: Présence Africaine and the Politics of Otherness 1947-1987*. Chicago: The U of Chicago P, 1992. Print.

Ndi, Bill F. *Gods in the Ivory Towers*. Bloomington, IN: Author House, 2008. Print.

Nyamnjoh, Francis B. "Cameroon: A Country United by Ethnic Ambition and Difference." *African Affairs* 98.390 (1998): 101-118. JSTOR. 7 Jan. 2013.

Ojo-Ade, Femi. "Of Culture, Commitment, and Construction: Reflections on African Literature." *Transition* 51 (1991): 4-24. JSTOR, 5 Feb. 2013.

Saïd, Edward W. *Representations of the Intellectual*. New York: Vintage Books, 1996. Web. 5 Feb. 2013.

Sontag, Susan. "The Aesthetics of Silence." Web. 2 Sept. 2013.

Section III:
Strangers at Home and Abroad

Chapter 8

A Costly Gift to the Receiver: Francis B. Nyamnjoh and the Alienation of the African

By
Benjamin Hart Fishkin

In the eighteen forties, when Benjamin Disraeli looked at the social degeneration of Great Britain in *Sybil*, he came to the conclusion that the nation was in serious trouble. Society had become polarized and underneath the appearance of prosperity were sharp economic and social divisions. England had become "Two Nations" and these fault lines, if unchecked, could literally break the nation in halves. What's more, these separate halves of rich and poor had little or no awareness of how the other half lived. Each was "as ignorant of the other's habits, thoughts, and feelings, as if they were in different time zones or inhabitants of different planets" (96). Life in modern Cameroon is equally perilous, but it is not for a fundamental lack of knowledge. Everyone knows all too well about the hypocrisy that has permeated every crevice of the capital city, Yaoundé, but all are too petrified to give voice to their criticisms.

Whether a Cameroonian belongs West or East of the River Moungo, it is clear that his or her success and survival are dependent upon a debilitating form of self-censorship. People hold back their innermost thoughts, and they are not all full-fledged members of the nation. The novel *Mind Searching by Francis B. Nyamnjoh* tells us of a wayward persistence in which the powers that be trudge on blindly in precisely the wrong direction. Those embedded within the system are selfish and mistrustful of outsiders. Those who are outsiders must desperately endure the unjustifiable caprices of "nitwitted leaders" (19). The well-to-do have western-style homes with fences around them. The impoverished who cannot see into the homes of the wealthy are not even worth their surveillance.

How did the country get here? Francis B. Nyamnjoh's tracing of Judascious Fanda Yanda is like the medieval play *Everyman* with Fanda Yanda showing us the ills that are all around him. In *Everyman*, God forthrightly tells the audience that people are not living right. When one is dead he/she does not take anything but his/her soul. Six hundred years ago people thought only of worldly riches and that is still the problem. *Mind Searching* updates the morality play as Fanda Yanda begins his censure in the church, telling all about the men who attend Sunday Mass "to honour their appointments with young women" (4). Instead of representations of genuine people, Nyamnjoh's poetic world shows only their flaws, and these are very old flaws.

The question is why are these flaws only being seen now? Aren't these the types of problems that should have been gone with the wind of Cameroon's independence from France and Great Britain? In *Mind Searching*, a sociological and ethnological study of modern Cameroon, Nyamnjoh reveals the frustration of a people who do not know if their collective identity lies in their colonial past, their ensnared present or their cultural future. They cannot even count on their priests. The hero, the "Everyman" within the church service, is a distinguished senior lecturer in sociology named "Dr. B." Just as Socrates prided himself on being a gadfly by posing upsetting or novel questions, Dr. B. reprimands Africans for being "carried away by every passing wind" (6). If the parishioner is a sheep within a flock, Dr. B. points out that sheep also possess less than desirable qualities and that is what is going on here. People seem not to know who they are. The Westerners have not left town. Postcolonial Africa is, in many ways, a political, social, cultural, economic, philosophical and historical misnomer. *Mind Searching* tells us that religion has "survived both the destruction of colonialism and the authentication of Africa" (8). This type of commentary is intended to be humorous because neither of these results has been realized. There is little camaraderie between the citizens. The nation has two marked linguistic divisions: French and English. The English and French speaking regions of the nation comprise a house divided against itself along inherited colonial linguistic lines. The Gospel of Mark, however famous it may be, has not reached Nyamnjoh's characters—most of who pride themselves as being devout Christians.

The rapidly forming question is why does Nyamnjoh even bother to address these problems? Surely, everyone knows that hypocrisy is part and parcel of the human condition. What *Mind Searching* does is wonder at the degree of such reckless lawlessness. The novelist recoils in horror at the gap between how things should be and how they actually are. There is no prescribed path for an orderly and efficiently running society. Those who take leading action are shouted down at and hounded into obscurity. The system is so fundamentally inefficient that people do not even pretend that there is or ever will be equity in their lifetime. Cameroonians have become "a beggarly bunch, desperados, doing all to survive right in the midst of affluence which seems, somehow, always to loom beyond the reach of the common folk" (Doh 17). In this elaborate pantomime, the average Cameroonian citizen must employ silence and judicious decision-making to negotiate the chaos, some would say the stranglehold, of national politics and globalization.

The mentally and morally confusing question is where do these seeds of discontent come from? According to Emmanuel Fru Doh, a Cameroonian born scholar who has left Cameroon and resides in the United States, this is explicated by the fact that revenue streams rarely flow into the national ocean (4). It is clear to Doh that imperialism has damaged and still continues to damage the nation to the point where there are so many problems that no one knows what to fix first. A once financially successful nation struggles unnecessarily. This is not a criticism of modern capitalism, but a lament of checks and balances that have broken down and rendered the skilled improvisationalist — the person who has no steady nine to five job, but must survive on the fringes of society — omnipresent. The structure is marked and distinguished by a permeable and porous legal system. If postcolonial Africa is an alleged paradise, the reality is far more worrisome. People on the street have weights attached to their feet in the like of Rousseau's proverbial "man is born free and everywhere he is in chains." Underneath this delusion of democracy in Cameroon lies a bureaucracy devoid of integrity. The resulting drunken sleep is one that is purposely corrupt, incoherent and nonlinear. No career guide can help and none will ever be published. British, French and African components combine to form the political equivalent of a science fiction horror. The nation's problem is an interwoven fabric replete with a series of intertwining threads that none of the disinterested authorities has taken the time to understand, let alone untangle (Doh 59).

While the people are unquestionably elegant and honorable, at the individual level, Cameroonian literature in English is about depreciation and disintegration, in short about Achebe's eponymous *Things Fall Apart*. The nation clutters and scrambles the human predicament. If Cameroon is truly a microcosm of Africa or Africa in miniature, it is enough to make an outsider weep and a national emigrate. Order is absent and Francis B. Nyamnjoh points out in *Mind Searching* that he is "just a nonentity" and, as such, has no power to help change Cameroon (35). He is like most people, and his dream to escape a dystopian society is punctuated by his novel's penchant for taking the perspective of the unnoticed. If it is true that the meek "shall inherit the earth," here is a text for those who are left only to aspire to meekness. The narrator looks to heaven, and I am not discounting the power of prayer, because no one other than God will listen. A true, comprehensive and authoritative direction in instruction—meaning political change—is practically unrealistic. There is no healthy development, and there is no clear national identity that is built from the ground up. The American linguist

Noam Chomsky once stated, "The intellectual tradition is one of servility to power, and if I didn't betray it I'd be ashamed of myself" (*Various Quotes*). In the aforementioned elaborate pantomime, the average citizen in Cameroon must quickly realize not only why he or she is so marginalized, but also why the nation is divided into groups that share only the weather. If the Britain of Disraeli and Charles Dickens was known for its filthy and wretched working conditions, the Cameroon of the twenty-first century is known for its confusion, corruption and its discrepancy of influences.

Nyamnjoh has not betrayed his convictions, but his bold stance has created an intellectual career for himself outside of his country of birth, Cameroon. He is a dissident with the most basic of objections In *Mind Searching*, when Fanda Yanda as a little boy complains to his grandfather that one of the other children has beaten him, the old man replies, "Those are the complexities of the world!" (43). In other words, even basic security is not guaranteed. No one cares about you. The famous Blues lyric of B.B. King states that "Nobody loves me but my mother..." but does not omit the refrain that "she could be jivin' too." The novel is one part informative track and three parts desolate lament for the rudimentary freedoms that do not exist in Cameroon, where "[t]o succeed to the throne of a king, one needs inordinate ambition, a dead conscience, an assassin, a God-sent opportunity, a lie and a malleable people" (44). Is it any wonder that Doh and Nyamnjoh as well as many others have left Cameroon? There are many Cameroonian dissidents who live and work overseas. Just in January of 2013, a lobby that refers to itself as Cameroonian Patriots demanded that Biya and his entourage be put out of a lavish Swiss hotel. The delegation, according to the *Africa Review*, spent roughly $ 48, 500.00 per night while the average citizen in Cameroon lives on less than one dollar each day (Web). The President seems more comfortable on vacation in Europe than at home with his people. Is this not the equivalent of Marie Antoinette's "qu'ils aient du gateau" i.e. "Let Them Eat Cake"?

One can almost feel the rage within Nyamnjoh's smooth and intricate text. There is a violent desire to eliminate obsolescence in Africa. Part of this has to do with race where white people have inflicted incalculable damage upon black people worldwide. This is undeniable, but part of this also has to do with the way problems are approached on the ground by Africans themselves. The people simply follow the examples set by their leaders. In Nyamnjoh's *Mind Searching*, "One must not postpone till tomorrow what one can eat today" is a popular saying or slogan (131). It is in keeping with this here-and-now mentality that Paul Biya has reigned with for more than thirty years, a focus on the immediacy. This desire to want things without the patience or discipline to wait for them has created a world of consumers. The enemy of such unwillingness to budget and plan for the future is the sheer indisposition to think. The dominant ideas of how to live and govern are external, but they are adopted too eagerly without the least scrutiny. The author, Nyamnjoh, in a research paper, "Potted Plants in Greenhouses" speaks of values and systems that are "transplanted" from the European world and then refracted on another continent (4). What Cameroon and most African countries fear more than anything else is a thought process that is organic and an educated and independent mind (Baldwin 260).

In the more than fifty years since independence Cameron has been dreaming. Everything is patched up, long-term solutions are quickly dismissed and "Nothing ever seems to get its deserved attention" (Nyamnjoh 19). There are many examples of behaviors that would perplex any outsider. The mere use of languages, which language to use in which location and under what circumstances, is enough to immerse one in a thick and impenetrable fog. Francis B. Nyamnjoh uses *Mind Searching* as a vehicle to talk about what he calls "linguistic cleavages," where French and English battle for dominance and leave the individual to fend for himself or herself (77). His assessment that one linguistic group verbally jousts with another, always "from "a room above" reminds one of adolescents in a schoolyard or territorial battles conducted by domestic household pets. One such instance occured in technical schools in West Cameroon, where English is spoken, but the majority of the teachers recruited to teach was French speaking, and they began to lecture in French. The political scientist Mufor Atanga, in his *The Anglophone Predicament*, tells us that recipients "had no previous knowledge of French" (86). The result of this was that the students had all sorts of difficulty with the examination, the test scores were frighteningly low and technical education in West Cameroon came to a grounding halt. Now surely this is not a question that parallels the riddle of the Sphinx in Thebes. It was very predictable that a student familiar with just the language that the British had imported only after the First World War was going to have trouble learning a lesson in French when still battling with his or her first foreign language. That said, an entire generation of young people miss an opportunity to learn and put these skills to work in a country that desperately needs skilled workers who can build new and fix existing infrastructures.

The culture gravitates towards instant gratification. People have a sense of entitlement to luxuries and material possessions on an individual basis and are reckless when it comes to using power and natural resources for posterity. Other problems that are not mysteries, like actually needing a roof for the church, never, in Nyamnjoh's world, get addressed. There is no personal gain to be had by retrofitting the infrastructure. This is not to say that there are no benefits to African culture—or distinct flaws with European stratagem. However, don't truly spiritual Christians deserve a better place of worship? Surely this should transcend the petty squabbles that make it easy for African countries to be dismissed as nations that are not proactive. Furthermore, if they are not genuinely devoted worshippers does this have some connection to why the parishioners are covered in sawdust? This is a form of mendacity. And Nyamnjoh, critical of it, portrays in *Mind Searching,* the Honourable Vice-Minister who frequently arrives "after the Gospel" and has a special seat reserved down at the front. Isn't the actual problem clear to anyone who is willing to open his or her eyes (26)? Or again, is his reserved seat on the account that he is a generous thinker trying to bribe his way into heaven through thinking?

Mind Searching tells us about a society where misery borders on psychosis and no one has the inner confidence to contradict an omnipresent government that borders on the Orwellian "Big Brother." This is a form of shellshock where the explosion is inside as opposed to outside i.e. implosion. At least a futuristic dystopian tract clearly identified the enemy. A person's mind searching must be "an internal mental process" (38). No one can permit his or her thoughts to become a matter of record. To curry favor with the dictator, everyone must play the game except for the "writer," though Africa is replete with rather than void of praise singers in the names of writers. The writer's refusal makes him an enemy of the state and compromises his liberty. Contrastingly, we see the sycophant of the state. A figure who arrives late to church, leaves early and refuses to kneel is not a political ingenue but a sophisticated and practiced graduate of the actor's studio, the player engaged in the art of survival. But in this circumstance the cabinet member has severely overplayed his part; in his haste to be ceremonial, he fools no one on either side of the altar. In Henrik Ibsen's play *An Enemy of the People*, everyone is terrified of being labeled an enemy of the "system." The Honourable Minister in *Mind Searching* represents such a "system" in which all discord is pushed under the surface. This emerges in Nyamnjoh's own personal brand of what I call effective sarcasm or disingenuous self-deprecation. Thus, Nyamnjoh, in *Mind Searching*, leaves Judascious Fanda Yanda to inform the reader of the minister's unscrupulousness in the passage that follows:

> Oh! Yes! It is now I understand that my mind might make things appear so different from what they really are. Wasn't it

silly of me to expect the impossible from the Honourable V.M? I stay right in the heart of Briqueterie, where there is neither house nor light, but where all is a bustling ghetto that booms with resistant life, defying the threatening cords of overdue death. How can one thus situated imagine such a fantastic an illusion as an address? (65)

The "address" in the last line refers to a postal box for mail delivery. This raises the question of why there isn't a governmental agency with the means and inclination to provide the people of Briqueterie with mail delivery. There are not even letterboxes. Surely the affluent have the latest Western conveniences. The first Post Office was founded in Scotland in 1712—more than three hundred years ago. This is a plan to create inconsistency. The idea is to widen gaps in terms of class and corruption rather than to narrow them. Basic problems, according to Nyamnjoh, are left "unresolved" and the job of *Mind Searching* is to reveal how these inexplicable shortcomings irrevocably alter the average person's thoughts and behaviors (65). If Judascious Fanda Yanda has an impaired reality, the novel reveals why his delusions and hallucinations have overtaken objective reality. The author is presenting a narrative that is chaotic because his surroundings are likewise. This is not the fruit of chance, coincidence or some accident. The fog exists to distract and disorient the human mind from the real problems at hand. There is an artificial conflict between how the mind sees things and how they really are, hence, the book's title, *Mind Searching*.

The search is for why the two gaps have such unbridgeable differences. Life in Cameroon is such that it "might make no sense to readers who are used to…clearly defined themes" (67). It is like a child's shoelace that has been double knotted several times. The poor are simply invisible. At least the autobiographies of Frederick Douglass and Benjamin Franklin honor the humble roots of the narrators. How can individuals apply for a job and begin their rags-to-riches travails, if they cannot easily receive a letter or a telephone call? While a citizen in the physical desert of New Mexico can find a relatively modern computer terminal at the local library in an effort to self-educate, the African in his or her circumstance can only rage internally (if they are so informed) at why they are so menaced by a society that is so byzantine. These sorts of problems are so embedded that there is no easy way of knowing why they have not been fixed. The very basics— an indoor bathroom, light fixtures, reliable bus service and access to easily attainable medical care—are all illusory. They have been since Cameroon's independence slightly more than half century ago.

People in Cameroon (unless they are of the power elite) march to the beat of a drummer that is not their own. It would be easy to say that the director of bands for the Cameroonian Marching Band is Paul Biya, but Biya is now eighty years of age, aloof and happiest overseas than at home. The citizen could easily read one of Franz Kafka's novels to cheer up. No one knows who is calling the tunes, but it is the French who are still paying the piper. *Mind Searching* states outrightly that the best way "to impress your foreign counterparts and friends is by giving them the only precious stones that can earn your country some foreign reserve..." (51). Having a foreign reserve is not compulsory. Nor is currying favor by sending silly souvenirs far away. Perpetuating a circumstance based on debt and dependence is offensive to decency. Francis B. Nyamnjoh uses his text to explain why publicly everyone is so nonchalant yet privately so miserable. The current situation requires a rebellion or a revolution, but the people are too frustrated, greedy, self-centered, and cannot even talk to each other. People's bodies are in a jail without walls and only their minds are free. However, one might still question, how free? Now that time has passed since the nation was freed of its colonial yoke, it needs a literature that is thoroughly its own. This possibility of free thought and change, a shared intellectual independence, is what so terrifies the well connected. Well, what is the chance or possibility of developing free thought and change and / or a shared intellectual independence in a nation that has never attempted "to develop an indigenous homogenous system" (Atanga 168). The nation is split down the center on any subject of importance. This includes all the administrative areas and the educational system. Similarly to what is said about large cities, one can be absolutely alone while literally surrounded by people with similar concerns.

Cameroon is a Democratic post-colonial state in name only. This is accomplished not by clear rules and regulations but by obfuscation and a bifurcated national consciousness. Opacity seems to be everywhere, especially in the world of Post-Independence Cameroonian Public Service. Many of the roadways constructed in the days of West Cameroon have been neglected (Atanga 97). According to *Mind Searching*, "... they are not streets in the real sense of the word. They happen to be footpaths which have gradually broadened up through the years. Everything in Briqueterie is muddled up" (64). The use of the Dickensian term "muddle" is tellingly appropriate as it describes a mystery or problem that has no answer or solution. Cameroon is a mix up, an untidy mess or confusion in which people do not know what they are doing or why they are doing it. If nothing else, *Mind Searching* is a tale of upheaval, where things will never be as they once were. This sense of quiet desperation bleeds into every facet of the citizenry. The government has let education deteriorate to the point that "the responsibility passed on solely to parents..." who had other pressing problems to deal with such as keeping their families together (Atanga 86). In "Cameroon: A Country United by Ethnic Ambition and Difference," Francis B. Nyamnjoh tells us that the "system is interested in nation-deconstruction, not nation building, national disunity, not national unity, disintegration, not integration. It finds comfort in chaos, and makes conviviality a subject mostly of rhetoric" (109). No African nations will be built without lucidity. Such transparency is very difficult when there are both anglophone and francophone regions within a culturally diverse nation. If Cameroon were a family, it would be a "blended" family with each parent bringing to a new union, children begotten with previous partners. That means a different history, a different language and a different literature in the hope that all will coalesce and grow together. Here, there is a total absence of written policy—or at least a written policy that has any realistic bearing on how things are and should be done. Much like a pre-Berlin Wall demolition in East Germany or the former Soviet Union, albeit without the actual violence, there are symbolic threats of harm to anybody who tries to promote single standards of clarity. Anyone who has been to the Department of Motor Vehicles has seen a glimpse of life in Cameroon. However, in an urban center such as Chicago or Los Angeles, one can step "out" of the building. It is a component of modern life, but not modern life itself. Bright people spend their time in an endless queue—a form of purgatory Dante Alighieri never dreamed of.

What is its Genesis? Nyamnjoh, in *Mind Searching* suggests his own playful and flirtatious banter, "I wonder if anyone is free from the feeling there is something wrong with African politicians (41)? He might as well be saying, "I wonder if it will be cold in Wisconsin in January?" A big part of the problem—an intentional occurrence—has to do with the collision of Western values of globalization with the more traditional African conventions including the French and British legacies that all predate the birth of modern Cameroon in 1960- 1961. With regards to the political and economic trends of globalization, Emanuel Fru Doh argues that it is "over-assuming for an outsider to think he or she has mastered a people and their values so well simply because of a number of years spent with them" (5). Not only do the Western overseers battle one another over which culture and which language will dominate the bureaucracy that they themselves have created; the Cameroonians are subordinate to the English subordinates. Someone else gets all of the crumbs of the "national cake" (*Mind Searching* 27). There is an Anglophone minority and a Francophone majority. No one wants a truly successful integration and exchange of ideas. What we have is a turf war where no one has a right even to be present upon the turf itself. The African population has had its own collective identity erased, ignored and violated, while foreigners decide both their fate and their form of government (Atanga xiv – xv). In 1959, Breitinger contends, France "was still controlling Cameroon as a U.N. trusteeship…" (567). Today, things are supposed to be different. *Mind Searching* replays on a continuous loop a melody that haunts the reverie of a bitter and disillusioned people. Prime Minister Ahmadou Ahidjo and later President was a French appointee. Cameroon under his successor, Paul Biya, has witnessed "…all the foreigners, especially from France, owning and managing Cameroonian institutions although there are qualified Cameroonians to own these businesses or fill these positions" (Doh 31). The implication is that the government today is unable to say no to the French. The power and the purse strings (and even the international mail) must run through Paris before they arrive in Cameroon. In an arrangement similar to a Punch and Judy show, Cameroon is a puppet whose neocolonialist roots reach back both chronologically and geographically to a foreign power. If France is a former colonial power, where is the precise line of demarcation between the nation's spheres of influence and that of the nation as a bystander? The impossible to answer question is when does colonialism end?

Like a parent who is too involved in the decisions of his or her now adult progeny, colonization has financial and psychological consequences. The mindset is more important than the money. It is felt in Cameroon, according to Nyamnjoh's *Mind Searching*, that a "Western education is prerequisite to good leadership" (73). This puts the mindset of one nation permanently in the back pocket of the other. Not only does the author not believe the premise—there are severe flaws to Western education—he chastises the African for taking in this message without a question, a bang or even a whimper.

There is an arrogance to presume that there is one type of civilized leadership and that it emanates from one place, and it is a place that you have never been. To question such a philosophy labels one a subversive. This is no different from the thinking of Rudyard Kipling in India more than one hundred years ago. *Mind Searching* points out not only the problem but how long it has been in place. The Africa's self-perception is that of an entity that continues to resist progress. The African postcolonial state, like the Republic of Ireland in James Joyce's *The Portrait of the Artist as a Young Man*, leaves nothing for the young upon whom youth is wasted. The Irish also suffer under the British, awaiting a rebirth in perpetual deferment. The mere passage of time is not the issue as Ireland has been independent for forty *more* years than Cameroon. A Cameroonian may be tempted to leave his village for the land of those who (without invitation) have done the colonizing to his own detriment. The questioning of the youth, in regard to their future, leads to travel. In "Cameroonian Bushfalling: Negotiation of Identity and Belonging in Fiction and Ethnography," Nyamnjoh states that "money is hardly all there is to relationships" (711). This is true, but healthy relationships are not the emphasis. In other words, Cameroonians suffer a double bind. The very fabric of their culture is damaged by a hypocritical and corrupt government that encourages its youth to flee, but the fleeing severs a social and anthropological link to the past. The distance is a price that cannot be measured as a medium of exchange. This has consequences as ties to the family become thinner and thinner. In the pursuit of more money family relationships suffer. The roles are reversed when it comes to financial providers. Children who are in the West become vehicles by which their parents and extended family members demand money. Furthermore, since this is the newfound role of the progeny, to send remittances home through the equivalent of Western Union, why come home at all? In "Cameroonian Bushfalling," Nyamnjoh states that rather than return "to a bleak and jobless future at the margins, most American Wandas elected to stay and make a home in the hunting grounds and farmlands of the United States" (705). The idea is to be away from one's home, away from financial crisis, and in a position to ostentatiously display newfound gain. The depletion of values is not unlike the 1920s America where the display, as opposed to the readiness, is all. The same thing, a misplaced emphasis or greed that is not an African trait, depletes Cameroon of its most powerful resources: its people. This is the same trait that caused generations of Irish to go abroad. It is a mainstay of James Joyce's literary career, and a century later, Nyamnjoh has focused his attention upon the same thing in a different locale. In return for migration is the hope that those who have "bushfallen" will send money back home. For money that cannot be earned within Cameroon's borders, the nation's youth are pushed into voluntary exile. The twenty-six year old who stays in his village in Cameroon is poor, whereas his peer who travels to Europe or North America is distant. The dynamic is such that none can win.

The psychological loss of African customs, values, and creativity renders postcolonial Africa still not free from the yoke of colonization. In Part Two of *Mind Searching*, *the* author states forthrightly that ideas of Cameroon are "forged in Europe and then flown in hot and ready to be put into practice…. How do we expect a plant grown in a test tube to be as firm as one with roots in the soil?" (76). Nyamnjoh points out that this is a relationship that is not about skin color, but about power. It is an unasked for relationship that lasts forever. When a marriage ends in divorce, is there ever any genuine separation when children are involved? This creates all sorts of problems, as it is a machine whose parts do not work together. Either the components work at different speeds from one another or the order of their steps is transposed. However you parse the facts, one thing is for certain: Nyamnjoh's claim in "Potted Plants in Greenhouses" that African cultures are "cut off from their surroundings" erects a barrier between Africa and the African (8). The native has been alienated without knowing how, when or why this has happened. The result is a nation with more than one personality.

The nation is thus left suffering from a kind of split personality disorder. Not only are things not simple and clear, but the frustration embedded within Nyamnjoh's text indicates that no one in Cameroon can remember precisely how things got this way. The desire to consume and display wealth is not an African trait. Still in "Cameroonian Bushfalling" the traveler "displays of the latest consumer gadgets and hard currency" so that he will stand out "like a peacock visible with beautiful feathers" (706). Also, values such as these come from elsewhere and they exist for a purpose. Since the early 1990s, when it became clear that there were real and permanent problems with the Biya regime, Cameroonians have become "the leading asylum seekers in Africa" (704). Bushfallers come to the United States and learn to spend like Americans only to come home during the holidays. The long lost travelers arrive back in his or her home village "Returning home at Christmas…appreciated for their bounty and detested for their arrogance as they step on the toes of rivals"(706). Early in *Mind Searching* Nyamjoh states, "I hate those who give in order to ridicule or show their superiority" (14). Commerce, all too often, takes the place of thought. Foreign customs take the place of clothing, language, and education. The result is a lack of belonging, albeit one that is self-inflicted and brought about by freewill. African Presidents, for all their talk of national pride and unity, "prefer to beg and bank in foreign currencies—ignoring even bank notes that bear their own faces and stamp of omnipotence" as Nyamnjoh suggests in "Potted Plants In Greenhouses" (9). Paul Biya spends a great deal of his time away from Cameroon's capital, Yaoundé. Why is it surprising that every student will do all he or she can to leave the country? Is it any wonder that the paths of thought, scholarship and professional advancement follow the course cleared by the franc, Euro, Pound, or Dollar?

Experience tells each and every one of us that we (Africans or those who believe in genuine independence) have been fooled. *Mind Searching* questions why it is that "Briqueterie is down in a valley while Bastos is situated on an elevated plateau…" and he does not come up with a clearly stated coherent answer (101). Nyamnjoh's reader must look behind the lines, beneath his sarcasm and between his clever irony for answers. Neither the nation's research nor its politics emanate from any transparent deductive thought. The novel excavates and unearths the consequences of this informational deficit. The practice since independence has been anything but self-supportive.

Cameroon has an active secret police. The title of this paramilitary unit, the Bureau de Recherche, illustrates the connection between intellectual thought and a regime bent on censorship. According to *Mind Searching*, it surprises no one that, "[w]hen the secret police raid in search of subversives, everyone is affected" (102). Cameroon is supposed to have more than one political party, but it does not, in spite of the more than two hundred registered political parties. Cameroon used to have more than ten independent newspapers at the time of the nation's independence from the French and the British, but it does not. This has to do with the passage of the press law in December of 1966 (Breitinger 558). Cameroon is supposed to have more than one advanced printing press, what Eckhard Breitinger calls SOPECAM, but it does not (565). As a result, controversial works that should be SOPECAM imprints, like René Philombe's *L'Ancien Maquisard* will never be printed. The publication of *L'Ancien Maquisard* has been delayed for ten years or more, much like the works of Mikhail Bakhtin in the former Soviet Union.

African leaders do not encourage uninterrupted information. They are not interested in the ideas of their own people. Like supply-side economics, the ideas that come to Africa "trickle down" from the West in an uneven and perfectly calibrated relationship. Allegedly, Eleanor Roosevelt is often quoted to have once said, "No one can make you feel inferior without your consent". Africans, specifically Cameroonians, seem to have granted this proxy willingly. There is little protest and too much eagerness in learning a thought process that renders one a second-class citizen in his or her own country. Intellectual thought that challenges is not valued as scholarship. The University of Buea has a library without a budget for buying books or academic journals. Instead the university relies on the benevolence of individuals and thus "…became a cultural toxic dumping site for unwanted and obsolete literature…" as highlighted by Nantang B. Jua and Francis B. Nyamnjoh in "Scholarship Production in Cameroon: Interrogating a Recession" (55).

A real thinker who wants to read, write, and think freely has no up-to-date resources and also has all sorts of obstacles to overcome. Current literature is repressed. Scholarly conferences are not attended. Critical voices in Cameroon are silenced. Nantang B. Jua and Francis B. Nyamnjoh state that "human relations are privileged over science…" (62). This means that no meaningful objective work is produced. By isolating himself or herself, an African scholar cannot compete with one in the West, and by subtraction, this is the source of any true academic work. The best students look to the academic equivalent of bushfalling and try to leave the country to bypass the impasse at home. The biggest problem is that the intellectual needs of the typical African are not being met or even listened to. The national finds himself increasingly a spectator in a land where someone else decides what justice is as well as what sedition is.

Judascious Fanda Yanda in Nyamnjoh's *Mind Searching* is so frustrated with his country, Cameroon, that it is a miracle that he does not erupt, spewing volcanic ash. The narrator's first name is likely a play on the word "judicious" for he is always calming himself down and conveying details in a writing style that would offend no one. The rhetorical style constantly disarms itself with phrases like "I am so silly" or "I am so foolish" to mask and conceal heat. Nyamnjoh borrows liberally from Falstaff in Shakespeare's *Henry IV Part I* who says, "The better part of valor is discretion" by attempting to appear passive (5.4. 118). This is how the alienated African is pushed into a form of self-censorship to avoid reprisals as an intellectual. He calls himself a "Chameleon," and surely this is a testament to how he deals with the twists and turns of the nation's political climate (3). *Mind Searching* reveals the perpetual tragedy of a nation that muzzles its best and brightest into silence. The worst thing a person can do is speak his or her mind. Everyone Fanda Yanda encounters is similarly trapped and is always under surveillance. Like a modern-day Icarus, he tries to fly above the labyrinth of hypocrisy, corruption, and triple talk.

Intellectuals in *Mind Searching* as well as in Nyamnjoh's other works seem to have it the worst as they try to solve problems that others would prefer remain unsolved. When Cameroon had its first multi-candidate presidential election on October 11, 1992, it was open in name only (Breitinger 557). Paul Biya remained in power despite all sorts of doubts about his legitimacy and fears that his stay would lead to an outright civil war. Genuinely kind people are not able to exchange ideas openly and cannot be truly supportive of the citizens themselves. Any study dealing with "sensitive political overtures" is marginalized or censored (Jua and Nyamnjoh 57). Thinkers are likely to become part of the diaspora or worse. The few who do feel this way, and vocalize it are divided from one another and easily trampled upon by others who are thinking of themselves and not the country as a whole. With its best underrepresented, Nyamnjoh's fear is that these very figures will be subject to erasure and that there will be no reconstruction no matter how great or desperate the need. He even goes as far as to pointing out in *Mind Searching* that it is widely thought that, "every Sunday, there is at least one member of the congregation with a walkie-talkie, gathering intelligence on and measuring the level of subversion in the rest of the faithful" (126). The interchangeability of "subversion" and "faithful" is surely an oxymoron and enough to tell any outsider that it is impossible to know which way is up. Even being in the right place, at the right time, can place one on an enemies' list and end one's career before it has begun. *Mind Searching's* portrayals of social dysfunction are so bleak that it is only some sort of implosion south of the Sahara that can treat this pathology.

A large portion of this internal ailment as made evident by Doh is that "what Cameroonians wanted on the eve of their independence was of little consequence" (12). In other words the African nations in such predicaments are crashing by design. There is a direct relationship between Cameroon's dependence on France and Nyamnjoh's bewildering appraisal of economic, political, social and cultural problems in Cameroon in *Mind Searching*. In a very real sense, if someone in Paris sneezes, then someone in the great African capital city catches a cold. This is not a relationship of equal partners any more than the Head Chef at a fancy Five-Star restaurant is on par with the Head Waiter. This uneven scale has been a problem for many years. The former colony continues to be a captive audience with French hands manipulating the marionettes that take orders, but are never in a position to make demands. Mismanagement, and not ill fortune nor outright nonchalance, is the culprit. Nyamnjoh's complaints are that he is surrounded by a bureaucracy characterized by exploitative criminals totally disconnected from the reality of the citizens they are supposed to govern. He states that "[s]ome however argue that only a mad fool who grossly ignores the realities of Cameroon would expect the Honourable V.M. [Vice Minister] to behave with integrity. 'Isn't he there,' they would ask, 'to fill his pockets with bits and pieces of the national cake by playing down radical criticisms?" (36 – 37). There are resources in abundance, but these goods are greedily and shamelessly stolen without remorse. A truly candid critic, if he or she values self-preservation, will keep his or her mental agility to himself and pretend that what has happened to his or her once solid and profitable country is a mirage.

Works Cited

Atanga, Mufor. *The Anglophone Cameroon Predicament*. Mankon, Bamenda : Langaa RPCIG, 2011. Print.
Baldwin, James. *The Price of the Ticket*. New York : St. Martins, 1985. Print.
Breitinger, Eckhard. "'Lamentations Patriotiques': Writers, Censors and Politics in Cameroon" *African Affairs* 92. 369 (Oct. 1993): 557 – 575. Print.
Chomsky, Noam. *Various Quotes*. Web. July 2013.
Disraeli, Benjamin. *Sybil: Or the Two Nations*. London: Penguin Books, 1985. Print
Doh, Emmanuel Fru. *Africa's Political Wastelands: the Bastardization of Cameroon*. Mankon, Bamenda: Langaa RPCIG, 2008. Print.
Jua, Nantang B., and Francis B. Nyamnjoh "Scholarship Production in Cameroon: Interrogating a Recession." Spec. issue of African *Studies Review* 45. 2 (Sept. 2002): 49-71. Print.
Nyamnjoh, Francis B. "Cameroonian Bushfalling: Negotiation of Identity and Belonging in Fiction and Ethnography." American *Ethnologist* 38.4 (Nov. 2011):701 – 713. Print.
_____. "A Country Unified by The Ambition and Difference." *African Affairs* 98. 390 (Jan. 1999): 101 – 118. Print.
Nyamnjoh, Francis B.. *Married But Available*. Mankon, Bamenda : Langaa RPCIG, 2009. Print.
_____. *Mind Searching*. Mankon, Bamenda: Langaa RPCIG, 2007, 2nd Edition. Print.
_____. "'Potted Plants in Greenhouses': A Critical Reflection on the Resilience of Colonial Education in Africa." *Journal of Asian and African Studies* 47.2 (2012): 129-154.
Roosevelt, Eleanor. *This Is My Story*. New York: Harper, 1937. Print.

Shakespeare, William. *Henry IV: Part One*. Baltimore: Penguin Books, 1957. Print.

Timchia, Yuh, "Cameroon Lobbyists want Biya Evicted from Geneva Hotel" *Africa Review,* Web. January 2013.

Chapter 9

Willful and/or Imposed Alienation in Recent African Emigration Narratives: Chimamanda Adichie's *The Thing Around Your Neck,* Fatou Diome's *Le Ventre de l'Atlantique,* and Henri Lopes's *Une enfant de Poto-Poto*

By
Robert Alvin Miller and Gloria Nne Onyeoziri

In discussing the notion of alienation in a West Indian context, Alain Brossat and Daniel Maragnès explain that

> often, in its development, we see the word "alienation" slip discretely from the classic meaning conferred on it by German philosophy (Entfremdung: the fact of being a stranger to oneself) to the sense of madness or mental illness. Everyone knows that Fanon was a psychiatrist and that his training influenced his views on the colonized, leading him to detect in the latter's behavior attitudes that he considered neurotic if not psychotic. (27)[21]

As Brossat and Maragnès go on to question the validity of applying a psychiatric concept of alienation to West Indian culture in general, their observation reminds us of the need to understand the varied and changing ways in which people become strangers to themselves.

As African writers become increasingly aware of the fact that the everyday experience of Africans is played out in a world where emigration to destinations in Europe and North America is a

---

[21] All translations from French in this study are ours.

common part of life, narratives focusing on the lives and witnesses of Africans living out their cultural identity in foreign cultural contexts are becoming more and more frequent. These are no longer the narratives of alienation and return, the "Ambiguous Adventures" of the early post-colonial period: the sense of radical separation between the native land and the foreign metropolis has been blurred by new forms of communication and new obstacles to "*enracinement*," forcing a new generation of African writers to reconceptualize the experiences of alienation of African men and women leaving their countries of birth. Alienation from one's community of origins becomes more of a negotiation, a game of frustration, deception and misunderstanding than an absolute existential rupture.

At the same time, alienation from and within the new community is becoming more complex and multi-faceted, involving not only rejection by that new community but also betrayal by the very people one imagines to be the closest representatives of one's origins. In the world of African Emigration narrative in the early 21st century, characters' cultural assumptions about the metropolis are confused with crumbling assumptions about themselves and those closest to them. Old languages compete in new contexts; futures and destinies get lost in a maze of conflicting and contradictory claims to cultural identity and moral value. None of the authors discussed in this study suggests, however, that this moral-cultural confusion occurs in a brave new world of reciprocal global acceptance: old forms of prejudice and systemic exclusion continue to find their place in the magma of changing experience.

Fatou Diome's *Le Ventre de l'Atlantique*, Henri Lopes's *Une Enfant de Poto-Poto* and Chimamanda Ngozi Adichie's collection of short stories *The Thing Around Your Neck*, all reflect these changes in African emigration narratives, but with remarkable diversity of style and political perspective. Careful study of this diversity will lead us to the conclusion that the history of African communities is being rewritten in newly imagined spaces of alienation and conflicted memory.

As a major new Nigerian novelist, Chimamanda Adichie has been placed by Susan Andrade in the tradition of African women writers who tell politically significant stories through family narratives: "Like novels by Nwapa, Emecheta, Bâ, and others, Adichie's novels represent a politics of the family while quietly but clearly telling stories of the nation" (91). Andrade goes on, however, to suggest that Adichie also represents a significant change in that she is prepared to "represent national imagery more directly" (92). This becomes, in Adichie's first novel *Purple Hibiscus,* an explicit juxtaposition of a private pater familias and a public persona: "By thematizing the schism between public and private, making the public man the opposite of the private monster, Adichie makes a simple correspondence impossible; the metaphor moves from out to in, and yet the interpenetration of the spheres is reemphasized" (99). The short story format of *The Thing Around Your Neck* allows Adichie not only to explore national issues such as dictatorship, police brutality and violence but also to broaden the spectrum of forms of oppression within family structures. At the same time, many of the stories in the collection are premised on the understanding that the daily realities of both family and nation in the Africa of the twenty-first century spread beyond national borders.

Referring to two of the short stories of *The Thing Around Your Neck* ("Imitation" and "The Arrangers of Marriage"), we will consider how Adichie traces variations on the alienation of Nigerian women emigrants living in the United States of America. The male characters represented have fashioned their own stereotyped narratives of adaptation and power in which the female protagonist has been given an assigned role she has gradually become unable or unwilling to act out. It is the protagonist's reflection on this resistance that forms the discursive material of Adichie's own implicitly ironic commentary on emigration narratives and their claim to cultural authenticity. In both texts there appears to be a direct connection between a failed or dysfunctional marriage contract and the way that the emigration narratives are interpreted by the narrator and the protagonist.

Chinaza, the protagonist/narrator of "The Arrangers of Marriage," has been pushed by the aunt and uncle who had cared for her after her parents' untimely death to accept a marriage proposal from a Nigerian medical student living in Brooklyn. When she arrives to join her husband, she is met with his maniacal drive to wipe out everything Nigerian about her identity, speech, culinary practices and thinking. Her name is forcibly changed from Chinaza to Agatha, she is discouraged from using any form of Igbo and even taught to greet in American ways. Her husband, Ofodile, demonstrates an obsessive fear of failing as an immigrant in America by missing out on the "mainstream" of the host country's consumer culture. While Chinaza is hardly enamored of the new culture she is being forced to ingest at an accelerated rate, she continues to acquiesce as layer after layer of her way of life is stripped away, not out of any romantic or physical attachment to Ofodile, but out of a sense of duty toward her surrogate parents who perceived her marriage and emigration as a form of redemption as much for themselves as for Chinaza herself. The acculturation contract seems to fall through when Chinaza discovers that Ofodile had previously married an American woman for immigration purposes and is now caught up in an awkward divorce procedure. Chinaza tries to move out with the vague intention of making it on her own, but soon realizes the practical necessity of staying with Ofodile, at least for a time.

Two forms of alienation are brought together in an uncomfortable and precarious marriage of convenience: Ofodile's frantic rush to shed all signs of cultural identity and Chinaza's gradual acquiescence to an arranged existence over-determined by cultural obligations, sexual subalternity and self-imposed silence. When Chinaza does protest her not being told about the previous marriage,

Ofodile responds by reminding her that her guardians and Nigeria's economic problems actually dictated her submission to the marriage in any case. When he explains that he chose her simply because her lighter skin held the promise of lighter skinned off-spring who would fare better in America, she describes her reaction suggestively: "I watched him eat the rest of the batter-covered chicken, and I noticed that he did not finish chewing before he took a sip of water" (184). The batter-covered chicken is a sign of Ofodile's "Americanity" that continues to evoke a psycho-somatic disgust in Chinaza's mind and body because she has never been a willing partner to his alienating version of the American dream. At this point, she goes one step further in allowing herself to look at his body as an alienated object, a being that functions as a human being but in fact only parades itself before her as a moving mass of unsightly gestures.

In case one might think that Adichie's representation of alienation centers exclusively on Africans pursuing American dreams at the expense of their "African identity," "Imitation" offers a very different version of the narrative of Nigerian women immigrating to America for Nigerian husbands. Nkem's husband Obiora is a rising Nigerian entrepreneur who buys a fine house in Philadelphia for his wife and children while residing in Lagos most of the year in order to pursue lucrative federal contracts. The arrangement has elevated Nkem from her lower class origins, and she has become accustomed to what she herself sees as the comforts and conveniences of her new American life-style. It is only when a friend informs her that Obiora is openly keeping a mistress in Lagos that Nkem becomes disillusioned. She turns cold in regard to what she had previously taken to be a felicitous marriage. As she announces to Obiora her decision to return to Lagos with the "Americanized" children, the narrator leaves us with the kind of ambiguous and doubtful conclusion that Adichie often chooses: "There is nothing left to talk about, Nkem knows; it is done" (42). We cannot know for sure if what is done is her marriage or simply the old illusion of a functional family covering an inherently dysfunctional mode of existence. What we can surmise is that in her act of rebellion itself, Nkem is demonstrating to what extent she has come to understand the dimensions of the imitation of self that her relationship with Obiora represents.

In many ways Obiora seems to represent an exact opposite to Ofodile's obsession with the American Dream. The narrator views him as one of those Nigerians who avoid living in the USA where they would not be treated as "Big Men." He clearly sees Americans as ignorant outsiders incapable of understanding Nigerian culture. He is highly conscious of both the riches of Nigerian cultural heritage and the historical reality that Nigeria was plundered by Europeans to fill the museums of the world. His art collecting is seeking to move from an initial level of imitation (a position he justifies by attributing the lack of "original" Nigerian art to colonial plundering) to a level of ownership where he approaches, little by little, the original artistic creation:

> After dinner, Nkem sits on the bed and examines the Ife bronze head, which Obiora has told her is actually made of brass. It is stained, life-size, turbaned. It is the first original Obiora has brought.
> "We'll have to be very careful with this one," he says.
> "An original," she says, surprised, running her hand over the parallel incisions on the face.
> "Some of them date back to the eleventh century." He sits next to her to take off his shoes. His voice is high, excited. "But this one is eighteenth-century. Amazing. Definitely worth the cost." (39)

As she listens to her husband, Nkem might wonder if his rising economic power has led him to acquire more prestigious women as well as statues. She is painfully self-conscious of the class differences between them. She also sees through the contradictions of seeking to valorize traditional culture through commercial transactions while ignoring the human imperfections embedded in all historical cultures. Thus she reminds Obiora that he had told her that the mask makers "killed people so they could get human heads to bury the king" (39).

Although Nkem may have more readily become acclimatized to life as an emigrant than Chinaza, the two women are far from being opposing figures. Whereas Chinaza reacts negatively to her husband's obsession with imitating all things American, including fraudulent behavior if necessary, Nkem suddenly realizes that her proud, politically conscious husband, so enthusiastic in his desire to possess the signs of authentic culture, is as much an imitation as the cheap imitation statues that her American neighbors shop for in pursuit of exotic African art. Nkem questions her husband's glorification of a Nigerian past not only because of the doubtful nature of cultural icons and idealized pre-colonial narratives, but also because he is asking her to sacrifice her identity as a Nigerian woman to complete his trophy collection of symbols of success. Her demand to return to Lagos is less a rejection of emigration than a refusal to be an imitation among imitations. America, for both Chinaza and Nkem, is neither a new land of opportunity nor a place of exile. It is something closer to the mythical and ultimately deceptive backdrop of a struggle with family, gender and class exploitation that, though they apparently cannot win in the immediate, the young exiled African women Adichie imagines are not willing to lose either.

The implicit irony of impasse that we have met in Adichie's characters such as Chinaza and Nkem turns to incisive reflection and analysis in the narrative voice of Salie, the narrator-protagonist of Fatou Diome's *Le Ventre de l'Atlantique*. Dominic Thomas underlines the fact that Diome's novel renews and reframes the tradition surrounding the alienation experienced by Africans coming into contact with metropolitan colonial cultures:

> Whereas writers during the colonial era such as Ousmane Socé, Cheikh Hamidou Kane, and Bernard Dadié (all of whom Diome alludes to in her novel) were concerned with the "ambiguous" nature of the cultural encounter with France—initially in colonial schools through the exigencies of the *mission civilisatrice* (civilizing mission) and subsequently through travel to the *métropole*—Diome extends and updates the implications and parameters of her work in order to situate her observations and critique within the contextual framework of a reflection on globalization and its impact on Africa. (244)

In a particularly revealing episode, Salie, who has been living in France for many years and has become a successful writer, recounts one of her infrequent visits to her home on the island of Niodior in southern Senegal. She frames her analysis of the "entre-deux" of the returning emigrant by putting into question the notion of the rootedness of native origins:

> Irresistible is the desire to return to one's source, because it's reassuring to think that life remains easier to grasp in the place where it has sunk its roots. Yet, for me, returning amounts to the same thing as leaving. I go home as one would go to a foreign country, since I have become the other for those that I still call family. (166)

Salie's sense of alienation, however, is not a simple, straightforward ostracism or rejection: her self-described predicament is far from that of a Samba Diallo in Kane's *Aventure ambiguë*. Her position is built around complex and, all too often, contradictory contemporary emigration problems that implicate both her own sense of estrangement and evolving, though sometimes persistent, problems within the society of "home".

Salie begins her narrative of return with a reflection on the multiple motivations of the many residents of Niodior who come to join the "killing of the fatted calf," the generous dinner parties celebrating her visit from overseas, of course, at her own expense. Acknowledging the fact that many people come simply to enjoy a free meal, she notes how communal ideology, with its assumptions of entitlement, even when that entitlement is paid for by individuals who are no longer truly accepted (if they ever were) as members of the community, trumps decency. Samuel Zadi interprets this turn of communal ideology as a breakdown in traditional values related to the problematic insertion of African communities into globalized market economies:

> The novel in fact takes up the crucial cultural question of the practice of "African solidarity" which in traditional Africa seemed to constitute a source of socio-economic stability, but which has been transformed in postcolonial Africa in to a source of dependency, exploitation and thus socio-economic regression. (171)

But this is a problem that only appears on the surface of globalized waters. According to Salie, the "greatest indecency of the 21st Century" is "an obese West facing a rachitic third world" (167). Neither endorsing the exploitation of an uncritical "communalism" nor willing to forget the global economic inequalities ultimately responsible for the loss of dignity that such exploitation implies, Salie is not just the outsider within; she is the outsider within thinking as an insider, even if that thinking is not understood or is yet to be understood by her neighbors and relatives.

Salie is particularly emphatic as she describes the effects of female solidarity when it isolates a fellow woman who has turned to other lifestyles and economic modes of existence. Although she is painfully aware of being rejected from the tight-knit circles of activity and conversation of the women of the Niodior she returns to visit, she suggests that the arrangement is mutually desirable since it frees her from overwhelming traditional constraints. Salie's narrative calls into question any idealization of belonging to a community of women, not because she denies its existence or even its social necessity, but because she feels that if belonging is not felt spontaneously, it becomes imposed and oppressive. At the same time, she has no illusions that her unusual acceptance in the circle of young men surrounding her brother is a sign of her having escaped the realities of patriarchy:

> In any case, macho from birth, [the young men] saw nothing out of the ordinary in my being able to go against the will of women, even if it included opposing their own mothers. On the other hand, they considered it legitimate to impose their will on me, without it occurring to them that when one is thirsty for freedom one could care less about the gender of the oppressor. (172)

Thus, during the brief hours and days of return without return that Salie spends in the company of young men who value her only as a sign-post pointing to self-exile, she is unable to exert the moral authority that she views herself as possessing as someone who has experienced firsthand the racial prejudice, degradation and marginalization of many Africans living in France. Despite the support of her friend and mentor, the schoolmaster Ndétare, she is faced with the futility of reconciling the returning emigrant's awareness of a racially hierarchical Europe and the aspirant immigrant's dream of change. Although the novel ends (perhaps some would say a little artificially) with a change of heart on the part of Salie's brother who decides to put his energies and talents into succeeding in business at home, there is little to suggest that Salie can ever escape the multidimensional alienation that characterizes her endless passage through circles of familiar, suspicious strangers. She will later draw the conclusion: "Rooted everywhere, always exiled, I am at home where Africa and Europe lose their pride and satisfy themselves with completing each other: on the written page, alloys like the life they left to me" (181-2).

Though there are examples of moments when Salie herself seems to give up any pride of un-belonging, as when she hears the music accompanying the traditional wrestling matches in M'Bour, it is difficult to see anything in Salie's experience of "homecoming" that confirms the existence of such alloys even in her own writing. Yet, the desire to belong does lead her to construct ideas and re-construct memories of stability that often seem to contradict her narrative. Her grandmother, who did indeed help her to survive as an illegitimate offspring rejected by her immediate family, was also, in Salie's own eyes, an ambiguous figure who could be as oppressive as any other member of a hostile community:

> Even my dearest grandmother, to prove her love for me, never stopped murmuring: "To raise an illegitimate child in this village, I had to accept all the dishonor: prove me right, be polite, brave, intelligent, above reproach." To make sure I was all those things, her severity was like her sacrifice: terrible. She didn't just hit, she thrashed. In the village, her punishments that always ended up revealing a biting bitterness beneath her anger were as legendary as her determination to protect me from all adversaries. (226)

Yet, the memory of her grandmother is necessary and unavoidable because, according to Salie herself, freedom amounts to nothing when it is not freedom from someone to whom we are in some way attached.

> [My grandmother] is the lighthouse planted in the belly of the Atlantic to give back, after every storm, a direction to my solitary navigation. […] Sedentary as she is, she is the last port

of call of the ship of my emotions, before it is thrown at random into the terrible immensity of freedom. (190-1)

Both the image of the lighthouse and that of the port differ from the language of rootedness because they do not imply the permanent belonging of the individual, but suggest a claim to shelter, protection and guidance. The lighthouse is also a marker of memory and so enables the new free subject to imagine returns to places that no longer constitute homelands, but seem to promise some measure of security though they fall short of, or steer clear of, any form of belonging.

Before the publication of *Une enfant de Poto-Poto* in 2012, Henri Lopes was already well established as a writer of a decentered, migrant world where displaced African characters struggle to understand their origins and identities, even putting into question sharp distinctions between Africans and others. Vincent Simédoh, discussing previous novels of Lopes such as *Chercheur d'Afriques*, probes further:

> Behind a question of personal identity, we begin to see a reflection on a whole continent. Who is today this African man without a compass, at the crossroads, at the confluence of multiple voices? What does Henri Lopes offer to the African man of today who is searching for traces that could help him find himself in the midst of world history? (3)

Henri Lopes's *Une enfant de Poto-Poto* poses a particularly provocative challenge to the dichotomies of home and exile as well as to the assumption that the most representative figure of African quests of identity would be an "African man." He ironically places his female protagonist's origins in the title of a book that documents her progressive disassociation from Poto-Poto, the popular quarter or neighborhood of a city she can now only claim as a remembered home. Kimia's disassociation is fore-grounded by another figure of paradoxical belonging: she is obsessively attracted to the figure of a white man who bears all the signs (both outward and inward) of a "native" of Brazzaville, so much so that even though he is truly and forcibly pushed into political exile, he maintains a concrete commitment to his African origins that she herself is barely able to emulate. He becomes not only the professor who teaches her the meaning of social and political consciousness through the great texts of African and universal self-affirmation, but also the lover who leads her to wonder about what she values in life and the focus of memory that continually brings her back to a country from which she has chosen to be estranged.

Kimia's alienation is not the product of her having travelled to the United States as a student, nor of her settling there as an academic marrying an African American. These displacements only complete a cultural alienation built into her childhood and upbringing as a member of what she calls the "les enfants dipanda," a generation of Africans who were reaching adulthood in 1960 when their country, among other African countries, became independent. Although they witnessed the birth of a postcolonial state, they were trained to understand themselves as colonial subjects with colonial values.

This training is alluded to early in the novel. For example, when *La Marseillaise* is sung at the independence ceremony, Kimia remarks: "At the sound of *La Marseillaise,* we came to attention. We knew it by heart, *La Marseillaise*. As well as the multiplication table" (11). When a chorus starts to sing the new national anthem, Kimia asks: "What's that thing?" (13). Even as a young woman, Kimia has to have words spoken "en langue" i.e. in an African language translated for her into French. She describes the speech of the first president (l'abbé Youlou) as "a patois as incomprehensible to me as Norwegian, Javanese or Quechua" (15).

But Henri Lopes is too subtle a writer to leave us with such a one-sided portraiture of "les enfants dipanda." In order to dissuade us from accepting the narrator's version as the last word on postcolonial alienation, he pairs her with Pélagie, a classmate in the high-colonial secondary school (le lycée Savorgnan-de-Brazza) where black students are just starting to slowly gain entrance ("au compte-gouttes" i.e. trickling in). Pélagie shares many of Kimia's alienating dreams of "escape" from their homeland:

> For me and Pélagie, it was the country itself that was becoming unbearable. We found ourselves scolding the climate in the same terms that the colonists used to affirm that Equatorial Africa was an accursed country that undermined one's health and the benefits of being an expatriate in that country were not equal to the costs. The only way out of our hell: to earn a scholarship, escape the country, enroll at the Sorbonne. (105)

Yet Pélagie is different from Kimia, or at least Kimia perceives her as being different, not just because she finally settles at home and Kimia does not (as much a result of circumstances as of any politically conscious decision), but because Pélagie comes to understand herself differently as an "enfant dipanda." Pélagie is the first translator who explains the independence ceremony to Kimia and corrects her friend's confusion of names of ethnic groups and languages. While saying little of her own parents, Kimia sees Pélagie's mother as an "illiterate with an innate sense of philosophy" (55). This suggests (perhaps with some condescension) that her friend's family is somehow more "native" than she is.

Although both Kimia and Pélagie succeed in travelling abroad to study, the former in the USA and the latter in France, they are both drawn to their place of origin by their shared attraction (often turning into a bitter rivalry) to their high school and later to university instructor Franceschini. When Pélagie becomes pregnant with what seems to be Franceschini's child, she leads her friend on an equivocal word-game by purposely confusing the word *metis* with the name of an ethnic group *Mbéti* (56) in order to suggest that Franceschini might be the father without clearly saying so.

As the two women continue forming and re-forming liaisons with Franceschini, all the while weaving in and out of exile and homecoming, they both develop (according to Kimia's narrative) a sense of identity that reproduces his discourse and his consciousness. When Pélagie questions Kimia's aspiration to become a writer, Kimia obsessively connects every one of her friend's arguments to Franceschini's influence: "The more I listened to her, the more I believed I was hearing Franceschini's voice" (101). She herself admits as her narrative draws to a close, after his death, "I too am Franceschini" (264).

What is the significance of this rivalry of two women, both capable of telling their own story of alienation and desire of re-attachment? They both spent the prime of their lives in the emulation and pursuit of a man who, according to Kimia "wanted to be of this country. If there had been beauty products to blacken the skin and make the hair kinky, he would have gone bankrupt buying them. At the same time he taught us to become human beings. Of here and of elsewhere" (263). Although one might be tempted to see in this strange imbroglio an affirmation of universal humanism, there is little in the text to support such a straightforward conclusion. Neither Kimia nor Pélagie could be seen as simply alienated beings: they do not lack political consciousness. If anything Kimia is excessively self-conscious, sometimes of her tendency to use Congolese turns of speech in speaking French, sometimes of her pedantry in trying to avoid such expressions. Though she aspires to be a French writer, her original dream is to write a novel called *Une enfant de Poto-Poto* which she ultimately succeeds in doing. Just as Franceschini's most memorable lesson, where he quotes Shylock's "When you prick me do I not bleed" speech from *The Merchant of Venice*, only substituting

Noir for Jew, tricks his students into reassessing the relevance of world culture, Kimia constantly observes herself on the edge of alienation, yet repeatedly drawn into a paradoxical wrestling match for an imagined authenticity with a fellow Congolese woman and a fellow child of independence. Both are slightly compromised by their need to be like the "white man," but if he is not really a "white man" but only the enigma of racial identity, that is not racial identity. Their identification with him can hardly make a case for racial alienation. Sexual alienation perhaps in that being (with) him at some point becomes more important than being themselves, but even that case is not totally clear since they both appropriate his voice without sacrificing their solidarity. The presence of Kimia's American husband at the end of her narrative further suggests that her sexual fascination with Franceschini represents a search for self-understanding rather than an abdication on Kimia's part of her right to sexual fulfillment and stable companionship. As children of independence, they had to forge the meaning of postcolonial being in the world, but they could not do so without coming to terms with their colonial upbringing. By "being Franceschini," the little Frenchman according to Franceschini himself, they do not exactly come to terms with their past, but they do play a surprising game with the most sacred assumptions of cultural belonging such as the primacy of racial and sexual solidarity and the recognizable face of identity.

What questions need to be asked, what assumptions need to be re-visited as we consider the possible implications of the narratives of alienation and emigration of Adichie, Diome and Lopes?

All three authors attribute a central role to women, not simply in the experience of displacement and alienation in the 21st century, but also in the internalized meditation on the relationship between the two. Displacement is not always, in these women's analyses, the sole source of alienation between individuals and communities: it can also be the result of alienation already built into interpersonal relationships or a screen designed to hide the real alienation that both underlies and sometimes escapes the notice of globalizing influences. Chinaza's physical aversion to an American culture that her obsessive African husband is imposing on her, Nkem's discomfort with her place in the collections of authenticity of her patriotic Nigerian husband, Salie's determination to bring self-understanding to her half-brother and his friends even through her own alienation and Kimia's self-conscious struggle with her own attachment to colonial values all reflect a growing charge of doubt as to the origin, meaning and locus of both belonging, and the failure to belong, for Africans in the global world.

The central role attributed in these examples to the inner narrative voice of women may reflect the increasingly important voice of African women authors. It may also suggest that the weight of patriarchy in contemporary forms of alienation is such that women are particularly well placed to think through the underlying contradictions and paradoxes of the present situation. On the other hand, Lopes's complex representation of identification across "boundaries" of gender and racial identity serves as a caution against any hasty election of standard-bearers of new forms of understanding.

Works Cited

Adichie, Chimamanda Ngozi. *The Thing Around Your Neck*. New York: Knopf, 2009. Print.
Andrade, Susan Z. "Adichie's Genealogies: National and Feminine Novels." *Research in African Literatures* 42:2 (2011): 91-101. Print.
Brosset, Alain and Daniel Maragnès. *Les Antilles dans l'impasse*. Paris: Éditions Caribéenes/L'Harrmattan, 1981. Print.
Diome, Fatou. *Le Ventre de l'Atlantique*. Paris: Éditions Anne Carrière, 2003.

Lopes, Henri. *Une Enfant de Poto-Poto*. Paris: Gallimard, 2012. Print.

Simédoh, Vincent. "Henri Lopes: d'une quête incessante à une identité plurielle." *Voix plurielles*. 3.1 (2006): 2-12. Print.

Thomas, Dominic Richard David. "African Youth in the Global Economy: Fatou Diome's *Le ventre de l'Atlantique*." *Comparative Studies of South Asia, Africa and the Middle East* 26. 2 (2006): 243-259. Print.

Zadi, Samuel. "'La Solidarité africaine' dans Le Ventre de l'Atlantique de Fatou Diome." *Nouvelles Études Francophones* 25.1 (2010): 171-188. Print.

Chapter 10

Blighting Companionship: Emmanuel Fru Doh's *The Fire Within*, A Tale of Passion and Alienation

By
Bill F. Ndi

In the micro context of Cameroonian literature, or again in the macro context of African literature, Anglophone Cameroonian Literature (ACL) as an emerging subset brings with it an array of writers. These writers, besides their desire to pursue the traditional trends expressed in the micro and macro contexts of African literature, take the colonial and postcolonial discourse therein to an all new level. In Emmanuel Fru Doh's *The Fire Within,* he broaches on every possible type of alienation imaginable through Mungeu's story: alienation from family, linguistic alienation, powerlessness, meaninglessness, normlessness, cultural estrangement, social isolation, existential and self-estrangement. Emmanuel Fru Doh (EFD) handles this recurrent concern in ACL from a holistic perspective. However, before probing into some of the trends of this emerging literature and the commitment of its writers, having recourse to one of the highlights of literary theory as expressed by Jean-Paul Sartre seems indispensable. Sartre sheds light on what he conceives as literature, most especially one produced in the unsettling kind of society from which ACL writers like EFD hail.

Questioning why writers write in his famous treatise, *What is Literature?* Sartre makes it clear that the reasons vary. Under the chapter "Why Write" Sartre highlights the following:

> Each one has his reasons: for one, art is a flight; for another, a means of conquering. But one can flee into a hermitage, into

madness, into death. One can conquer by arms. Why does it have to be writing, why does one have to manage his escapes and conquests by writing? [...], behind the various aims of authors, there is a deeper and more immediate choice which is common to all of us. (38)

Pursuant to this view on the explicit or implicit reasons for writing, the critical question here is: do ACL writers like EFD conceive writing as an art of flight, conquering, or conscientization? Are there structural, thematic, stylistic, investigative elements and concerns of human existence in their works that would lead one to believe in their works qualifying as committed writing? Are there any historical correlations with their stories? What purpose do the issues of human existence raised in their work serve? And what do they say of the real world and the writer's poetic universe? How does one accommodate a child not his/her biological child, as in *The Fire Within*? This last question is replete with political undertone given that the minority English/British Cameroons appended to *"La République du Cameroun"* faces the same if not worse challenges and harassment than those suffered by Mungeu', EFD's protagonist. One could also pry into the question as to why it should be impossible for any to make plans and follow them through to realization in contemporary Africa in general and Cameroon in particular. Is it that the forces out there are too powerful to be averted? Are they man-made, natural or supernatural? Over and above, it would also be judicious to explore in depth those who people this novelistic universe to account for their conscious or unconscious role in the fate that befalls them. This chapter thus proposes to attempt an answer to these questions and follow up on how they all point towards the writer's resolve to committed writing and conscientization of the oppressed masses made strangers at home.

Structurally, EFD's novel follows a pattern of investigative exposition of ills and evils in the Caramenju society. His title *The Fire*

Within becomes, thus, a metaphor for psychic and physical alienation consuming his people from within. In EFD's prologue, which turns out to be the epilogue of his story, he skillfully draws from the postmodern trend of blurring the margins or again the mathematical theory of intersections in which, at certain points, the margins cease from being margins to becoming the center. The focal point in this prologue is Pa-pa, a marginal character who chooses to occupy the central location in the narrative space, the city of Batemba in the Republic of Caramenju. Not only is Pa-pa at the center of this city, but also he becomes the center (itself) of attraction and discussion among Pa' Anye, Ndomnjie, Yefon and her uncle Dr. Wirghan, a medical practitioner from Sweden.

In Pa-pa's story and plight is embedded the politics of alienation that plagues the writer's fatherland, Cameroon, though in the fictional narrative Caramenju. Both Cameroon and Caramenju do not only share the similarity of having alienation as a burden on the English-speaking citizens, but are social environments given to characters whose predicament would prick any committed writer to decry everything that would push a loveable character like Adey to end up as Pa-pa in a state of acute depression. The lamentations on the lack of psychiatric units in hospitals in the country or the mere mention of the only one in a country purportedly bilingual and where nobody speaks English is telling of the plight of the English-speaking minority Cameroonians as linguistically ppressed. This is a true cause for committed writing as EFD does through one of his characters Yefon: "First of all nobody speaks English there, and so we could barely communicate" (3). This is followed by a description of the treatment the patient received, which is none, in effect. Thus, this leaves the patient and his parents with no choice but prayers. Could EFD just be projecting his emotions on paper (as Sartre suggests) while managing to give them this languishing extension? (42) In this episode as in many elsewhere in the novel, EFD's words are more than this languishing extension. They become, as Sartre posits, paths of transcendence [that] shape feelings and name them as well as attribute them to imaginary personages who take upon themselves to live these feelings for the readers and have no other substance than these borrowed passions.... The writer therefore confers objects, perspectives and a horizon upon these words (45).

EFD's is a very simple storyline, yet this must not be treated with oversimplification. To untangle the storyline, EFD tells the story of a girl, Mungeu', brought up by a stepmother and a father who both, but most especially the stepmother, seem determined to crush any ray of hope in her. Her representation seems to stem from a logic following a process of reasoning akin to the workings of the mind of an observer and critic and not just a spontaneous, irregular firsthand character creation. Through her own determination to make a place for herself in the sun, she volunteers her services in partial payment for her own education at Holy Rosary Home Craft Centre (HRHCC). Upon graduation, she establishes her own business. Unbeknownst to her, she falls prey to the amorous advances of her one-time Economics teacher at the HRHCC, Fon. She gets pregnant, and she is made aware of her pregnancy by her stepsister, Mabel. They both try to handle this delicate and thorny issue of pregnancy with care. Mabel gets involved in a car accident and is evacuated for treatment abroad.

Unable to stand the mistreatment her society inflicts on her as an unmarried pregnant woman and in the absence of her stepsister, Mungeu' leaves the city of Batemba for Njunki. Mungeu' thus cuts herself off from her past, thus alienating herself from what might be called her natural place in the world. At Njunki, she reestablishes her own business once again, and the business thrives. In-between her business trips to neighboring Nigeria, she is involved in an accident that cost her one of her arms. She then resorts to doing business by buying from Batemba to sell at Njunki. During one of these trips to Batemba, she meets Adey and eventually falls in love with him. With Adey, they both give in to their passions at an untimely moment.

Mungeu' becomes pregnant once again. Determined not to keep this child, she opts for an abortion in spite of the resistance she meets from Adey. Adey's objection to the abortion is contained in his fears, doubts and joys of belonging/not belonging. His dire wish is to belong to the circle of fathers/married men. His fears include getting Mungeu' through the same woes that come with having a child out of wedlock, a thing Mungeu' has already experienced. And his joys are found in his finding Mungeu' (his Love) and loving her dearly and in turn having this love reciprocated. Conversely, Mungeu's obstinate insistence on the abortion is nothing but her attempt to spare Adey the trouble (suffered by many a young man caught in a similar situation). However, she fails to take into account the alienating consequences that can be brought about as a result of any accidental death occasioned by an act of abortion. In the process of aborting, she loses her life, yet not before she confesses to Adey and pleads for forgiveness while in her dying bed in hospital.

EFD's tale cages the conscientization of a people through the passion and alienation of the central character, Mungeu', a figment of EFD's imagination. EFD does this "to make an appeal to the reader that he leads into objective existence the revelation [...] undertaken by means of language" (Sartre 46). Besides, this ties up with what Terry Eagleton in theorizing literature and specifically in striving to validate psychoanalysis says of literature:

> It is a crisis of human relationship, and of human personality, as well as social convulsion [...] anxiety, fear of persecution and the fragmentation of the self are experiences [...] found throughout history. (131)

EFD crafts Mungeu' from nothingness to a tragic heroine. She is, from the very beginning, a partial orphan. She loses her mother shortly after she is born and has never had the opportunity of knowing her. This hampers Mungeu's capacity to communicate as she is brought up in a hostile environment that challenges her own sense of self and leaves her with anxiety and fear of persecution. Thus, she is exposed to what Ernest Mandel qualifies as "the ultimate and most tragic form of alienation" i.e. the inability to communicate. (web.)

The pernicious consequence of this is the fact that Mungeu' is brought up on the fringes of her own family and the broader society. In terms of relationship, both her father and stepmother tend to be oblivious to her sufferings. They would rather inflict more sufferings upon her. Unflinching in her determination, Mungeu' develops a strong personality and rises from rags to riches. But had she survived in Caramenju (a poetic space like in EFD's Cameroon) where talents are not allowed to flourish, a critical question would readily be asked: how judicious would it have been for EFD as a writer to allow this to happen? Would it not have been, in a way, defying any logic of narrative realism and commitment? Would this not have been an attempt at growing fruits other than dates in the desert? The heightened emotions and tragedy which close the novel are nothing short of catharsis for the writer.

Like his character, EFD won't stay at home to bear the humiliation of being alienated by those who, out of envy or pure ignorance, would not recognize and reward talents. From birth to death, Mungeu', in spite of episodic success in education and business, seems to know no other life than that of alienation, estrangement and tragedy. In this instance, and in a world so full of seeds of alienation and estrangement, one cannot but question whether successes in education and business are worth anything. Or, again is tragic death the only way out of this social convulsion? EFD's preference for tragedy over the hapless continuation of such a struggle underscores the writer's desire to have readers purge their passions, looking at themselves in total disbelief that this could be happening to them. In sum, the degree of realism, commitment and truth of EFD's narrative thus matches that of "Kafka's mythology which is not given" (Sartre 45) even if Eagleton asserts "an alienated personal identity is confirmed by a 'given' inevitable world" (162).

EFD weaves tragedy in his novel in a typical Hardyan twist. He intensifies the alienation looming in the air for the already estranged Mungeu' who has found favor in her stepsister, Mabel. Through an "estrangement effect" used for political ends (Eagleton 118), EFD sends the latter to a market in a neighboring village, Bansei. On her way back, she is involved in an accident which leaves the reader with a bitter taste in the mouth. The reader cannot but lament Mungeu's loss of her sole source of support that is likely going to leave her exposed to the taunts, torments, humiliation, torture, whims and caprices of an intolerant society hostile to any innocent girl who (by no fault of hers) is untrained in the art of sleeping around with men while avoiding by the same token the crucial/fertile period during which she could become pregnant. The narrator captures this moment very clearly:

> News of Mungeu's pregnancy had already spread around like brush fire. Even Sister Anne-Frances had heard and had personally written a letter to find out from Mungeu' herself if it was true. The talking had been too much with people pointing her out furtively when she went past, while others visited her to find out for themselves whether it was true or not. Their pretext was that they came to find out if she had heard anything about Mabel. It pained Mungeu' to think of how mean people could be, even those girls who slept with men as often as they ate in a day were now talking of how terrible she was, just because she slept with a man once and, because she did not know what to do, got pregnant. Nevertheless, Mungeu' made up her mind that nothing people said was going to bother her. It was true she was pregnant, but she knew she was several times well behaved than most of the girls who went around laughing at her and pretending to be better behaved. Mungeu' wondered if indeed these girls

were mocking the fact that she was pregnant or that she did not know what to do to continue operating like one who had not slept with a man before. [...] she knew she was alone, and alone she meant to face the tide of events coming her way. (35-36)

Hypocrisy here becomes intrinsically linked to alienation and in EFD's world, this results in people prying into other people's private affairs and birthing gossips that leave saints painted as devils and devils made angels. Again most people sleep around, yet when an innocent girl does it once and by accident falls pregnant, she is treated as if she has contracted a deadly contagious disease. This convinces Mungeu' "of the wicked and poisonous nature of humankind as people pried into the affairs of others not to give a helping hand but to gossip and paint a more unfortunate picture of the culprit" (25).

Moreover, the event of pregnancy in EFD's world becomes an alibi to expose a society in which out of wedlock pregnancies are ruthlessly exploited and the treatments meted on such a pregnant woman become a nightmare no woman wants to live in the first instance and worse still relive it. Mungeu' clearly explains why her "so-called parents" are interested in finding the father of her unborn child. He "would be condemned to try and win over my so-called parents by giving them repeated gifts of money and drinks." (37). With this, one cannot help but question if this shockingly unfamiliar rendering of the most-taken-for-granted aspect of socio-political reality of this society (Eagleton 162) is so done for its own sake or to create contradiction within the reader. This estranging literary device becomes for EFD a means to "denaturalize" and "de-familiarize" a political society (Eagleton 118).

EFD does not make of these acts of alienation and estrangement isolated cases here and there in his creative space. It is politically orchestrated and borders on all forms of alienation, including linguistic alienation, which to the author stands on the way of everything that can guarantee a society in which freedom thrives. This springs from EFD's contemplation of a world which is familiar. To clearly highlight how linguistic alienation can be a hindrance to everything as well as an ideological illusion of nationhood, the author does not hesitate to hint at the dominant linguistic code used in the capital city, Nayonde. As a result of the linguistic alienation, it comes as no surprise, be it in EFD's Cameroon or in his imaginative space Caramenju, that beside Pa-pa's challenges as a marginal depressive, the only hospital that could take care of his condition is situated in this capital city wherein to survive and communicate, fluency in French becomes an absolute necessity. It is clear from the prologue that Pa-pa cannot gain any access to treatment only for the simple fact that he cannot communicate in French. It is this worst form of alienation as asserted by Mandel ("Causes of Alienation") that fuels Adey's behavior at Mungeu's funeral. It marks the beginning of his insanity. EFD, through this, unsettles readers' conviction by reshaping and dismantling their received identities while exposing Adey's selfhood as an ideological illusion (Eagleton 162). Does this translate into Adey's passion for his love lost? Far from it. The fire within Adey (Pa-pa) burns with consummating passion, even if the person for whom the flames were lit is no more. This is EFD at best exploring the alienating aspect of death. Pa-pa's condition is occasioned by the parting and the vacuum created by this death, the oppressiveness of the Caramenju political and social structures, which are all EFD's target.

The author's despair and helplessness, in a typical Vaclav Havelian description of postwar Czechoslovakia, are echoed through the dialogue between Yefon and Dr. Wirghan. When informed of the fact that in the whole country, there is only one mental health hospital, Dr. Wirghan does not hide his bewilderment and questions, "So you say there is only one mental health hospital in the whole country?" (3). And Ndomnjie clarifies this by specifying the geographical location and the name of the institution: Centre

Bonaparte in Nayonde. Symbolically, Bonaparte, the grand confiscator of the ideals of the French Revolution, is memorialized with an institution which deprives patients of the ideals of psychological equilibrium just like Napoleon frustrating the efforts and aspirations of the revolutionaries. Hearing all of this and the fact that both men could not even help the young man as a result of their lack of communication skills in the language spoken in Nayonde, Dr. Wirghan's tersely expresses his haplessness as well as that of the multitude of Caramenjuans/Cameroonians in these three words: "what a shame!" (4).

In this vein, the political happenings in the country become ornaments of literary creativity and EFD makes the most use of these. His writing thus becomes a trough of political concerns for the Anglophone Cameroon cause. Creating the sense of nostalgia in his characters, he mentions with sarcasm and mock irony the founding of the United Republic of Caramenju. Historically, the founding of the United Republic of Cameroon in 1972 was no different in its arbitrariness from the founding of the United Republic of Caramenju. EFD using this literary technique to rouse the reader to new critical awareness writes:

> She thought of the days just before the arbitrary establishment of the United Republic of Caramenju when people worked from 8:00 to 3:00 pm straight, with only thirty-minutes of break and wondered who changed those hours that gave one enough time for one's family. (16)

Here, estrangement is made manifest in the change in work culture which leaves the English speaking minority questioning the logic in disrupting the fact that the people of West Caramenju lived in harmony in the past. This working culture was breached by the advent of the arbitrary establishment of the United Republic of

Caramenju and this left people feeling like foreigners in their own country.

EFD does not also miss to seize any opportunity afforded him to castigate the rampant corruption and malpractices in all the echelons of the Caramenjuan society. As in the broader scope of African colonialist and post-colonialist writings looked upon as literature of contestation by Kasteloot in her seminal 1967 publication, ACL distinguishes itself in its form of contestation as does EFD here in tackling issues of everyday life in a country plagued by alienation of its English speaking minority. Alienation in EFD's world mirrors the widespread political, social, economic, cultural and linguistic tensions, with the aim of awakening the sleeping consciousness of the oppressed (Sartre 1947). However, against this backdrop the sequels and negative effects of colonialisms also come under scrutiny.

EFD writes with the conviction and passion that is his people's. In their country they are robbed of freedom and autonomy by centuries of colonization and neo-colonization. This country, on several occasions, has been the victim of colonialist desire and has been treated with condescension and contempt by its various colonizers. In EFD's work, the death of Mungeu's mother shortly after Mungeu's birth could be likened to the historical occurrence in the Grassfield (Savannah) Regions of Cameroon/ Caramenju. Here one is tempted to look at EFD's scenario as on a par with the hasty departure of the last but one colonizing nation (Great Britain in 1961) which left the region orphaned. Such a departure is not different from a sudden death (that of Western colonization) engendered by the clamor for independence in the late 1950's and early 1960's by African nations amongst which was the former British Southern Cameroons. With that hasty departure by Britain, West Caramenju/Cameroon was then relegated to East Caramenju/Cameroon, its French speaking counterpart, only a year after its own independence. The wanton mistreatment suffered in the hands of the new colonizer has been executed under the watch of the supra–national organization (The United Nations), which should have been playing the role of a polygamous father overseeing the well-being of all his children and wives. As a result, EFD's novel transcends the role of a mere address of the ills that plague Caramenju/Cameroon to leave one with the question of how this kind of ills exist while humanity does nothing to stop them. Furthermore, this challenges any argument that would attempt to validate the workings of divine retribution.

Again as stated prior, Caramenju, a fictional theatre in which EFD unfolds his world view, is far from the real world of his country of birth, yet it becomes a "medium/place where the truth of the world speaks itself…" (Eagleton 56). However, any informed reader would not find it hard to draw parallels between these two in spite of the work's universality and timelessness. Both worlds are replete with corruption. In keeping with Sartre's idea of commitment in writing, i.e. tasking writers to name, shame and change, to take the reader into the future where poetics have no place and art for art's sake is discarded (Sartre), the scathing critique in EFD's *The Fire Within* tells of the novelist desire to urge or effect change for the better in a *La République du Cameroun* which is oblivious to its own ills and foibles. This rampant corruption in both Caramenju and Cameroon has been brought to the fore by the novelist and an organization like Transparency International respectively. This latter organization in recent years has crowned Cameroon on about 3 occasions as the most corrupt nation in the world. EFD's venom against such a society is a timely reminder for the citizens to see their own filth and ultimately clean it. It is with this Pascalian twist that EFD's work dwells on the idea of human misery.

Mungeu's dependency on her father's concern and her constant acknowledgement of this can only be comprehended as a means of signifying her demands as Roland Barthes claims in his *A Lover's Discourse* in which he writes, "[I]n the realm of love, futility is not a "weakness" or an "absurdity": it is a strong sign: the more futile, the more it signifies and the more it asserts itself as strength" (82). In effect, this dependency is the alienating force driving Mungeu into venturing her abortion, which in the end culminates into a fatal blow for her. This further reiterates another Barthesian quote: "What I am excluded from is not desirable to me" (88). Mungeu' seems not to realize her experience of reality as a system of power. This constitutes a gesture of Mungeu's own unhappiness (130) and long after perceiving the world hostile, she still would like to remain linked to it (89). This reading evokes many more questions than answers. What relationship can one have with a system of power if he/she is neither its slave nor its accomplice and much less, its witness? Even though Mungeu's desire for freedom casts her out of any of these categories, it is evident that her tragedy results from her fears, doubts and joys of either belonging or not belonging. Is it the result of the education Mungeu' has received? Or is it a sequel /relics of colonial and post-colonial machinations?

Amongst the colonial and post-colonial ideological arguments resonating in EFD's work are his criticisms of socio-political structures, educational systems, historical fallacies, etc. Education comes under scrutiny in EFD's work. EFD uses education in his literary world to examine some of the shortcomings of Christian education without sex education. Religious education counts among the causes of alienation. This take on education has been reiterated by anthropologists and historians of ideas and mentalities. In exploring the impact of colonial and postcolonial education on Africans, Nyamnjoh writes:

> When the values are not appropriate or broadly shared, the knowledge acquired is rendered irrelevant and becomes merely cosmetic or even violent. In Africa, the colonial conquest of Africans – body, mind and soul – has led to real or attempted epistemicide – the decimation or near complete killing and replacement of endogenous epistemologies with the

epistemological paradigm of the conqueror. The result has been education through schools and other formal institutions of learning in Africa largely as a process of making infinite concessions to the outside – mainly the Western world. Such education has tended to emphasize mimicry over creativity, and the idea that little worth learning about, even by Africans, can come from Africa. (1)

The whole tragedy in EFD's novel stems from such education which prepares girls for the world without giving them the necessary tools to face the challenges the world presents. Through Mungeu's dialogue with Mabel, the writer lashes out his frustration with this kind of education which fosters mediocrity as it prepares girls for everything else but for the most important thing they would certainly need in order not to fall victim as the protagonist does. If Mungeu' meets with her fate in the end, the author seems to blame this, to an extent, on the educational system. This, however minimal an aspect of education as it is, is representative of the things that are wrong with the educational system in Caramenju/Cameroon. At Mungeu's confused lack of understanding about her being safe after she had slept with a man, Mabel thus expresses her concern for the education Mungeu' received in this terms:

> O my God! You mean you are that naïve? You mean all your time at the Holy Rosary Home Craft Centre was spent on all the other things of the world and nothing about your own body? Nothing about men? Nothing about men and women? (17)

By presenting Mungeu' at the graduation ceremony ruminating on her loneliness and plight, the author seems to infer that in spite of her academic achievements, the challenges ahead of her are far worse than what she has overcome so far. This moment is pivotal not only because the writer uses it as an excuse to reinforce the protagonist's estrangement suffered thus far and that to come, but it is, in that the narrator tells the reader it is an unforgettable event and in several ways it evokes what Lenin once called "the reality of appearances" (qtd. in Eagleton 97). The narrator says:

> Mungeu' would never forget her graduation day – June 30th 1975. When at last it came and all the formalities were done with – speeches, awards, and the handing of diplomas and prizes won – the loneliness of her life struck her once more, like a blow in the face. While the parents of other students rushed to congratulate their daughters and walk them home, Mungeu' found herself searching the faces of visitors in vain for her father. He was nowhere to be found. Not one of her stepmothers had come to congratulate her on her day of success. (7)

From this, a haunting sense of estrangement grips both Mungeu' and the reader. It is a clever reminder of what happens in a socio-political context which frowns at success. Mungeu's is nothing short of the feelings of estrangement and powerlessness. EFD gets into the mind of the alienated to unveil human haplessness in the face of oppressive forces. The tyranny of education leaves the educated with alienating consequences. By probing into Mungeu's psyche the writer has the reader live and experience the internal trauma of the feeling of being estranged. He does so on several occasions, such as on one occasion when Mungeu' chooses to rush to her father and expose her fears and doubts after her concerns for her stepsister, who has been away to a village market at Bansei and has not returned. The welcome she receives leaves her mind wandering on her way back from her father's, as captured by the narrator:

> As Mungeu' walked back home, she tried to figure out what really she had done to Angwi but could hardly put her finger on anything concrete; or was it her late mother? She wondered. Were

her mother the second wife, such profound hatred could have been justified. The impact of the arrival of a second wife is usually more powerfully felt by the first who finds herself face to face with an archrival against whom her anger is impotent as she now controls at least half of the husband's attention, which all used to be fixed on the first wife. However, her mother was the fourth and did not have the fortune of having a baby as soon as she would have loved to. When the baby came, at last, it claimed her life and as if that was not tragic enough, it was a baby girl. Her only regret, however, was that her mother died while giving birth to her. She sometimes wondered if Angwi hated her for being a girl and for taking after her mother so much. For people who knew her often talked to her and claimed if one saw Mungeu' then there was no need trying to look for her mother. "Again, Mabel her daughter, is better placed than I am…." As Mungeu' walked home, all efforts to seek the cause of Angwi's profound hatred for her were futile and so she resolved never to let that bother her again. (24)

This quotation also brings to the fore social issues that are at the core of the ills EFD aims at redressing in his poetic universe as well as in the real world. How could being born a girl be tragic? Does it mean that girls are not much appreciated by parents? The root of Mungeu's problem is her being a woman, and EFD has the narrator point out that:

She smiled alone as the real problem became obvious to her. It was like the light of an electric bulb rescuing someone who had been groping about in the dark room loaded with many pieces of furniture. The real problem, it dawned on Mungeu', was not with the town as a whole but with a particular sex – the female. […] being a woman in this town is the problem. Women hate one another, for no reason in particular, so much so that they would go to any length to shatter the integrity of a woman they've only seen and admired even though they've not met before. (36)

Again, in the dialogue that ensues when Mungeu' is convened by her father, the reader gathers the same. The overbearing weight of a male chauvinistic society becomes, for the writer, a disturbing trend that needs to be changed. EFD expounds on this at length and shows how it is so widespread. As if the male dominated society did not do enough to crush women, this is supported by other women (38-41). This only intensifies the protagonist's resolve to avoid her status of the estranged. She thus endeavors to reply to her father and is made to understand that monologue is what her male dominated society requires when a man speaks in the presence of woman/women, much less of a female child.

This binary opposition of new trends and traditional values is EFD's way to clearly point out that where tradition should redress such issues as alienation, estrangement and oppression, tradition chooses to victimize its own children, thus alienating them more and leaving them with no choice but that of drowning in all sorts of torment and misery which are engendered by such inconsiderate victimization. His narrator says:

> After all, her father had barely been in her life whereas all Angwi had done was tell lies about her and torture her emotionally. Now she was a woman, and she would not take any nonsense from anybody. Mungeu' wept as she lamented Mabel's absence. Had she been around, all would have been different, at least under control. Now, here she was alone to wage a war against a family that never cared about her, and a tradition that seemed to go all the way out to victimize rather than redress. (37)

Another social concern that EFD tackles is polygamy. To live in the context of polygamy, and without a mother, is tantamount to living in a world of strangers or, better still, to accept the status of a pariah in society. Such a child is unwanted either by society itself or by its family members. It becomes evidently clear that the estranged relationship between Mungeu' and her father (who should be her source of comfort) and that between her and Angwi are the main sources of her alienation more than anything else. EFD seizes this opportunity to go a step further in highlighting how this marriage custom is responsible for plights such as Mungeu's. Her plight is not just the result of the fact that her mother died while she tried putting to bed the only child she would never live to see. It is the marital practice of polygamy, "where the impact of the arrival of a second wife is usually more powerfully felt by the first" (24). In the end, Mungeu's choice to abort the child she is carrying for Adey depends on her thinking that her father still cares. Ironically, this same father, all the while his daughter has been away, never lifts a finger to find out her whereabouts. All Mungeu' longs for is to be part of her father's family, and she does make her choice because she thinks it is the way to win her father's love and acceptance.

In *The Fire Within*, EFD traces the emergence of tragedy in post-independent West or British Southern Cameroons as a new epistemology to warrant a better understanding of the predicament in which the ordinary Anglophone Cameroonian is caught. EFD's heroine experiences marginality, alienation, estrangement and isolation. These become the central constitution of the novel. He explores characters who feel painfully alienated from social institutions, from family members and loved ones, and from their community. EFD's world is one fraught with tales of passion and alienation. They become such powerful forces to move the characters to impulses that lead to the ultimate tragedy. These characters, therefore, become agents and mediums through whom the harsh reality of estranging social and human relationships uncover themselves. In one of the tales, beauty, a universal cause for admiration, becomes the impending doom to drive the last nail into the coffin of any such admirer and make of beauty an object fit for the margins. Personal contentment, in a strange twist in EFD's world, leads to envy and consequently alienation and tragedy. In the relationship between Ngwe and Musa, the latter is led to believe that his wife's beauty is the result of her "emptying [his] ... wealth" (48). He, then, complains and requires explanation from a wife who has none. As a result, she is forced to leave him. The consequence is that he (Musa) is "found hanging from the roof of his bedroom" (48).

Furthermore, EFD weaves his narrative around the attempt of purging oneself and/or getting rid of an unwanted seed, even if this were contracted in the name of love. This narrative leaves such attempts with a devastating consequence. Mungeu' attempts to abort her baby with Adey, and in the process, she loses her life. To EFD, when the citizenry is reduced to wretchedness, vagrancy and to a point where they become hapless apatrides in their own country, death becomes by far, a better option. If not why should the creative writer EFD raise a suffering child, Mungeu', from her stead of an orphan, outcast/alienated, exile, undesirable element, yet, nobler and grander in character etc. to the height of prosperity only to let her fall in the end? Is it because of some innate flaw in her character? Has she the wherewithal to change her fate? Is she just a scapegoat for the errors of her own people? The answers to these questions project Mungeu's sufferings as instrumental in the resolution of the problems of passion and alienation that plagued her society at the outset. EFD does this by bringing Mungeu's entire family and friends together as a result of her funeral. In this instance, after Pa' Anye breaks down upon seeing the daughter's corpse, his instructions to the women and children to get the compound ready brings a sense of unity and purpose, as " together they went to work arranging the compound to accommodate the crowd that was already gathering" (204).

Again, in EFD's work which is never completely divorced from politics, he seems to be making a statement for his people. He highlights the union between West and East Caramenju, the result of which union is absolute corruption like the child Mungeu' carries for Adey. The child is the product of an unsanctified union or an illegitimate act. This calls for abortion. It is also something worth dying in its course as it conflicts with the rigors, moral rectitude and dilemma the tragic heroine has already faced in the past. Her death in the end spells the quest for absolute freedom which for the author and his world view for his people is something to be attained at all cost, even at the cost of one's life. This concurs with a popular Cameroon Grassfield proverb that "a true warrior dies fighting and not kneeling with his cap in hand." As such, even though Adey's behavior at Mungeu's funeral marks the beginning of insanity, this leads one to probe whether this means his desire for Mungeu' is dead. Not at all, for the fire within Adey burns with consummating passion and pushes him in the depths of folly that he cannot contain.

Once more, the tragedy that befalls Mungeu' at the end of the novel is not different from that which befell EFD's West Caramenju/Cameroon shortly after independence in 1961. Historically, the union between the English-speaking and French-speaking Cameroons, which to this day remains contentious, has been seen as a kind of forced and unsanctified union in which the English speaking minority is estranged. However, this union was the result of some misconstrued form of mutual love and passion like the one between Mungeu' and Adey. Mungeu's fatal end is the author's refusal to live to see a failed union contracted with all the good intentions. The author is conscious of the fact that the offspring of any such union is unwelcomed to the society after which his people aspire. This reflection should not come as a surprise to any reader with fore knowledge of the fact that EFD is the author of *Africa's Political Wastelands: The Bastardization of Cameroon* (2008). By and large, EFD is one of the promoters of meaningful contracted unions (conjugal or political) and as a writer, he is more concerned with navigating the impossibilities to get the possible without having recourse to shortcuts that lead people nowhere near happiness. He does so by mirroring the outward condition of his literary inspiration in what he has written (Clark 333).

Life at Njunki symbolizes business and only business even if Mungeu' in this process creates a semblance of human relationship with the Ndomnjie's. Again, one might be tempted to see her relationship with Yefon, her apprentice, as one, yet this is nothing short of business or the fact that birds of the same feathers flock together. Mungeu' and Yefon share a similar plight. They are orphans without a guardian. Mungeu' expects love from her father, stepmother and society at large. She embarks on a very dangerous mission to abort Adey's child. With all the risk it entails, given her choice of a quack for a practitioner, she ends up dying. The critical question and concern here is whether there is any real reason to lose one's life for those who, in the first place, care little or nothing for one. Furthermore, the reader is presented with a Mungeu' from start to finish who seems to possess a rare brand of virtue for mortals, that of believing her father cares even though he has been silent all through her plight. For her, this silence does not entail lack of concern. Even though alienated, Mungeu' is without bitterness, an admirable character trait. However, one is tempted to find out why, if Pa' Anye does care for Mungeu', for the several years of Mungeu's imposed self-estrangement, he has not endeavored to find out where she could be? Is this an outlet for the writer to reprove this form of estrangement? Once again, can Mungeu's attitude be attributed to the powerful force exuded by alienation that leaves the estranged hapless and inclined to negative self-destructive impulses? Is the author here attempting to spell out to the reader the violence that a sense of alienation which, once bred in an individual, will drive such an individual or a character to, as a result of his/her findings through introspection and understanding of both intellectual and economic freedom?

By confronting new trends and traditional values in his novel *The Fire Within,* EFD does not only revert to the primal affirmation of unrest and possibly tragedy engendered by such an endeavor, but he goes a step further to explicate the process of alienation in a country where two inherited colonial cultures (one from the French and the other from the English) stand at variance with the English-speaking minority plagued with woes brought about by estrangement. From the opening of the novel to the end, EFD strives at driving home alienation and its effects not only on individuals but on society as a whole. He structures the plot of his novel around the birth and death of his protagonist, Mongeu', and concludes the novel with these last words:

> The thought of going back to his room crossed his mind every once in a while, but there was a certain overpowering feeling of estrangement which convinced him he could not face the room, in fact, the entire compound with occupants, in this present state of mind, and so he kept on walking, walking and talking to himself. (209)

This hardly conceals the lamentations of a writer, conscious of the alienation suffered by millions of people in his home country. In EFD's poetic universe, Caramenju, a cross section of the people, most especially the English-speaking minority, suffers from estrangement as a sequel of colonization. Likewise, in his fatherland, Cameroon, colonization left a similar burdensome linguistic imposition on the English-speaking West Cameroon, formerly known as British Southern Cameroons.

In the end of this novel, EFD, with tact, warrants Mungeu's passion to survive through Adey. Nonetheless, Adey's plight, which in the end culminates into "madness," is a telling reminder of the pervasive and irrefutable trauma left upon the marginalized, estranged, isolated and alienated as well as their loved ones. This end also marks EFD's frustration with a country in which the only alternative to its English-speaking citizens is to die or live with insanity on the fringes of society and with the fire of freedom burning undeterred within. This bitter note of frustration is akin to the one felt by many a young West (British) Cameroonian who on the eve of independence were just as passionately in love as Mongeu' and Adey, both enthralled by the ideal of true and everlasting love. Adey ends up suffering from severe depression. This replicates the violence distilled from real life that lay the foundation for alienation in EFD's work. This violence takes various and multiple forms: psychological, physical, emotional, etc. It affects the multitude of West Caramenjuans who are unhappy and hapless in their stead and in their union with East Caramenjuans, yet they can't do anything about it. *The Fire Within* thus becomes what G.N. Clark, in explicating literature, qualifies as "the sensitive and responsive apparatus by which the world of imagination is adjusted to the most complex and most personal requirement of the human soul" (333). It would, therefore, not be misleading to assert that EFD's work is about fears, doubts and joys of belonging/not belonging in contemporary Anglophone Cameroon coupled with her relationship with her neo-colonizer, *LRC*, who took over the territory after the British abandoned it in the wake of independence in 1961. The relationship between British Southern Cameroons and *LRC* from then till date has been as alienating as Mungeu's and her stepmother's. In short, it is as Mandel would have it in his 1971 publication, "Causes of Alienation":

> A society which is turned toward creating a systematic frustration [that] generates bad results recorded in the crime pages of the daily newspapers. A society which breeds worthless dissatisfaction [… and] all kinds of antisocial attempts to overcome this dissatisfaction. (web.)

Having explored the causes of alienation in contemporary Anglophone Cameroon from EFD's prism, this chapter has covered the distinguishing causality resulting in the psychological make-up of both writer and his characters to unveil a compelling tale of passion and alienation brought about by a blight in companionship in a world peopled by characters who, like the writer and his people, are forever strangers either at home or abroad.

Works Cited

Doh, Emmanuel Fru. *The Fire Within*. Mankon- Bamenda: Langaa RPCIG, 2008. Print.

——————. *Africa's Political Wastelands: The Bastardization of Cameroon*. Mankon- Bamenda: Langaa RPCIG, 2008. Print.

Barthes, Roland. *A Lover's Discourse,* New York: Hill & Wang, 2010. Print.

Clark, G.N. *The Seventeenth Century*. Oxford: Clarendon, 1957. Print.

Eagleton, Terry. *Literary Theory: An Introduction,* Minneapolis: U of Minnesota P, 1998. Print.

Heidegger, M. *Time and Being*. New York: State U of New York P, 1996.Print.

Kasteloot, Lylian, *Anthologie négro-africaine:Panorama critique des prosateurs, poètes et dramaturges noirs du XXème siècle,* Paris : Marabout Université, 1981. Print.

Mandel, Ernest. "Causes of Alienation." *The Marxist Theory of Alienation: International Socialist Review* 31.3 (1971): 19-23, 59-50. Print.

Mufor, Atanga. *The Anglophone Cameroon Predicament*. Mankon-Bamenda: Langaa RPCIG, 2011. Print.

Nyamnjoh, Francis B. "'Potted Plants in Greenhouses': A Critical Reflection on the Resilience of Colonial Education in Africa." *Journal of Asian and African Studies 47.2* (2012): (129–154)

Sartre, J.P. *What is Literature?* New York: Philosophical Library, 1947. Print.

INDEX

A

Achebe, Chinua 39, 93, 107, 187
Adichie, Chimamanda Ngozi .. 207, 209, 210, 211, 212, 214, 223, 224
Ahidjo, Ahmadou 11, 15, 197
Alembong, Nol 35
Ambanasom, Shadrack...........39, 45, 53
American Dream 125, 127, 130, 212
Amuta, Chidi 39, 53
Andrade, Susan Z. 209, 224
Anyangwe, Carlson 156, 157
Aristotle......................................4, 60, 63
Armah, Ayikwe 134
Asaah, Augustine H. 165, 180
Ashcroft 35, 53, 137, 139
Ashcroft, Bill 138, 140, 147, 154, 158
Ashuntantang, Joyce 39, 54, 135, 136, 145, 158
Asong, Linus T 45
Attardo, Salvatore 106, 110

B

B. W. Vilakazi, ... 41
Ba'Bila, Mutia 35
Badiou, Alan................................. 36, 54
Bakhtin, Mikhail 65, 82, 83, 201
Balladier, George 132
Baraka, Amiri........................... 102, 110
Barfield, Owen 26, 30
Barthes, Roland 238, 250
Bate Besong........................13, 35, 56
Benjamin Franklin 193
Berlin, Isaiah 36
Biya, Paul... 8, 11, 14, 15, 189, 194, 197, 200, 203, 206

Bjornson, Richard 175, 176, 178, 180
Blake, William 27, 30, 41, 46, 48
Bly, Robert 25, 30
Bobda, Simo 136
Bradbury, J.G.............................. 27, 30
Brée 18, 30
Breitinger, Eckhard ...196, 201, 203, 205
Brewster 44, 54
Bridgwood, A 34, 54
Brockbank, Elizabeth......................... 83
Brossat, Alain 207
Browning, Robert 41, 56
Bruccoli ...113, 115, 117, 118, 119, 120, 121, 124, 125, 126, 128, 129, 130
Bryer, Jackson R. 130, 131
Burroughs, Edward...........75, 76, 80, 81
Butler, Marilyn 47, 54
Byron, Lord 41, 43, 52, 56

C

Casaliggi 37, 54
Chew, Shirley.................................. 158
Chirac, Jacques 20
Chomsky, Noam..................... 188, 205
Chopra, Ramesh. 60, 83
Churchich, Nicholas 76, 84
Clark, G.N. 69, 70, 84, 247, 249, 251
Coleridge 42, 48, 54
Collins, Peter 64, 65, 83
Commissaire Mbida 5
Cory, Richard..................................... 88
Coxere, Edward ...58, 59, 60, 61, 62, 63, 64, 65, 66, 67, 68, 70, 71, 72, 73, 74, 75, 76, 77, 78, 79, 80, 81, 82, 83

D

Dadié, Bernard 214
Davies 37, 54, 60, 68, 69, 76, 78, 84
Denby, David 124
Diasporic 148
Dickens, Charles 188
Dickensian 195
Dieudonné..... 88, 90, 91, 92, 93, 94, 95, 96, 97, 98, 99, 100, 101, 104, 105, 106, 107, 108, 109, 111
Dieumerci.. 99, 100, 101, 104, 105, 106, 109
Dinka, Gorji 13
Diome, Fatou ..207, 208, 214, 223, 224, 225
Disraeli, Benjamin.............184, 188, 205
Doh, Emmanuel Fru.....3, 12, 30, 32, 35, 37, 38, 39, 40, 41, 42, 43, 44, 45, 46, 47, 48, 49, 50, 51, 52, 53, 54, 186, 187, 189, 196, 197, 204, 205, 226, 250
Douglass, Frederick 193
Dover... 60
Duff 44, 45, 55

E

Eagleton, Terry 231, 232, 234, 235, 238, 241, 251
Ebini, Atem Christmas................. 12, 30
Echu, George. 170, 171, 180
Ehling.. 41, 55
Emmanuel Fru Doh 226, 227, 228, 229, 230, 231, 232, 233, 234, 235, 236, 237, 238, 239, 240, 241, 242, 243, 244, 245, 246, 247, 248, 249, 250
europhonism 40
Eyoh 32, 55

F

Fanon, Frantz 90, 91, 96, 110, 134, 146, 149, 158, 207
Fantouré, Alioum................................ 4
Fellini, Federico 119
Fisher, Samuel 75, 76
Fitzgerald F. Scott....113, 114, 115, 116, 117, 118, 119, 120, 121, 122, 123, 124, 125, 126, 127, 128, 129, 130, 131
Fox, George 58, 84
Franceschini 221, 222
Frost, Robert 37
Fru Ndi 13
Furst.. 42, 55

G

Galvin 27
Galvin, Rachel 30
Gikandi, Simon..........132, 133, 139, 158
Gillin, Edward 120, 131
Gioia, Dana 34, 55
Glasgow University......................... 7, 31
*Gods in the Ivory Towers*161, 162, 174, 180
Gramsci, Antonio 147
Great Gatsby, The....................... 126, 130
Greene, Diana................................ 6, 31
Griffiths 35, 53, 137, 139
Griffiths, Gareth 138, 154, 158
Gwangwa'a, Gahlia 35

H

Heaney, Semus 34
Heidegger, Martin 251
Henry IV 203, 206
Hill, Christopher.............58, 59, 84, 250
Hillis Miller, Joseph 34, 55

Hitler 23
Hooker, John Lee 102
Hugo, Victor 3, 31
Hugo's 3
Humanist Vision 3

I

Ibsen, Henrik 192
Innes, Stephen 67, 71, 84
Irele, Abiola 89, 110, 158, 179, 180

J

James, Henry 122
James, William 120
Janowitz 39, 40, 56
Joycean 19
Jua, Nantang B 202, 203, 205

K

K'cracy 3, 5, 6, 11, 27, 31
Kafka, Franz 194, 232
Kamangola 134, 135, 137, 142, 143, 144, 145, 146, 147, 148, 149, 156, 157
Kandel, Lenore 25, 26, 31
Kane, Cheikh Hamidou 214, 215
Kasteloot, Lylian 236, 251
Keats, John 41, 47, 54
King, Adele .. 47, 71, 104, 157, 158, 173
King, B.B. 188
Kipling, Rudyard 197
Kotchnig, Elined P. 84
Kourouma, Ahmadou 107
Kremlin 20

L

La Dolce Vita 119
Labang, Oscar C. 33, 56
Lacoue-Labarthe, Philippe 36, 56
Larrissy 37, 56
Laura Rice 107
Levertov, Denise 31, 37
Lopes, Henri 207, 208, 218, 219, 220, 223, 224
Loukes, Harold 59, 83, 84
Lowell, Robert 37

M

Makowski, Veronica 127, 131
Malaga 73
Mandel, Ernest 64, 84, 231, 235, 250, 251
Mandela, Nelson 16
Mantell, Humphrey 74
Maragnès, Daniel 207, 224
March-Russell 37, 54
Márquez, Gabriel José García 7
Marx, Karl 60, 89, 94, 110
Matson, I Wallace 60, 84
Mayakovsky, Vladimir 6
McGann, Jerome 36, 56
McKaig, Alexander 116
McLeod, John 133, 134, 144, 158
Meyerstein, E.H.W 82
Miller, Arthur 4, 29
Miller, Daisy 124
Mimboland 92, 93, 94, 98, 100
Mind Searching ... 184, 185, 186, 187, 188, 189, 190, 191, 193, 194, 195, 196, 197, 199, 200, 201, 202, 203, 204, 206
Morton, Stephen 138, 158
Moscovici 37, 56

241

Mudimbe, V. Y. 110, 180
Mufor Atanga .. 190, 194, 195, 196, 205, 251
Muna, Solomon Tandeng 11

N

Nancy, Jan-Luc 36, 56
Napoleon 14, 235
Ndi ... 3, 4, 5, 6, 7, 9, 10, 11, 12, 13, 14, 15, 16, 17, 18, 19, 21, 22, 23, 24, 25, 26, 27, 29, 30, 31, 35, 58, 83, 161, 162, 172, 175, 178, 180, 226
Negritude 89
Neruda, Pablo 7
Newfoundland 62
Nfah- Abenyi, Juliana 32, 56
Ngong Kum, John 35
Ngwane 35, 56
Nkam, Giftus 35
Nkengasong, John N. 132, 134, 140
Nyamnjoh, Francis B. 88, 90, 93, 95, 98, 101, 107, 109, 111, 132, 159, 164, 165, 166, 167, 170, 180, 184, 185, 186, 187, 188, 189, 190, 191, 192, 193, 194, 195, 196, 197, 198, 199, 200, 201, 202, 203, 204, 205, 206, 239, 251

O

O'Neill, Michael 37, 43, 52, 56
Oakley 40, 56
Odyssey 41, 44
Ojo-Ade, Femi 161, 162, 177, 180
Oke Akombi, Sammy 35
Onyeoziri, Gloria 107, 108, 111, 207
Oriki'badan 38, 41, 42, 43, 55
Orwellian 191
Ousmane, Sembène 4

Owen, Wilfred 37

P

Parini 24, 26, 31
Philombe, René 201
Plato 3, 31
Plymouth 62
proletarianization 67

Q

Quaker 58, 59, 60, 62, 64, 68, 71, 75, 76, 77, 78, 79, 80, 83, 84

R

Rand, William E. 128, 131
Rapport, Nigel 83, 84
Reid, Jimmy 7, 31
Richards, David 145, 146, 158, 159
Ritz .. 115, 117, 118, 120, 121, 124, 126, 128
Robinson, E.A. 88
Roderick Hudson 122
Romanticism 32, 36, 37, 39, 40, 42, 44, 45, 53, 54, 55, 56
Roosevelt, , Eleanor. 202, 206
Rothstein, Arnold 126
Roy, Christopher D. 161

S

Saïd, Edward 139, 146, 168, 180
Saro-Wiwa, Ken 174
Sartre, Jean-Paul 145, 226, 227, 229, 230, 232, 237, 238, 251
Sartre, Jean-Paul 18, 30
Sayre, Zelda 116, 117, 121, 122, 129
Schlegel, Friedrich 51, 57

Schmitt, Richard 88, 92, 100, 111
SDF.. 12, 14
Seeman, Melvin.........66, 84, 89, 99, 111
Sethi, Rumina 138, 159
Shakespeare, William 29, 34, 41, 203, 206
Shelley, P.B....40, 41, 43, 46, 49, 51, 52, 54, 55, 57
Simédoh, Vincent. 219, 224
Siskin, Clifford.............................. 43, 57
Sklar, Robert 116
Smith, Bessie 102
Socé, Ousmane 214
Social Angst 3
Somerset.. 60
Sontag, Susan............................ 178, 180
SOPECAM 201
Southern Cameroons 134, 156, 158, 237, 244, 249, 250
Soviet Union............................. 195, 201
Soyinka, Wole 6, 39, 41, 93
Steinbeck, John 125
Subalternity.......................147, 157, 211
Swift, Jonathan 17
Switzer, Robert 102, 103, 111
Sybil 184, 205

T

Takwi, Mathew 35
The Fire Within.......38, 55, 226, 227, 228, 238, 244, 248, 249, 250
The Smart Set 115, 124
Things Fall Apart.............................. 187
This Side of Paradise........................... 115
Thomas, Dominic............................. 214
Thoreau, Henry David 128
Tiddeman, Edmund................78, 79, 80
Tiffin 35, 53, 137, 139
Tiffin, Helen 138, 140, 147, 154, 158

Tilly, Captain 63
Tilly, Captain John 66
Turnbull 116, 122, 131

U

Ubley.. 60
Unger, John T...115, 117, 124, 127, 128
University of Yaoundé 4

V

Vakunta, Peter Wuteh 35, 170
Venn, Couze.................... 148, 156, 159
Voltaire.. 6

W

wa Thiong'o, Ngugi 40, 57, 93, 162
Wakai, Kangsen Feka......................... 35
Walcott, Derek 23, 34
Washington 20, 128
Washington, George 126
Washington, Percy 119
Wegener, Frederick 121, 131
Westley, David............................. 41, 57
Westminster....................................... 20
Wexler, Bruce 34, 57
Wharton, Edith 118, 120, 123
Whitman, Walt................................... 6
William Thomas................................. 60
Wordsworth, William.39, 41, 43, 47, 48, 57

Z

Zadi, Samuel............................ 215, 225
Zoggyie, Haakayoo 88

www.ingramcontent.com/pod-product-compliance
Lightning Source LLC
Chambersburg PA
CBHW050901300426
44111CB00010B/1325